THE FIRST PHYSICAL CULTURISTS:

Ancient Greek Athletics, Training, and Competition

...

Dr. Alex Daulat

© 2020 by Dr. Alex Daulat

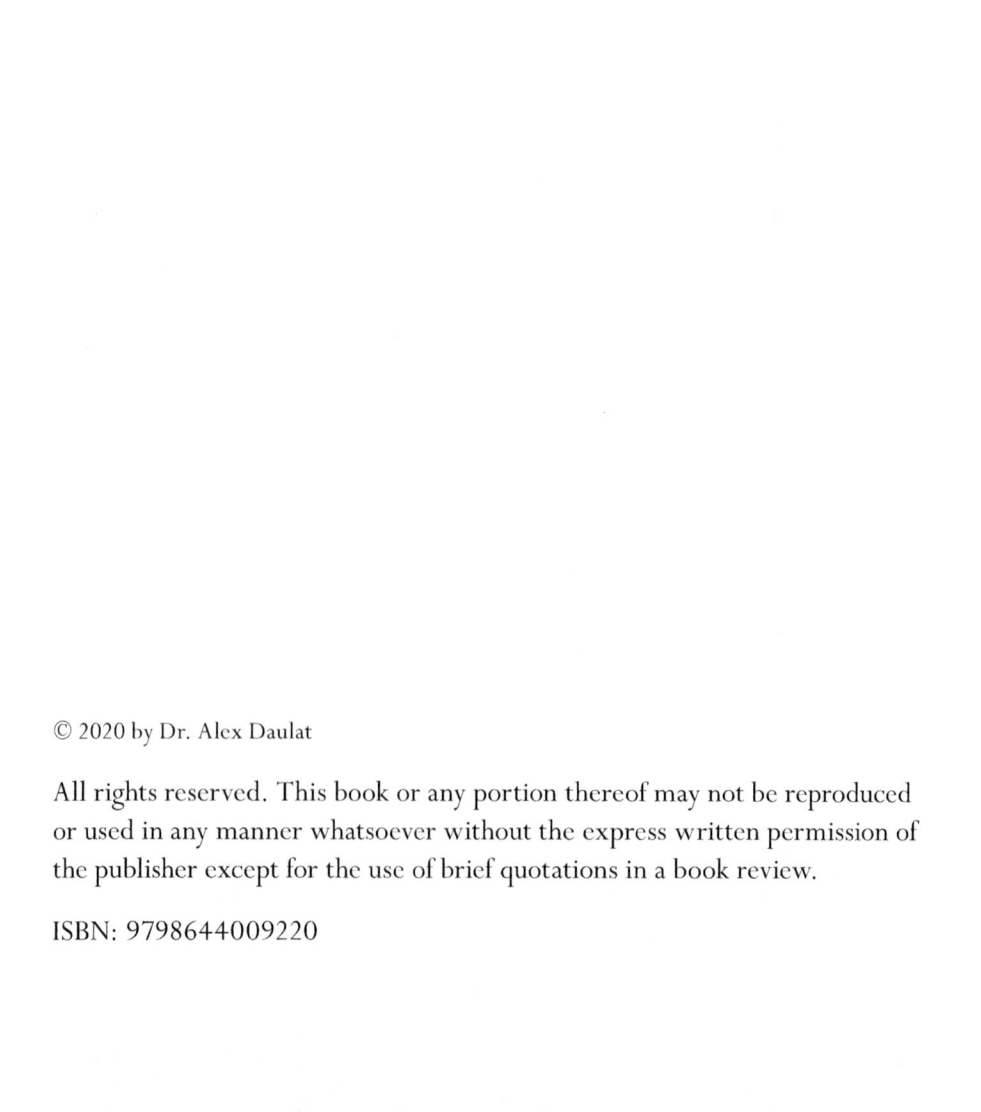

All rights reserved. This book or any portion thereof may not be reproduced or used in any manner whatsoever without the express written permission of the publisher except for the use of brief quotations in a book review.

ISBN: 9798644009220

THE FIRST PHYSICAL CULTURISTS

CONTENTS

List of Figures · vii
Introduction · ix
Chapter Overviews and Synopses· xiii

Chapter 1   The Beginnings of Exercise and Sporting Contests in the Ancient World· 1
    1.1: Sport from Early History to the Ancient Greeks · · · · · · · · · 1
    1.2: Professionalism in Greek Athletics · · · · · · · · · · · · · · · · · · 12

Chapter 2   The Olympic Games in Ancient Greece · · · · · · · · · · · · · · 19
    2.1: The Olympic Games · 19
    2.2: Nudity · 22
    2.3: Olympic Events · 24
        2.3.1: Chariot Racing · 24
        2.3.2: Pentathlon · 25
        2.3.3: Running · 30
        2.3.4: The Jump (Halma) · 31
        2.3.5: Discus · 34
        2.3.6: Javelin · 35
        2.3.7: Wrestling · 36
        2.3.8: Boxing · 36
        2.3.9: Pankration · 38
        2.3.10: Other Running Events · 38
    2.4: Homer's Games · 41
    2.5: Female Exercise and the Olympic Games · · · · · · · · · · · · · 48

Chapter 3   Gymnasium, Equipment, and Trainers · · · · · · · · · · · · · · · · 53
    3.1: Gymnasium · 53
    3.2: The Athlete's Equipment · 57
    3.3: Ancient Greek Trainers · 59

Chapter 4   Modern Principles of Exercise Training · · · · · · · · · · · · · · · 65
    4.1: Strengthening · 65

	4.2: Training Volume	68
	4.3: Power and Exercise Intensity	69
	4.4: Endurance	70
	4.5: Progressive Overload	71
	4.6: Interval Training	72
	4.7: Plyometrics	73
	4.8: Periodization	75
Chapter 5	**Gymnastics, Exercise, and Training in Ancient Greece**	**83**
	5.1: Gymnastics and General Exercise	83
	5.2: Galen on Health and Exercise	88
	5.3: Galen: On Exercise with the Small Ball	94
	5.4: Specific Aspects of Exercise Training in Ancient Greece	95
	5.4.1: Strengthening	*95*
	5.4.2: Running and Walking	*101*
	5.4.3: Jumping	*103*
	5.4.4: Throwing	*104*
	5.5: Diet in Ancient Greece and of the Athlete	105
	5.5.1: Greek Diet	*105*
	5.5.2: Athlete's Diet	*107*
	5.6: The Tetrad System	110
	5.7: An Alternative Interpretation or Theory of the Tetrad System	119
Chapter 6	**The Greek Body and Physical Culture**	**135**
	6.1: The Greek Body	135
	6.2: Applied Anatomy	141
	6.3: Achieving the Ideal Body	158
	6.4: Physical Culture from Ancient Greece to the Twentieth Century	162
Epilogue		**171**
Acknowledgments		**173**
Bibliography		**175**
Index		**195**

LIST OF FIGURES

Figure A: Torso of Apollo, probably after a statue of Onatas from Aegina (ca. 460 BC)

Figure B: ***Doryphoros, Spear-Bearer***

Figure C: ***Discobolus***, by Lancellotti Massimo

Figure D: The anterior abdominal muscles

Figure E: The external oblique muscle

Figure F: The internal oblique muscle

Figure G: The human torso representing the anterior muscles, including pectoralis major and minor

Figure H: The superficial muscles of the upper body, including pectoralis major and deltoid

Figure I: Male torso, circa 470 BC Torso Miletus, Louvre

Figure J: Muscular torso

Figure K: ***Heracles and His Child Telephos***; marble, Roman copy of the first to second century CE after a Greek original of the fourth century BCE

Figure L: The muscles of the anterior thigh highlighting rectus femoris

Figure M: The muscles of the anterior thigh highlighting vastus lateralis

Figure N: The soleus muscle

Figure O: Marble statue of the so-called **Apollo Lykeios**, AD 130–161, Roman

Figure P: So-called **Thermae Boxer: Athlete Resting after a Boxing Match**; bronze, Greek artwork of the Hellenistic era, third to second centuries BC

INTRODUCTION

> *But I imagine that in a little while you will be filled with a greater desire, if you see the rightness of truth lighting some other road more beautiful than the one you now seek, for I see that you are in a state of divine inspiration regarding the discovery of the truth in whatever material form it might appear.*
>
> —Galen, *On the Constitution of the Art of Medicine*

My Biography

I have over thirty years' experience working in health and fitness. I am a sports science graduate and a UK-chartered physiotherapist with qualifications as a sports coach (squash leaders) and a gym and Pilates instructor. I am currently specializing in musculoskeletal conditions with an interest in managing back pain. My research at the postgraduate level has looked at exercise therapy for managing chronic lower-back pain. This has led to a professional doctorate and publications in the *Journal of International Musculoskeletal Medicine*. This was an internationally recognized and highly regarded peer review journal. My first self-published book, *A History of Exercise Therapy: From Ancient to Modern Times*, was a rather ambitious attempt to cover the origins of some of the most popular forms of exercise used therapeutically in clinical practice, such as yoga and Pilates. This book looked at the history of exercise therapy and the medical systems of ancient civilizations. The feature of this book was that it took the reader through a chronological history of exercise therapy to the present day. It aimed to lead the reader to think about exercise prescription in clinical practice, why clinicians are prescribing certain types of exercise, and how adherence can be improved. I linked the past, present, and future and related past philosophies of exercise with current thinking and how this could benefit us today. There was a focus on the management of lower-back pain. Throughout this previous book, as in this current text, I provided the current literature as well as my own analysis and opinions. In the final chapter of my first book, I had outlined a holistic model of exercise therapy based on what I had learned from the past and how this could be implemented for improving health and rehabilitation. This was in keeping with the NHS Five Year Forward View originally set out in October 2014, aiming to take more action on prevention of musculoskeletal (MSK) conditions. MSK conditions are a diverse group of conditions that affect the bones, joints, muscles, and the spine, associated with pain as well as impaired physical function. These conditions have an enormous impact on the quality of life of millions of people in the United Kingdom, with the worst quality-of-life impact after neurological conditions and mental health. The Joint Strategic Needs Assessment (JSNA) aimed to assess the health needs of the local population to improve the physical and mental health of individuals and communities (Bernstein, 2014). The plan was to support people in managing their own health by staying healthy, managing conditions, and avoiding complications. The overall objective outlined in my first book was to encourage self-management for MSK conditions and promoting a healthy lifestyle through exercise. A second edition of this book is not warranted, but this current work aims to expand with further research on the history of athletics and exercise in ancient Greece, which was included in a chapter of my previous work.

Physical Culture

Physical culture can be regarded as a philosophy, regimen, or lifestyle aiming to achieve maximum physical development by exercise, diet, and athletic competition. The objective is to improve general health, appearance, and attributes of physical fitness such as strength, endurance, speed, and flexibility as well as success in sport-related activities. The ancient Greeks were the first to cultivate their bodies to achieve the ideal physique and use physical culture as a form of preventative medicine. Physical culture through exercise was a fundamental aspect of life in ancient Greece. They were the first physical culturists. Bruce Sutherland, a Scottish physical education specialist, comments that the ancient Greeks had achieved a state of perfect health and beauty through physical education (Sutherland, 1917). The physical culture movement reemerged during the nineteenth century in Germany, England, and the United States. Kirk (1999) defines physical culture as a range of practices concerned with the maintenance, representation, and regulation of the body centered on three highly codified, institutionalized forms of physical activity: sport, physical recreation, and exercise.

Sources for Ancient Greek Athletics

The fragmentary nature of ancient Greek evidence may create an incomplete and even inaccurate history. It may also be difficult to separate history from myth. Information regarding ancient Greek athletics and exercise comes from many sources, both written and visual. These include archaeological artifacts, such as athletic equipment, illustrations on coins, shields, ornaments, vases, sculptures, and bas-reliefs. The most abundant are the vase paintings, but these are almost exclusively restricted to the sixth and fifth centuries BC. It is not known for certain whether the depictions seen on these vases are actual athletic competitions or training events in the gymnasium. These are studied in conjunction with written evidence from other eras. Most of the information regarding this topic is taken from many ancient Greek and Roman authors and provides the largest single group of evidence. Written contemporary ancient testimony does exist but is rare. An example is a second century AD Egyptian papyrus (Papyrus Oxyrhynchus III 466) showing a fragment of a wrestling manual (Miller, 2004). These texts have been passed down to modern times, usually in the form of later manuscripts. These manuscripts have been copied and recopied over the centuries and may introduce an element of uncertainty. An exact translation from other languages, such as Greek to English, is not possible. There are many translations of these authors available and several interpretations. For example, in Homer's *Iliad* Book 23, some describe a pigeon as the target in the archery contest; others describe a dove. We do not know whether some of these authors were even interested in athletics and how accurate the information is. My main research for this book looked at how ancient Greek athletes trained, including the types of exercises used, and how they resemble modern training regimens. E. Norman Gardiner says, "There is little in our modern systems of physical education which we will not find anticipated in Greek medical writings" (Robinson, 1955).

My Sources for This Current Work

I have used a variety of sources for this book accessed online or from books. This has included original translations of writers from antiquity on exercise. These have included Homer, Plato, Galen, Philostratus, Lucian, and Pausanias. I have sourced books from some of the eminent academics in the field of athletics in ancient Greece, such as Gardiner, Harris, Sweet, Robinson, Young, Miller, Kyle, Scanlon, and more. I have also accessed journals and postgraduate research. The Wellcome Library has also been a useful resource, particularly for nineteenth- and early twentieth-century works on ancient Greek exercise, medicine, and physical culture.

CHAPTER OVERVIEWS AND SYNOPSES

Chapter 1 covers the historical origins of exercise and sport through to the early Greek periods, Hellenistic, and Roman eras. This chapter mentions the emergence of Greek city-states, which coincided with the rise of sport and the need to have a fit military force, as earlier cultures had. The origin of the Olympic Games, which remains controversial, is also discussed as to whether the accepted date of 776 BC is accurate or whether they were a revival of earlier cultic festivals. Finally, the concept of professionalism in ancient Greek athletics is debated as to whether this was a decline, a transformation, or the fact that Greek athletics were never amateur.

Chapter 2 introduces the Olympic Games, describing the oath that had to be taken before Zeus, the prizes, and the order of the events. The origins and purpose of nudity in Greek sport are discussed, bringing together the opinions of academics in this field. Several views are proposed, including the training of the warrior athlete in preparation for war, cultural and religious origins, the emergence of pederasty, improving performance, and the incentive to keep in good condition. The various events of the Olympic Games are described, from chariot racing to the running events and pentathlon and the heavy events, such as wrestling. The order of events in the pentathlon has been widely disputed. This chapter also includes debate on the pentathlon, providing alternative theories as to how a winner was decided. There is also an updated analysis on the jump event and a discussion of whether it was a single jump, or a series of jumps performed. For the first time in a book of this genre, there is a detailed comparison of the athletic events described by Homer in *The Iliad* and *The Odyssey* with those in the ancient Olympic Games. Finally, there is a section on female athletics and their contribution to the Olympic Games.

Chapter 3 includes the origins and structure of the ancient Greek gymnasium, describing it as a place for both physical and intellectual culture. Vitruvius's textbook on architecture is used to describe what a gymnasium would have looked like architecturally and what the key sporting facilities were. The equipment used by Greek athletes is included in this chapter, highlighting the importance of oil and powder often applied before athletic activity or competition. Finally, there is a section on the various ancient Greek trainers, including the paedotribe, *gymnastes*, *aleiptes*, *spheristici* and *xystarches* often not fully described in other texts. The role of the gymnastes is also discussed as specialized trainers or athletic experts who possessed medical knowledge relating to anatomy and athletic experience, as well as someone who understood the laws of hereditary and could affect sport performance.

Chapter 4 introduces the historical background of the basic principles of modern training and provides scientific evidence from the literature. Training principles such as strengthening, training volume, power, intensity, endurance, progressive overload, interval training, plyometrics, and periodization are mentioned. This gives the reader a basic level of knowledge to apply to their own exercise training but also provides a background for modern comparison with ancient Greek exercise techniques in *Chapter 5*. This is a novel idea to include this chapter in a book on Greek athletes but provides the reader with explanation of common exercise terminology and how this might be relevant to exercise in antiquity.

Chapter 5 provides a comprehensive account of ancient Greek exercise techniques from the literary works of Philostratus, Galen, and Lucian. There is a detailed account of Galen's writings on exercise and his defined three categories of exercise. There is a reference to *Chapter 4* on how Galen's theories of exercise suggest a knowledge of modern exercise principles and sports-specific training. This chapter highlights that there were a variety of weight-training type exercises designed by the Greeks to develop and strengthen the muscles, achieving the bodily ideal, which suggested a rudimentary understanding of the progressive overload principle. Not usually covered extensively in a book of this genre, there is a separate section on diet in this chapter. The Greeks recognized the importance of diet for health and treating illness. The diets of the Greek citizen and athletes are discussed. Different perspectives on the tetrad system of training described by Philostratus are also discussed. It is highlighted how this system incorporated different exercise intensities, rest, and technical aspects of training and was organized around modern theories of periodization. An alternative interpretation of the tetrad is proposed, which may change current thinking regarding this training system.

Chapter 6 discusses the ideal Greek body and how it was portrayed in Greek sculpture. It is suggested that some Greek and Roman sculptures were true representations of the athletic body, but there was also disproportionate physical development of athletes brought on by sporting specialization. Unique to this book genre, there is a section on applied anatomy and training methods for developing specific muscles. The relationship between applied anatomy and Greek sculpture is also discussed. The manners in which muscular development and low body fat were achieved in ancient Greece with early plyometrics and strengthening are described. An account of physical culture in ancient Greece through to the twentieth century is included. This chapter outlines how the ancient Greeks were the first physical culturists by achieving their superior body condition with hard work and sacrifice as well as holding competitions promoting outstanding bodily beauty. The chapter concludes with Greek revivalism and how the likes of Bernarr Macfadden, inspired by the ancient Greeks, were significant in the physical culture movement of the twentieth century.

This current work provides a different perspective on Greek athletes compared to similar books on this topic by Miller (2004), König (2010), Scanlon (2014), Kyle (2015), and others. My background as a sport scientist as well as a researcher in rehabilitation provides a unique fusion of sport history and science. This book covers the rise of early Greek sport and competition, the Olympic Games, and physical culture up to the twentieth century. The works on Greek athletics mentioned above have a very academic focus, whereas my book is targeted more at a novice level in this field, written so those with little or no knowledge regarding ancient Greece can follow very easily. Beale (2011) has written an informative introductory text on Greek athletics aimed at A-level students and undergraduates and is similar in format to an earlier book by Sweet

(1987). My book, at a similar introductory level to these, has a different focus and covers a greater depth on athletic trainers, types of training used, and diet in antiquity. In addition to these previous books, I draw on perhaps "forgotten authors" on Greek athletics of the nineteenth century, such as Blundell (1864), Adams (1844), Taylor (1880), and Plummer (1898), most of whom are not usually included in contemporary works in this field. I contribute further analysis and findings to this subject using my research experience on Homer's writings on athletes, the pentathlon, ancient Greek training methods, the tetrad system, and the athlete's diet. My book also compares ancient Greek exercise techniques with modern exercise principles using my knowledge of sport science, which is not covered extensively in other books. This current book is aimed at exercise enthusiasts and sport historians who may wish to know the origins of some of the most popular exercise forms used by the ancient Greeks that are still applicable today. This book may also be of interest to undergraduate students of the history of exercise and ancient Greece.

There are several writers from antiquity that are included in this text whose work has contributed to ancient Greek athletics, health, and exercise.

Hippocrates (440–370 BC)

Hippocrates is the most important name in medical history, and he is credited as being the father of medicine. He was associated with the theory of the four humors. The continuum theory originated with the Greek philosopher Empedocles (494–434 BC). This theory stated that the substance of bodies is a mixture of four elemental substances: fire, air, water, and earth. The four elemental qualities are associated with the elements, namely hot, cold, wet, and dry. The Greeks believed that related at a macroscopic level, the four elemental qualities were the four humors, or important fluids, contained in the body. A person was healthy if these humors were in balance but became ill if they were imbalanced. The four humors were blood (hot and wet), phlegm (cold and wet), yellow bile (hot and dry), and black bile (cold and dry)—all of which were linked to illness because doctors observed them when people were sick. For example, they observed blood when people had nosebleeds, phlegm when a patient had a cold, and bile when people vomited. Galen's main authority was Hippocrates; his work *Hygiene* contains several quotes from the Hippocratic corpus.

Important works from Hippocrates include *Aphorisms* and *Epidemics* as well as a regimen for athletes. Hippocrates also facilitated the growth of exercise to improve fitness and founded the theory of medical gymnastics. He suggested that exercises were not merely for sport, but along with diet and massage, they were essential in preventive medicine. He felt that activities such as running, and wrestling were important for health. He advised against exercising too long and promoted having frequent rest periods.

Plato (427–347 BC)

Plato was born in Athens, which in his time was the greatest democracy in the ancient Greek world. In approximately 375 BC, he wrote *The Republic*, one of the fundamental texts of Western philosophy. Plato considered athletics, along with music, a core element in the raising of virtuous citizens (Spivey, 2012). In his younger days, it is said he competed as a wrestler at the Isthmian Games. He was a keen advocate of physical training and had proposed a new system of athletics based on the requirements of war. He suggested in the ideal state that the young should build gymnasia for themselves and their elders. The Academy was an Athenian gymnasium and workplace for Plato. The Academy was the school of Plato and came to be known as the Academics (Harris, 1964). Several of his dialogues took place there. Plato provided many insights regarding Greek athletics, including the origins of nudity, duties of Olympic officials and legislation, as well as his views of pentathletes as being second-rate performers who would not triumph in individual running or combat events. He was forward thinking for this time, promoting female sport by advocating that unmarried females should take part in footraces of various lengths. We think of Plato as more of a philosopher, but his Academy was foremost a place for exercise.

Aristotle (384–322 BC)

Aristotle was a philosopher in the fourth century BC. His teacher was Plato, and he was Alexander the Great's tutor as well as being the founder of the library in the Lyceum of Athens. Aristotle's writings covered many subjects, including the natural and physical sciences. His treatises made a significant contribution to Greek athletics, with his insights described throughout this text. He included a revision of the list of Olympic victors among his works. Aristotle, in his *Politics*, recommended that children up to the age of puberty should apply a hard diet and compulsory light exercises in their development. In the *Constitution of the Athenians*, Aristotle or one of his pupils provided evidence on the two years training of the *epheboi* (adolescent males in Greek cities). Aristotle made contributions to motion analysis and physiological aspects of the jump, as well as running events. For example, in *Physics*, he suggested the jump in the pentathlon was an example of motion that was not continuous and suggested it was a series of jumps. He also suggested that athletes jump further with weights than without.

Aristotle in *Rhetoric* stated that pentathletes are most endowed with beauty because they are naturally built for speed and strength but condemned the exaggerated one-sided development of athletes.

Asclepiades of Bithynia (130–40 BC)

Asclepiades established Greek medicine in Rome from 91 BC. He was a friend of the great Roman orator Cicero and was very influential in the field of medicine. None of his writings survive, but he is quoted by many ancient writers, including Celsus and Galen. He initiated a methodist movement that rejected the Hippocratic theory of the four humors, much criticized by Galen. Methodist physicians instead developed a theory of atoms to explain disease, which originated from Leucippus (fifth century BC) and Democritus of Abdera (circa fifth or fourth century BC). In this theory it was suggested that the human body is composed of molecules or corpuscula, which in turn are made up of atoms, all similar, existing, and moving in an empty space or void. The proper arrangement of atoms led to good health, whereas obstruction in the atoms led to diseases classified as acute or chronic. Asclepiades was a supporter of the hygiene lifestyle. He prohibited strenuous exercise used by athletes. He advocated mild therapeutic methods, including regulation of diet, massage, passive exercise, thermal treatments, cold baths, and drinking wine.

Celsus (25 BC–AD 50)

Cornelius Celsus was an author probably during the reign of the Roman emperor Tiberius (AD 14–37) of a general encyclopedia of various subjects, including medicine (eight of his books on medicine survive). He was not a professional doctor or a surgeon but quoted from several physicians in antiquity, including Hippocrates and Asclepiades of Bithynia. Celsus may have been a source for later writers like Galen with his access to the works of Asclepiades, now lost. Wealthy Romans owned medical encyclopedias, such as Celsus's *De Medicina*, which would advise them on health matters. He advocated exercise for keeping healthy and wrote, "A man in health should more often take exercise which ought to come to an end with sweating" (Spencer, 1935). He said it is better to walk in open air than under cover unless the body is thoroughly weak. Celsus, like Galen, criticized athletes and suggested both their training and diet were carried out to excess. Due to this training, their bodies aged very quickly and became infirm. The example of athletes should not be followed by others, according to Celsus, with their fixed rules and immoderate labor.

Pausanias (AD 110–180)

Pausanias was a Greek writer in the Roman period and provided us with substantial knowledge regarding ancient Greek athletics. Pausanias wrote a guide to the cities and monuments of Greece, *Description of Greece*. His writings can be dated around AD 175. He visited the most important historical sites of classical antiquity hundreds of years after their prime. Two of his ten books are concerning Olympia, and he devoted more space to Olympia in his work than other site. Pausanias describes the buildings and monuments of Olympia, offering an architectural outline of the site. He saw statues of hundreds of athletes and read the inscriptions on their bases. He also accredited the work of these statues to famous Greek sculptors such as Lysippus and Polyclitus. His works provide details of names, dates, events, and procedures of the Olympic Games. For example,

Pausanias provides details of female running events, the first female owner to win a chariot race, and how the Hellanodikai matched wrestlers according to age and skill. He mentions famous athletic winners such as the runner Hermogenes of Xanthus, who won eight Olympic titles between AD 81 and 89 and the wrestler Leontiscus, who won in 456 BC by breaking his opponents' fingers rather than throwing his opponents (Pausanias, 6.4.3). He also tells the story regarding the demise of Polydamas, a pankration champion at Olympia in 408 BC. He was crushed to death while helping his companions escape from a collapsing cave (Harris, 1964). As with other accounts on ancient Greek athletes, this current work takes many examples of Pausanias's recorded observations.

Lucian (AD 125–180)

Lucian was a contemporary of Pausanias in the second century AD who provides a valuable source on the evidence for ancient Greek athletics. He was a writer who came from Mesopotamia. Lucian's work *Anacharsis* (Volume IV), from around AD 170, is an imaginary dialogue between Solon and Anarcharsis regarding Greek athletics. This conversation is supposed to take place in the Lyceum at Athens. Solon was a chief magistrate in Athens, and Anacharsis was a Scythian who visited Greece in the sixth century BC. Anacharsis, who belonged to a people classified as barbarians, is a spectator at the Lyceum, the Athenian gymnasium. Solon defends the practice of athletics, whereas Anacharsis criticizes it. Anacharsis finds it difficult to understand that Greeks would engage in violent activities such as wrestling in the nude and in the full sun for only symbolic prizes. Lucian's account provides us with information regarding the athletic training of young Greeks to turn them into stout guardians of the city. For example, Lucian mentions athletes running in deep, soft sand to make them good runners, the use of *halteres* (a type of hand weight) to make the jumping exercise more difficult, and the throwing of the discus to strengthen the upper body.

Galen (AD 129–216?)

Galen made a significant contribution to ancient Greek exercise and features prominently in this work. Claudius Galen was born in AD 129 in Pergamum (modern-day Turkey). He traveled to Alexandria to study at the medical school and wrote works on anatomy and physiology. Galen became a physician to the gladiators and later was appointed as court physician to the Roman emperor Marcus Aurelius. As a physician to the gladiators, Galen would have learned much about diet, exercise, and rehabilitation. Hence, he was considered as the first sports physician due to his role as a surgeon to the gladiators (McMaster, 2005). Galen was a prolific writer on an astonishing number of subjects with strong opinions including exercise. His treatise *Hygiene*, also known as *Preservation of Health* (*De Sanitate Tuenda*), consisted of six books. Books one and two were concerned with the benefits of exercise on health. Galen saw the importance of exercising at the right intensity for health benefits. He wrote, "To me, it does not mean that all movement is exercise, but only when it is vigorous. The criterion of vigorousness is change of respiration. Those movements that do not alter respiration are not called exercise" (Callaghan, 2004). His shorter treatise *Thrasybulus* explored the theoretical question of whether hygiene is part of medicine or gymnastics. A substantial number of writings regarding exercise were available to Galen, which are now lost. Galen's work is sporadic, sometimes repetitive, and difficult to read, but it provides valuable insights into how the ancient Greeks exercised.

Philostratus (AD 170–250)

Philostratus was born in the second century AD. He was a Sophist and writer. His work *Gymnasticus* is the only surviving ancient treatise on sports. Philostratus explores the history of the Olympic Games and other sporting festivals, athletic training, and the tetrad system, as well as the ideal proportions of the athletic body. Philostratus provides important information regarding ancient Greek exercise and training. He also features prominently in this work. There is no evidence that Philostratus was a trained athlete, and it could be argued that we should not rely so heavily on his treatise for our history of Greek exercise. Harris (1964) had criticized this author as having little evidence of athletics or acquaintance with its techniques.

Philostratus did use information from other ancient writers, some of whose works are now lost. For example, Pausanias's record of the Olympic Games may have provided much of Philostratus's information regarding Olympic victors mentioned in his text. Philostratus also suggests his use of other sources for his work: "For it is important in such matters to make reference to the most accurate sources possible" (Phil, *Gym* 2).

CHAPTER 1:

THE BEGINNINGS OF EXERCISE AND SPORTING CONTESTS IN THE ANCIENT WORLD

Drives, through a stream of dust, the charioteer. High over his head the circling lash he wields; his bounding horses scarcely touch the fields.

—Homer, *Iliad* 23

1.1: Sport from Early History to the Ancient Greeks

It was the aristocrats in the societies of Sumer, Babylon, and Assyria who engaged in sports such as boxing, wrestling, and swimming. Physical fitness through exercise was important for early civilizations such as Assyria, Babylonia, Egypt, and Persia to improve physical performance in war and not for sport or health benefits. For example, the Persian empire had a strict mandatory training program for boys from the age of six. This program was aimed at improving strength and stamina to provide recruits for the army and not for sporting pursuits. Physical activity was less important for the rest of society particularly as the empire became more affluent (Shephard, 2012). In Mesopotamia during the third millennium BC, physical performances were staged at festivals as well as at court.

These included military exercises, hunting, and supposedly feats of strength performed by Mesopotamian kings to demonstrate their prowess. Artwork shows that Mesopotamians were also familiar with wresting and boxing (Kyle, 2015).

There is no evidence of organized team sports or individual competition in ancient Egyptian society before the arrival of the Greeks, although Shephard (2012) suggests that international games may have been organized in upper Egypt around 1200 BC. In the Middle Kingdom of Egypt (2050–1710 BC), wrestling had become a ceremonial sport alongside dance and stick fighting, but these activities were mainly used for religious and secular celebrations. Running was an important aspect of military life and was perhaps included in regular army training. Couriers were required to deliver urgent messages by foot, and bodyguards seen on tomb reliefs ran alongside the royal chariots to provide protection for the king.

The Hittite empire (1400–1200BC) had funeral rituals with games, evidence of which was found in Hittite texts (Puhvel, 1988). These games had at least six of the eight athletic events that Homer (see chapter 2) had described in Patroclus's funeral games (namely running, archery, jousting, weightlifting or stone throwing, boxing, and wrestling). The Greek civilization started around 1800 BC. The earliest Greeks were the Bronze Age Mycenaeans. The Mycenaeans were Indo-Europeans who spread into northern Greece from the Peloponnese and into many of the islands of the Aegean and Ionian seas. They dominated mainland Greece by 1600 BC and peaking around 1450–1200 BC. The Mycenaeans, by about 1400 BC, may have been responsible for the destruction of the Minoan civilization of Crete. The physical evidence for Mycenaean sport is fragmentary and unclear (Kyle, 2015). They probably had chariot races and boxing performances. Athletics may have originated from the Minoan age of Crete (2000–1200 BC). They had bull leaping and combat sports such as boxing (Christopoulos et al., 2003). The *Boxers* vase from Hagia Triada, a Minoan settlement, has been dated around 1600 BC. The Dorians also came to Greece as the Mycenaean civilization collapsed. They were the last wave of invaders between the twelfth and eleventh centuries BC and, with a union of cultures from the Mediterranean, gave rise to the origin of the Greek people. It was under Doric influence that Greek athletics evolved in the Geometric period in approximately 900–700 BC (Miller, 2004).

Early Iron Age Greece, or the Homeric age, was between 1100 and 750 BC, including the so-called Dark Age from 1100 to 900 BC, prominent for its absence of writing. The setting of the Trojan War is estimated to be in the late Bronze Age, around 1225 BC (Kyle, 2015). After the Dark Ages, by the eighth century BC, the Greeks had spread over the whole of the Aegean and founded prosperous cities on the shores of Asia Minor (modern-day Turkey), including Miletus, Ephesus, Smyrna, and Halicarnassus. In North Africa, the Greeks founded Cyrene, which exploited the fertility of Libya. The Phoenicians prevented any effective Greek settlement off the coast of Spain.

There was no country or single state called Greece in the ancient world, but the area that we know as Greece today consisted of city-states. The Greek language was the main unifying influence of the Greek world. The Archaic period of Greece was between approximately 750 and 480 BC, a period from which the city-states started to emerge. Greek city-states were fiercely independent and constantly at war with each other. Despite these frequent civil wars, there was a mutual consciousness that the city-states constituted the Greek nation. That is why they were always united when it came to conflict with an external enemy, such as the Persians. The rise of sport coincided with the need to have a fit military force ready to defend their city-state. According to Gardiner (1930) functional exercises were performed in various athletic events, which translated to the battlefield. Spivey (2012) describes the practice and participation in Greek athletics as war minus the shooting.

Olympic events, though, according to Miller, were individual actions and had little in common with military practice (Philips and Pritchard, 2003). City-states in Greece may have arisen as early as the ninth century BC, and by 550 BC, Greek settlements spanned from southeast Spain to the Crimean Peninsula. Kyle (2015) quotes that in the Archaic period, "Greek city-states had incorporated, expanded or refounded earlier cultic games to the gods and heroes as local athletic festivals with prizes of material value." Each one of the city-states had their own legislation, quite different from the others.

The Spartans were arguably the most physically fit society in history. The period from 720 to 576 BC marked the most development for the city-state of Sparta. Physical education was realized to be the care of the state, but intellectual education was not encouraged, although education of the young was multifaceted, including not only gymnastics but also dancing, music, and poetry (Christopoulos et al., 2003). It was a very military-dominated culture that underwent economic reform around 640 BC. The government imposed a law that obliged Spartan males to undergo training that equipped them as soldiers and citizens. This allowed the Spartans to retain superiority above other Greek states. According to their harsh laws, the refusal to fight was considered the worst treachery, and children handicapped by birth were sent to death. At age seven, boys were taken from their families and sent for special hard training regimens and austere diets. They progressed through defined age groups with selection and competition at each stage to ensure they would become highly fit adult soldiers. At twenty years of age, some were selected as knights in the king's bodyguard. The knights were the famous three hundred, who fought against the Persian Army at Thermopylae in 480 BC (Fox, 2006). The Spartans were largely responsible for the growth of athletics in Greece. This was partly due to their habit of stripping naked for games and their use of oil. According to Thucydides,[1] the Lacedaemonians[2] (Spartans) were the first who rubbed their bodies with oil before wrestling (Adams, 1844). They dominated the Olympic events for 150 years until 576 BC. They recorded forty-six victories out of eighty-one in that period (Gardiner, 1930).

Olympia was not a city-state itself, as it passed no laws, issued no coins, or pursued any independent foreign policy. The accepted date of the Olympic games in honor of Zeus is 776 BC, with the *stadion* race as the only event (Dawson, 2005). There is disagreement about this date.

The tethrippon was introduced in 680 BC as one of the earliest chariot races. The chariot race was possibly staged before this period, as it was prominent in the funeral games for Patroclus in Homer's *Iliad* (see chapter 2). There have been finds of bronze statuettes of chariots among the lowest levels of Olympia, also suggesting an earlier period for chariot racing (Scanlon, 2014a). Pindar (see 2.1), in this tenth Olympic ode, mentions Herakles as establishing the first Olympiad as a five-year festival. In this festival, the young were given wreaths for victory. In addition to the footrace, this festival featured wrestling, boxing, javelin, discus, and the chariot race won by Samos of Mantinea. "In the path of which ancient

---

1. Thucydides (460–400 BC) was an Athenian historian and general. He is known for his history of the Peloponnesian war between Sparta and Athens.

2. In antiquity the city-state of Sparta was known as Lacedaemon.

traditions, now also, for grace in this namesake and exalting victory, we shall sing the thunder and the firehanded bolt of Zeus of the loud stroke" (Pindar, Olympic Ode 10). Was, then, the Olympic program already an established ancient tradition? The inclusion of just one event at the first Olympiad of 776 BC is in sharp contrast to the completeness of the Homeric program for the funeral games in *The Iliad*, but did these disciplines described by Homer exist in the eighth century BC? This may all suggest the traditional chronology of Olympic events to be implausible. Hippias of Elis, a local historian, in the fifth century BC started an Olympic register that was later revised by Aristotle in the fourth century BC (Sweet, 1987). This contained a list of victors in the games and later became the basis of Greek chronology. Another chronicle of Olympic history from 776 BC to AD 140 was compiled by Phlegon of Tralles, one of the Roman emperor Hadrian's freed slaves. There are also doubts regarding the accuracy of these dates. Lee (2002) notes that some of the numerous tripods[3] found at Olympia dating from 1,000 BC to the seventh century BC may have been votive offerings by victors in athletic contests held at Olympia before 776 BC. Preliminary results of German excavations at Olympia suggest that the cult of Zeus was established in the late eleventh century BC (Philips and Pritchard, 2003). Kyle's (2015) theory is that any early games at Olympia were, at best, minor contests consisting of footraces in a cultic festival with symbolic cult prizes.

There was an unstable period in Greece around 884 BC. It is said the games had been neglected and forgotten. Iphitus, king of Elis, had consulted the Delphi oracle and according to the oracle the old games should be revived. Cleosthenes, king of Pisa and Iphitus, made a truce and revived the festival. The terms of this sacred truce were engraved on a bronze *diskos* that still existed in the time of Pausanias (Gardiner, 1930). The diskos was kept in the temple of Hera in the Altis. The Altis was the sacred grove of Olympia rich in plane, oak, pine, and wild olive trees. The quoit of Iphitus is mentioned by Pausanias: "The quoit of Iphitus has inscribed upon it the truce which the Eleans proclaim at the Olympic festivals" (Pausanias, 5.20.1). In König's 2010 work on Greek athletics, it is suggested that this quoit was a later forgery designed to legitimate the Elean claim

---

3. Tripods in ancient Greece were frequently used as supports for cauldrons or as bases for other vases but could also function as ornaments, trophies, and sacrificial altars. They were awarded as prizes for athletic competitions.

of the custodians of the games. The truce may have been applied much earlier than 776 BC. It is not known why the date was fixed at 776 BC. The truce imposed to the city-states abstained from any kind of armed conflict among them. Armed soldiers were not allowed to enter in the wider area of Olympia, courts were not permitted to convict death, and death penalties were not conducted during the truce. Even thieves used to make a vow that they would not commit any thefts during this period. Therefore, all the athletic games in ancient Greece were linked with a temporary inhibition of armed conflicts. External countries were not included in the scope of the truce. Greek city-states were free to be in a conflict with any country outside Greek territory without violating the truce. The period in which the Olympic Games were held was sacred, so no form of conflict, human humiliation, or confinement was permitted.

To spread the news of the truce before the Olympic festival, three heralds were sent out from Elis to every Greek city-state. These heralds become known as truce bearers, or Spondophoroi, and sometimes the Oroi (Miller, 2004). They would wear olive wreaths and carry staffs, which symbolized their power. It was the function of the Spondophoroi to announce the exact date of the festival, to invite people to attend, and to declare the Olympic truce. Initially, the truce lasted for one month, but it was extended to two and then three months to protect visitors who would come from further afield (Gardiner, 1930). This truce, though, was never a time when all Greek nations ceased all wars throughout the actual time of the games but really forbade invasions of Olympia itself (Young, 2004). The truce was respected by all the city-states, with only a few violations reported. Violations were considered disrespectful to the gods. Violations were perceived as crimes and subsequently were followed by strict sanctions. These sanctions included fines and a ban on attending the games. One example of a truce breach was in the 420 BC Olympic Games. The Spartans had sent heavy infantry into the city of Lepreon and attacked Fort Phyrkos during the Olympic truce. The Eleans considered the maintenance of this garrison to be a breach of the sacred truce, as they considered Lepreon as part of their governance. The Spartans were excluded from the games, as they refused to pay a fine imposed by the Eleans and specified by Olympic law. Another breach occurred during the reign of Philip II of Macedonia (359–336 BC). In 348 BC Macedonian soldiers took an Attic citizen[4] prisoner while he was on his way to the games. They set him free only when a ransom was paid. Philip settled the matter immediately and restored the victim's property (König, 2010).

Major games were not an original part of the earliest festivals at Olympia and did not emerge until 680 BC with the addition of equestrian events. Athletics were only part of the festival to Zeus at Olympia. This event, which took place every four years, also consisted of worship with processions, sacrifices, prayers, and feasting. Exhibitions of athletic prowess at the Olympic Games were looked upon favorably, as they brought both honor to the victors and the towns or cities from which they came.

By the sixth century BC, the games had become pan-Greek. The expansion of civic athletics featured an increased degree of state involvement, such as the official administration of contests, prizes, and facilities. This era saw the golden period of the Olympic Games from the sixth century BC. *Arete*, or excellence, a notion to dominate and achieve, was fortified in Greece. The ancient Olympics stressed the idea of *kalos kai agathos*, translated as the beauty of the mind and soul as well as sporting excellence. The athletes, with their beautiful and vigorous bodies through training, were regarded as heroes. These athletes were led to represent the desires and aspirations of the Greek people. Olympia was the greatest of four Panhellenic games, along with the Pythian Games at Delphi (founded in 582 BC), the Isthmian Games dedicated to the god Poseidon near Corinth (around 581 BC), and the Nemean Games at Nemea, also in honor of Zeus (instituted in 573 BC). It is said that Plato once competed in the Isthmian Games as a wrestler (Harris, 1964), but this is unlikely to be true. The Olympic and Pythian Games were held at four-year intervals. The Isthmian and Nemean Games were biennial, the Isthmian held in the Olympic and Pythian years, and the Nemean in the years in between.

Victories in these four games, later known as the *periodos* or circuit, brought the athlete the highest of honors (Kyle, 2015). The famous athlete Theogenes of Thasos[5] in the fifth century BC had won at all four games; an inscription was

---

4. "Attic citizen" is pertaining to Attica, a region that encompassed the city-state of Athens.
5. The island of Thasos was in the northern Aegean.

found at Delphi recording his career (Harris, 1964). The runner Ergoteles, also in the fifth century BC, won the circuit twice (Young, 2004).

The prizes at these games were initially crowns or garlands. At Olympia, the prize was a garland of wild olive; at Delphi of laurel; at Isthmia of pine; and at Nemea of wild celery. The Olympic games of 480 BC were featured in *The Histories* of Herodotus.[6] The festival was taking place in the middle of the Persian invasion. After the battle of Thermopylae, the Persians learned that the Greeks were celebrating the Olympic Games. The fact that the first prize for victory was just a wreath of olive leaves had shocked Xerxes's[7] courtiers. One had said, "Good heavens, Mardonius commander of the Persian troops, what kind of men are these that you have brought us to fight against men who compete with one another for no material reward, but only for honour!" (Herodotus, *Histories* 8.1–39).

Stadia were built all over Greece, with both athletes and cities winning glory for themselves. The aristocrats in the early years of the games had the most leisure time in which to train and the resources to pay for a healthy diet. Harris (1964) suggests there was no evidence that any city subsidized an individual athlete to the attend the games. The Panhellenic Games still had entry restrictions of gender, ethnicity, and social class, but every potential competitor was subject to official scrutiny. If they did not meet the entry standards, they were sent home.

The Pythian Games was the second-greatest crown games, which was part of the Pythian festival to the god Apollo at Delphi. Athletic events very similar to those at Olympia were added in 586 BC when it emerged as a city-state (Kyle, 2015). These games took place every four years in the middle of each Olympiad. Delphi was known throughout ancient Greece as the home of an oracle of Apollo, which surpassed the oracle of Zeus at Olympia. Homer possibly mentions the wreath of Apollo at Delphi, but he does not mention the Olympic Games. In Book 1 of *The Iliad*, the priest Chryses serves as a priest to the god Apollo: "And his hands charged with the wreath and golden sceptre" (*Iliad*, Book 1). This wreath might have been a laurel crown. The oracle was functioning by the late eighth century BC but well before the Pythian Games had started. In *The Iliad*, Agamemnon consulted the oracle before the Trojan War. Delphi had held earlier

---

6. Herodotus was an ancient Greek Historian in the fifth century BC.
7. Xerxes was a Persian king who ruled from 486 to 465 BC.

musical competitions, with music being a specialized profession in early Greek history.

The four festivals shared Olympic elements, including crowns, truces, envoys, and multiple cults. Ancient Greece had hundreds of local games put on by the city-states or local sanctuaries. The sanctuary of Asclepius in Epidaurus was known as a center for healing but also held athletic and musical games. Like the crown festivals, the Asclepius Games had judges, envoys, a procession from Epidaurus, and a sacrifice. This sanctuary gained an athletic complex with a new stadium, a tunnel, as well as a changing room in the fourth century BC (Tomlinson, 1983; Gesler, 1993). The Panathenaic Games held in honor of Athena, the goddess of civilization, started after 566 BC. Athens had more festivals than other city-states, celebrating 144 days of festival a year (Mikalson, 1975). These festivals often included musical, dramatic, and athletic competitions as well as torch races. Pericles[8] in the fifth century BC proclaimed Athens a city open to all (Thucydides, 2.39.1), and non-Athenians were invited to attend and take part in the program. Athens had become a rich city succeeding under Pericles's leadership to 430 BC. Pericles was responsible for the building program on the Acropolis, including the Parthenon. Numerous gymnasiums with halls, baths, and palaestrae were built for the training of young people. This allowed the right of all citizens in Athens to receive physical education rather than the privileged few. Pindar notes several non-Athenian victories at Athens, probably at the Panathenaic Games. During Solon's period in the sixth century BC, symbolic prizes of olive oil gained substantial material worth. Each amphora contained ten gallons, or forty liters of oil. Young (2008) suggests a Panathenaic men's stadion victor won one hundred vases of oil.

In the Hellenistic period (323 BC–31 BC), there was a shift from independent city-states to larger kingdoms and empires. Philip II of Macedonia's victory at Chaeronea in 338 BC in northern Greece against an army mainly of Athenians and Thebans virtually ended the epoch of the independent city-states. The ancient kingdom of Macedonia lay between Greece and the Balkans, consisting of an ethnic mix of Dorians, Thracians, and Illyrians. It was Alexander the Great who expanded the Macedonian empire he inherited from his father. Alexander

---

8. Pericles was a famous Athenian politician born in the 490s BC.

intended to conquer the whole of Asia. He defeated the Persian Army under Darius III at the battle of Issus in 333 BC. The battle of Gaugamela in 331 BC was the decisive battle in which Alexander again defeated Darius III, leading to the end of the Persian empire (Badian, 2000). Victory at the battle of the Hydaspes in 326 BC against the king Porus had opened the Indian subcontinent to the Greek world, but Alexander's army went no farther.

Instead, Alexander secured the banks of the river Indus as the border of his empire. Alexander was a fine horseman, athlete, and warrior but may have rejected the Greek passion for athletics. His tutor Aristotle criticized excessive athletic training, particularly by the Olympic victors, as severe gymnastic exercises exhausted their constitutions (Aristotle, *Politics* 8.4).

Alexander scorned his father's (Philip II's) pride in Olympic victories (Adams, 2014). He supposedly criticized him for competing and for publicizing his wins on new coin issues. Philip had won equestrian victories at Olympia in 352 BC and 348 BC, but it is questionable whether he took part in these events himself. Alexander never competed in formal athletic or equestrian contests, perhaps because, according to Alexander, kings should compete only against kings. A story from Plutarch[9] mentions on one occasion, Alexander ran a race against a leading sprinter of the time who, no doubt with the best of intentions, eased up to allow the king to beat him. During his campaigns, he organized several sets of games, both formal and informal. For example, at Soli in Cilicia in 333 BC, he organized a sacrifice to Asclepius with a military parade, a torch race, and athletic and musical games. In 324 BC, Alexander honored his friend Hephaestion (356–324 BC) with spectacular funeral games consisting of three thousand competitors in athletic and musical contests. Two of his generals, Perdiccas and Craterus, carried with them on their campaigns a huge marquee, which was two hundred yards long, to enable training to be continued under all conditions of weather. They took baggage animals laden with wrestlers. Strabo[10] wrote that as soon as Alexander's army entered India, the native craftsmen were required to make strigils and oil flasks, which were equipment for the Greek athlete (see chapter 3). Throughout the newly Hellenized territories of Alexander's empire, stadia were constructed,

---

9. Plutarch (AD 46–120) was a Greek writer and biographer.
10. Strabo (64 BC–AD 24) was a Greek geographer, philosopher, and historian.

and cities instituted new athletic festivals. After Alexander's conquests, wealth was abundant in the Greek world. In many of these new festivals, the winners received many prizes of considerable value.

In the Hellenistic period, increasing numbers of people were making athletics their vocation. Athenian Ephebeia had been a compulsory public system of physical and military cadet training for young men eighteen to twenty years old, perhaps from the fourth century BC, but the date of origin of this system is debated (Lynch, 1972). Aristotle described the two-year training of epheboi as part of the present state of the constitution of Athens (Aristotle, *Constitution of Athens*, 42).[11] The physical training of the epheboi was distinct to competitive athletic training (Young, 2004). The two years of training of the epheboi was extremely hard and strict. Their training not only included gymnastic exercises but also riding and the use of weapons during the second year. For practical experience, they were required to serve as patrols on the frontiers of their state. Teaching in wrestling was the most important part of physical education. It was taught progressively as a drill. This instruction was given in pairs or in a group arranged in pairs. Once the pupil had thoroughly learned the movements and techniques, they would be allowed to combine them in loose play or in bouts. Similarly, the preliminary movements of throwing the discus or the javelin would be taught as a drill. The training of the epheboi may have been an important influence on the Greek physique (Gardiner, 1930). Hellenistic cities and monarchs began sponsoring promising young athletes who lacked adequate financial resources for high-level competition at prestigious games.

Civically sponsored training and festival games for citizen epheboi in local gymnasia provided a foundation for further competition and possible careers in athletics (Pleket, 1975). Although athletic and military training were closely related to each other, a man who lacked military skill was viewed as a negative, even if he had prowess as an athlete. Greek athletics flourished and continued to influence festivals and education in the Roman empire. Newby (2005) suggests Greek athletics had a place in Roman leisure and private life with depiction of athletic activity on mosaics in Roman baths, statues of sportsman in elite Roman villas, and the admiration of famous Greek athletes of the past. Greek sport was

---

11. The constitution of the Athenians is a work by Aristotle or one of his pupils. This treatise describes the political system of Athens and was written in the 320s BC.

a prominent and contested topic in Roman imperial literature, such as the works of Pausanias, Lucian, and Philostratus (König, 2005), all of whom feature in this text. High-level Greek athletics found an occupation and a means of social mobility in the Roman empire. Victories brought both fame and wealth. Athletes had to hire specialized and expensive personal coaches who trained and traveled with them—this being equivalent to those professional tennis players of the twenty-first century on the ATP tour. Athletic competitors came from the elite as well as the less-well-off families.

The Romans introduced a new ideal to the games. They were characterized mainly in the boxing events, in which it was not uncommon to see a fighter lose his life or be seriously hurt. No Roman, though, ever entered an athletic event at Olympia (Young, 2004). The Olympic games may have been abandoned in the fourth century AD when the emperor Theodosius I ordered all pagan sites to be destroyed (Sweet, 1987). Young (2004) suggests the Olympic Games continued until at least AD 385 and even into the fifth century AD until Theodosius II reinforced his father's ban on paganism.

1.2: Professionalism in Greek Athletics

Gardiner (1930) described a transition from a golden age of aristocratic amateur athletics in Greece from approximately the sixth and fifth centuries BC to a pattern of decline from the early fifth century BC and onward, when advances in training, specialization, and rewards produced professionalism. Athletics had become more of a spectator sport regarding full-time professionals. Young men could devote more of their time to training due to increasing monetary rewards. The result of increased wealth meant that athletes could employ professional coaches. It was common from the fifth century BC for athletes who were wealthy enough to commission poets to compose odes in celebration of their achievements (Harris, 1964). In the Hellenistic period at many new sporting festivals, winners received prizes of considerable value.

The word *athlete* had come to mean "a professional." Young (2004) suggests the word *athlete* meant "competitor for a prize." A different form of training arose to produce specific body types rather than all round even development, such as the "perfect athletes" in the pentathlon. Trainers prescribed meat diets for the boxing and wrestling events, counteracted by excessive exercise. This regimen aimed at producing more strength and bulk but sacrificed health and beauty. Eating, sleeping, and exercising occupied the athlete's whole time. Plato commented, "The athlete in training is a sleepy creature and his health delicately balanced. Haven't you noticed how they sleep most of their time, and how the smallest deviation from their routine leads to serious illness" (Plato, *Republic* 404a). Plato went on to suggest that there should be a new form of training to produce men fit for war.

Xenophanes[12] also criticized the professional athlete by saying those who had won in sporting events would be little use in war. Gardiner (1930) suggested this degeneration of the physical type was reflected in Greek art. Boxers, according to Gardiner, were represented in fourth-century Panathenaic vases as typical heavyweights with small heads and heavy, clumsy bodies. This is different to boxing scenes represented in fifth-century vases showing a more balanced muscular physique. The absence of weight classification meant that boxing was monopolized by the heavyweights. The second-century BC bronze statue of a seated boxer in the Terme Museum in Rome shows a typical bruiser with his scarred face and cauliflower ears (see chapter 6). According to Gardiner, professionalism led to the sport of boxing being less scientific and more brutal. He suggested the games was degraded by lower-class professionals motivated by profit. Perhaps Gardiner's views on ancient Greek professionalism in sport was slightly biased, as he believed in his own lifetime (1864–1930) that the sport of wrestling had been killed by professionalism and boxers would not fight unless guaranteed a huge purse. He had embraced the Victorian ideologies of athleticism, amateurism, and Hellenism (Kyle, 2015). H. W. Pleket (1975) later challenged Gardiner's views on professionalism. He suggested that ancient Greek athletes regularly competed for valuable prizes and that Olympic victory brought wealth.

Lower-class professionalism arose after Pindar's time. Pleket also suggested Greek athletic contests became open to the lower classes due to the proliferation of the culture of the gymnasium. Athletes saw prizes as gifts, not wages, and not profits; they were a matter of glory. Kyle (2015) interprets professionalism not as a decline but rather a transformation.

---

12. Xenophanes (570–475BC) was a Greek philosopher, poet, and social and religious critic.

Gardiner had said that increased specialization had started to occur in Greek athletics. Young (1996) in König (2005) suggested that the fifth century BC had marked the start of increased diversity in Greek athletics rather than specialization. He gives the example of the athlete Xenophon, who in 464 BC won both the pentathlon and the stadion race (approximately two hundred meters; see chapter 2). The stadion was part of the pentathlon in ancient Greek athletics. In modern athletics, an athlete may have one stronger event in a multievent competition such as the decathlon (consisting of a ten track and field events). This was the one-hundred-meter, in the case of Daly Thompson, who won the Olympic decathlon in 1980 and 1984, although as Young (1996) notes, no modern athlete has won the decathlon and the one-hundred-meter at the same competition. Daly Thompson's personal best (PB) time in the one-hundred-meter was 10.26 seconds. In the 1980 Olympic one-hundred-meter final, his PB would have been good enough to win the bronze medal. The race was won by Alan Wells in a time of 10.25 seconds. In my view, the feat of Xenophon was not an example of increased diversity over specialization. Pausanias also mentions the Greek runner Polites from Ceramus in Caria, who won the equivalent of the modern two-hundred-meter, four-hundred-meter, and five-thousand-meter approximately all in the AD 69 Olympics on the same day (Pausanias, 6.13.3). No athlete in modern athletics of the twenty-first century could achieve this feat. The female athlete Sifan Hassan in the 2019 World Athletic Championships won both the fifteen-hundred-meter and ten-thousand-meter races, which demonstrates that some diversity from middle- to long distance is possible in running events. We may also need to consider that the feat described by Pausanias was an exceptional example and not the norm. Young (2004) suggests that Polites's feat was truly unique in antiquity.

Professionalism in modern sport is related to better training, expertise, and specialization. A modern example of this is the professionalism of rugby union from 1995 onward. Rugby players prior to this period had other jobs and were not able to devote all their time to the sport. Young (1984) argues that the ancient Olympic Games were never amateur. Winners were rewarded in some way financially, providing more time for them to train. Pritchard's (2003) view was that Greek athletics was elitist and only the wealthy had the resources needed for training and gymnastic instruction. It was Plato who commented that selecting a trainer was important, and those able to secure and continue physical training as well as education were the wealthiest:

> Then they send them to the master of gymnastic, in order that their bodies may better minister to the virtuous mind and not be compelled by the weakness of their bodies—This is what is done by those who have the means, and those who have the means are the rich; their children begin to go to school soonest and leave off latest. (Plato, *Protagoras* 325c–326e)

Certainly, family tradition was a factor for equestrian and athletics whereby there was the opportunity and expectation for the wealthy to pursue these activities. This is emphasized by Pindar in his *Pythian Ode for Thrasydaios of Thebes, Winner in the Boy's Short Foot-Race*, Thrasydaios's family had raced chariots in previous games: "Of old for victories in the chariot-race they had bright glory at Olympia in the famous games for the swiftness of their steeds" (Pindar, *Pythian* 11.46). To conclude on professionalism in ancient Greek athletics, it was victory that gained wealth, but wealth helped to gain victory (Kyle, 2015).

CHAPTER 1 SUMMARY

Physical fitness through exercise was important for early civilizations to improve physical performance in war. In Mesopotamia during the third millennium BC, physical performances such as feats of strength were staged at festivals as well as at court. The Hittite empire (1400–1200 BC) had funeral rituals with games like those described by Homer.

Greek civilization started around 1800 BC. The earliest Greeks were the Bronze Age Mycenaeans. They probably had chariot races and boxing performances. Athletics may have originated from the Minoan age of Crete (2000–1200 BC). They had bull leaping and combat sports. A union of cultures from the Mediterranean gave rise to the origin of the Greek people. By the eighth century BC, the Greeks had spread over the whole of the Aegean. In the Archaic period between approximately 750 and 500 BC, city-states started to emerge. Greek city-states were fiercely independent and constantly at war with each other. The rise of sport coincided with the need to have a fit military force ready to defend each city-state. Greek city-states incorporated, expanded, or refounded earlier cultic games to the gods as local athletic festivals with prizes for the victors. The Spartans were arguably the most physically fit society in history. They dominated the Olympic events for 150 years until 576 BC.

The accepted date of the Olympic Games in honor of Zeus is 776 BC, but this is uncertain. A truce forced the city-states to abstain from any kind of armed conflict among them and violations of the truce were considered disrespectful to the gods. By the sixth century BC, the games had become pan-Greek. There were four Panhellenic games: the Olympic, the Pythian, the Isthmian, and the Nemean.

In the Hellenistic period, there was a shift from independent city-states to larger kingdoms and empires. Throughout Alexander's empire, stadia were constructed, and cities instituted new athletic festivals. In many of these new festivals, the winners received many prizes of considerable value. In the Hellenistic and Roman periods, increasing numbers of people were making athletics their vocation. Athens in the fourth century BC had established a compulsory public system of physical and military cadet training for young men eighteen to twenty years old. Greek athletes found an occupation and a means of social mobility in the Roman empire. Victories brought both fame and wealth. The Olympic games were finally abandoned in the fourth century AD.

According to Gardiner, there was a transition from a golden age of aristocratic amateur athletics to a pattern of decline, which produced professionalism. Both Plato and Xenophanes had criticized the professional athlete by saying that their attributes would be little use in war. Kyle interpreted professionalism not as a decline but rather a transformation to produce better trained athletes and specialization. Young suggested that the fifth century BC had marked the start of increased diversity in Greek athletics rather than specialization. Young also argued that ancient Greek athletics were never amateur, and winners were financially rewarded in some way, whereas Pritchard's view was that Greek athletics were elitist and only the wealthy had the resources needed for training and gymnastic instruction.

CHAPTER 2:

THE OLYMPIC GAMES IN ANCIENT GREECE

But if, my heart, you wish to sing of contests, look no further for any star warmer than the sun, shining by day through the lonely sky, and let us not proclaim any contest greater than Olympia.

—Pindar, *Olympic Ode 1*

2.1: The Olympic Games

Athletes attending the games at Olympia had to present themselves at the Sanctuary or at the city of Elis for extensive training a full month before the games. Elis was located about thirty-six kilometers northwest of Olympia. The athletes had to take an oath that for ten successive months, they had strictly followed the regulations for training (Pausanias, 5.24.9). The training period was sometime between early July and early September. This rule may have been introduced during the fourth century BC to ensure the quality of the competition, as athletes in that period started to come from further afield. There were twelve officials appointed to supervise this scrutiny. They were known as the Hellanodikai, or Greek judges. Their responsibilities included the conduct of various purificatory rites, the refereeing of events, the levying of fines for offenses, and the assignment of prizes. Hellanodikai were instructed by the guardians of the law as to their duties at the festival (Pausanias, 6.24.3). They would assess the ability and levels of fitness of competitors so that opponents could be matched accordingly. According to Pausanias, the runners were matched before sunrise, and at midday for the pentathlon, and then later for the heavy events (Pausanias, 6.24.1). This may have ensured fewer one-sided contests and hence better entertainment for the spectators. All those participating in the Olympic Games, including the trainers, athletes, and judges, were required to take an oath in the presence of the statue of Zeus before the competition commenced. The athletes would vouch that they had been in training for the past ten months and would do nothing to bring the games into disrepute. The judges would promise to do their duties fairly and not accept any bribes. This procedure and other sacrifices during the Olympic festival was overseen by three elected priests, or Theokoloi. The judges would make regular checks on athletes and create various categories of size, experience, and ability, for example. The method of assigning the order of bouts, heats, or lanes for racing was not based on ability but decided by the drawing of lots. The date of the Olympics was consistently the second full moon after the summer solstice. The order of events agreed by scholars at the Olympic Games[13] were the chariot racing and the other equestrian contests. Second was the pentathlon, third the footraces, followed by the wrestling, boxing, and the pankration known as the heavy events. Finally, there was a race in armor. The festival lasted five days in total (Christopoulos et al., 2003). A separate day was set aside for all the boys' competitions. The program also included further sacred rites and processions, a grand banquet for all participants, and the prize-giving ceremony (Spivey, 2012).

No victory prizes were on offer for the first five Olympic games. The king of Elis was Iphitos, who, according to Pausanias, did much to formalize the games. After consulting the oracle at Delphi, he decided to award a garland from an olive tree to victors in the Altis of Olympia. The first athlete to be awarded this crown was Daikles, a sprinter from Messene. The victors would make their way to the temple of Zeus, and in the presence of the image of Zeus, they would be presented with their crown of olive leaves. The statue of Zeus was one of the

---

13. This was the order of events when the Olympics was fully established as the "first" Olympic Games in 776 BC only one staged event: the stadion race.

ancient Seven Wonders of the World. It was erected by Pheidias[14] at Olympia in 435 BC. In Zeus's outstretched right hand was held the figure of Nike, the Greek goddess of victory. The victors would also receive a winners' parade on their return to their home cities. Pausanias recorded many Olympic statues in the mid–second century AD. Many of the inscribed bases upon which the statues once stood have now been excavated, and many others have survived as Roman marble copies or adaptations. In the fifth century BC, it was customary for victors of the games to commission poets to compose odes in celebration of their achievements (Harris, 1964). Epinikion poetry, which is a categorical term of reference for the Greek victory ode, would emphasize the effort and exertion required for athletic victory. The earliest Epinikion poet was Simonides of Ceos, who wrote at the end of the sixth century BC, but only a few fragments of his work survive. Pindar was the greatest Epinikion poet of the fifth century BC, with his last poem written in 444 BC (Gardiner, 1930). He only wrote for those who could afford to pay him. According to Pindar, victory did not come without toil, and an athlete needed to develop with hard work the natural talents given to him. This is summed up in Pindar's eleventh ode in honor of Agesidamos, a boxing champion at Olympia: "If one be born with excellent gifts, then may another who sharpeneth his natural edge speed him, God helping, to an exceeding weight of glory. Without toil there have triumphed a very few" (*Olympic Ode* 11). Euripides and Bacchylides were other famous ancient Greek Epinikion poets. In Athens victors would also receive substantial financial awards in addition to their glory of winning the event.

An Athenian inscription dated from 370 BC suggested that between 80 and 120 jars of oil were awarded to the winner of the males' stadion race. There were no prizes for second place. In Athens, beyond this financial award, victors would receive other honors and privileges, including tax exemptions and front row seats at the theater. These benefits of success may have been also extended to the victors' families and even descendants but were paid for by the state. This fact was suggested by Plato in *The Republic*:

---

14. Pheidias (490–430 BC) constructed the figure of Zeus and also constructed the Colossus of Athena for the Parthenon.

Their victory is more distinguished, and their maintenance by the public more complete. Their victory brings security to the whole community, and their reward is that they and their children are maintained and have all their needs supplied at public cost, that they are held in honour by their fellow-citizens while they live and given a worthy burial when they die. (Plato, *Republic* 465d–e)

2.2: Nudity

Male athletes trained and competed in the nude, which was regarded as the norm, but to the Greeks, being naked elsewhere in public was shameful (Kyle, 2015). The exceptions were the chariot riders with their white gowns. "Gymnasium" is translated as "an exercise for which you strip" (Gardiner, 1930). The word *gymnos* means *naked*, and *gymnasion* was a place for nudity (Miller, 2004). There is uncertainty regarding the origin of nudity in Greek athletics.

Mouratidis (1985) suggests that nudity in Greek athletics may have had its roots in prehistoric Greece and was connected with the warrior athlete whose training and competition in the games was at the same time his preparation for war. Thucydides (*Histories*, 1.6. 4–5) believed that the Spartans set the example of competing unclothed and anointing themselves with oil for gymnastic exercise. Thucydides wrote this account around 420 BC but states it was not many years since the custom began. There are a small group of vases dating to the end of the sixth century BC which show all athletes wearing white loincloths. Vase paintings and art after that period may suggest that being nude was a rule in Greek sport. Gardiner (1930) suggests that there may have been an attempt to reintroduce the loincloth at the close of the sixth century; hence, this temporary fashion was mentioned in Thucydides' account. Plato had commented that is was not so long ago that Greeks thought as most of the barbarians still thought: that it was shocking and ridiculous for men to be seen naked.

He goes on to say that first the Cretans and the later the Spartans began to exercise naked (Plato, *Republic* 452c). In Scanlon's view (2014a), athletic culture, including training, nudism, and competition, led to the emergence of pederasty in

Sparta. This spread to other Greek states in the seventh and sixth centuries BC. Certainly, there was a homoerotic component to nakedness, as the gymnasium was a favored place for making approaches between the adult and the younger male. Bonfante (1989) suggests a cultural or religious origin of Greek nudity. She associates nudity for its origin in eighth century religious ritual to a gradual transformation, from initiation rites to a "civic" nudity in the classical period.

This custom of athletic nudity set the Greeks apart from the barbarians. Ancient accounts suggest that Greek athletic nudity began at the Olympiad from 720 BC. This is when the sprinter Orrhippos from Megara won the stadion race but lost his loincloth en route. Pausanias wrote that Orrhippos won the footrace at Olympia by running naked when all his competitors wore girdles, according to the ancient custom. He suggested that Orrhippos had intentionally let the girdle slip off him, realizing a man can run faster without one (Pausanias, 1.44.1). It may have been an advantage to be naked, as a Spartan runner called Akanthos won the diaulos event naked in 724 BC (Scanlon, 2014a). There has been a suggestion by W. E. Sweet, based on experimentation, that the cremaster muscle under certain conditions lifts the testicles and tightens the scrotum during nude workouts, thus reducing the risk of injury, pain, or discomfort (McDonnel, 1993). The cremaster is a loose arrangement of muscle fibers looping around the spermatic cord and testis, forming a cremasteric fascia. It is continuous with the internal oblique muscle and the adjacent part of the inguinal ligament attaching to the pubic tubercle. Contraction of the cremaster pulls the testes toward the superficial ring. The cremaster has a significant role in testicular thermoregulation. The cremaster muscle can be contracted voluntarily together with the lower abdominal or pelvic muscles. Some athletes may have the ability to voluntarily raise their scrota to protect themselves against injury while playing sports, but not all males have this ability (Özdemirkiran and Ertekin, 2011). It is unlikely, though, that the origin of athletic nudity was for pragmatic reasons only. Lucian suggested nudity in athletics could inspire fitness, pride, and military worthiness among the Greeks. It has been generally agreed that nudity at Olympia was not introduced before the late eighth century BC, but by the mid–sixth century BC, it was standard athletic practice (Kyle, 2015).

Another story by Xenophon[15] regarding nakedness also came from Sparta. The commander and king Agesilaos were fighting against the Persians in Asia Minor in 395 BC. He and the rest of his soldiers had just returned from the gymnasium having trained themselves for the deeds of war. Agesilaos gave orders that the barbarians who were captured by the Greek raiding parties should be stripped naked. The Greek soldiers saw these men as white skinned and soft because they were never without their clothing or used to toil. They had not trained in the gymnasium or palaestra. This increased the soldiers' morale because they concluded that the war would be no different from having to fight with females (Xenophon, *Hellenica* 3.4.17–20). From 700 BC onward, statues of young males or kouros figures appeared in their physical prime, usually naked. There was an incentive for the Greek youth to keep themselves in good condition. It was disgraceful to be seen to be flabby, out of condition, or pale skinned (Gardiner, 1930). In chapter 6, we see the anatomical accuracy of these statues showing the musculature of these trained athletes. The Romans despised Greek athletes and were revolted by their nudity. The Etruscans[16] also disliked nudity, and vases for the public market had painted loincloths to cover the athletes' genitalia. They felt it was degrading to strip and compete naked in public. The Christians also had a prudishness about nudity.

2.3: Olympic Events

There were no team competitions in the Olympic Games. Every event was athlete against athlete. Winners were not decided by points, but simply who crossed the line first in the race or who threw the farthest.

2.3.1: Chariot Racing

Chariot racing was the most prestigious event at the Olympic Games and the sport of kings in the Greek world. These races took place in a rectangular area called the Hippodrome, which was to the south of the Olympic stadium. German

---

15. Xenophon (431–354 BC) was a historian, writer, soldier, and student of Socrates.
16. The Etruscan civilization existed from the eighth to the third and second centuries BC. They founded city-states in northern Italy and expanded their influence from the sixth century BC onward.

archaeologists in 2008 using modern geophysical methods possibly discovered the site of the ancient Hippodrome at Olympia. Our knowledge of the Hippodrome at Olympia comes from Pausanias's detailed description in the second century AD. Horse ownership and horse display were features of high social status in Greek society. It was only the rich who could afford the expense of a racing stable. It was the owners of the horses and chariot who claimed the prizes for victories rather than the hired drivers. The *tethrippon* was established in 680 BC (after most of the athletic events had already been established) and was the first event in the Hippodrome. Surviving vase paintings make it possible to see the type of chariot used for racing (Beale, 2011). This was a four-horse chariot race over twelve double laps of the Hippodrome, equivalent to nine miles. There were two central horses attached to a yoke and two outer horses attached by ropes. The one-driver chariots were light, two-wheeled vehicles with metal or wicker cages. The charioteer was usually a slave or professional driver. He would wear a long white robe and would carry a whip. There were as many as forty chariots competing in a single race. The chariots had to race to a turning post, sometimes called a *kampter*, at the far end of the course. In total, twenty-three turns had to be negotiated by the charioteer.

This required great skill, and few chariots were able to complete the race. The next race was the horse race, but the distance was only one lap of six stades (about 1.2 kilometers). This was added to the Olympic program in 648 BC. The jockeys were small boys who rode without shoes or stirrups. In early vases these jockeys are portrayed in the nude. The four-horse chariot race and the horse race were the only events at the Hippodrome in the fifth century BC. In 408 BC, the two-horse chariot race, or *synoris*, was added. This race was over eight laps of the hippodrome, about 9.5 kilometers.

2.3.2: Pentathlon

Homer does not mention the pentathlon. In his funeral games, he mentions the jump, discus, and javelin as separate events with separate prizes. Philostratus also states that before the time of Jason and Peleus, the jump, discus, and javelin were all separate events. In Greek mythology, Jason and the Argonauts were sent by king Pelias of Iolcus to retrieve the Golden Fleece (Waterfield and Waterfield,

2013). On the island of Lemnos, the Argonauts competed in athletic events. Jason, to please Peleus, joined five athletic events together to form the pentathlon, which was such a warlike event that it included the javelin (Phil, *Gym* 3). Plato described the pentathlon as an opportunity for a second-rate performer; for others, it was the supreme test for the all-around (Crowther, 1985). Aristotle states, "Bodily excellence in athletes consists in size, strength and swiftness of foot; for to be swift is to be strong…He who excels in all for the pentathlon" (*Rhetoric*, 1361a). In Etruscan sports, a type of pentathlon may have been performed, including the events of the footrace, discus, long jump, javelin, and wrestling. These five events have never been found painted together. The lost Tomba di Poggio al Moro (in the town of Chiusi, 470–450 BC) shows four of them (Gori, 1986) in Scanlon (2014a).

The pentathlon was introduced into the Olympic Games in 708 BC and had five events: running, jumping, discus, javelin, and wrestling. The jumping, discus, and javelin were only part of the pentathlon and were not separate events. The sequence of events within the pentathlon has been widely disputed. Aristides, the Athenian statesman, stated that only three wins were needed for victory in the pentathlon. "Victor in the first triad" is a frequently occurring inscription (Kyle, 1990). As soon as one competitor had won three events, the others were abandoned, which is a similar format to a five-set match in tennis. Harris (1964) suggests the two throws and the jump were the first three events. This is supported by Matthews (1994) who suggests the '*first triad*' must refer to these events as they were peculiar to the pentathlon. If no competitor won all three, a stadion race was held. If still no winner, then Harris (1964) provides the possible outcomes: Two men with two wins each; one with two wins and two with one each; or four with one win each. In the first scenario the two men wrestled, and the winner has three victories to be crowned champion. In the second scenario the two men with one win each wrestled and the winner of that wrestled the one with two wins in the final. Those wrestling in the preliminary match for the right to challenge the one with two wins for the pentathlon title were at a disadvantage according to Kyle (1990), as they had already wrestled. This may create a one-sided final due to fatigue. Kyle had proposed that the two single event winners would run another footrace to determine the right to wrestle for the title. This event would be quick and still leave the victor in decent shape to contest the wrestling (Lee, 1993).

Sweet (1983) had also rejected the preliminary wrestling contest. He suggested the two single winners would contest an event neither had won, and this would be determined by lot. The use of lots was common in Greece. The opportunity to compete for the second time is known as repechage in modern sport (Sweet, 1987). There is no evidence for these theories. I would agree with Harris's view that a preliminary wrestling match between the two single-event winners would be much more of a spectacle than watching the reprise of an event in which the athletes had already competed.

Finally, in the third scenario, there were two wrestling semifinals and a final to decide the winner. The Spartan Tisamenus (who migrated from Elis) fought Hieronymus of Andros in a wrestling match at Olympia. Herodotus (*Histories*, IX 33.3) says that Tisamenus trained himself for the five contests and came within one wrestling bout for winning the Olympic prize but was conquered by Hieronymus. Pausanias also tells us that Tisamenus trained for the pentathlon at Olympia but came away defeated. He was first in the two events, beating Hieronymus in the footrace and in the leaping match, but he lost the prize because he did not win the wrestling match (Pausanias, 3.11.6). From Pausanias's account this may suggest the footrace and the jump were the first two events of the pentathlon. Was Hieronymus a victor in the discus and javelin and then defeated Tisamenus in the wrestling? Matthews (1994) suggests the possibility that Hieronymus only won one throwing event and contested a wrestling semifinal to reach the final against Tisamenus. Further evidence that the last event was the wrestling comes with Bacchylides in his ninth ode celebrating the victory of Automedes of Phlious in the pentathlon at Nemea:

> That is how he displayed his marvellous physique in front of the huge surrounding crowd of Greeks when throwing the wheel shaped discus and he brought a roar from the spectators when launching from his hand the shaft of dark-leaved elder high in the air; of when wrestling with a flashing move at the end, with such great spirit and strength he brought strong-limbed bodies to the ground. (*Ode* 9. 21–39)

Bacchylides's ode supports the theory that winning three events gained overall victory in the pentathlon as Automedes had won the discus, javelin, and wrestling. This ode also suggests the discus throw preceded the javelin. A very fragmentary inscription from Rhodes indicates the discus event was first followed by the jump and then the javelin (Miller, 1991). Gardner (1880), from his ancient sources, suggests the order of the pentathlon was the jump followed by the discus, javelin, running and finally the wrestling. The order of the events in the pentathlon prior to the wrestling is still uncertain, in my opinion. Also, it has been suggested that if an athlete won two events, he would only have to wrestle once in the final. Bacchylides's ode states, "He brought strong-limb bodies to the ground," (*Ode 9*. 21-39), which may suggest Automedes had to wrestle more than one opponent. If correct, this would dismiss the theory of Kyle, stating that athletes would be too tired to wrestle twice.

The same combination of events as Automedes brought success in the pentathlon to an Ephesian athlete of the second century AD whose name is lost. His incomplete inscription records twenty-seven victories, and he claims he was never beaten in the discus, javelin, or wrestling. Egan's (2007) hypothesis differs slightly from Harris's scheme for deciding the winner. He suggests the whole field competed in all events of the first triad. At the end of the triad, there were three scenarios:

- In the first scenario, one competitor had won all three events and is the overall winner. Therefore, there was no reason to hold the stadion race or the wrestling.

- In the second scenario, one competitor, Alpha, has two victories, and Beta has one. With only two events left, Alpha and Beta are the only ones with a chance to gain the third victory, and the rest of the field is eliminated. Alpha and Beta contest the fourth event. There are two possible outcomes in this case: Alpha wins the stadion and is the overall champion with three victories, or Beta wins the stadion, and the two are tied with two wins each. They proceed to the wrestling, and the winner of this is the champion.

- In the third scenario, three competitors, Alpha, Beta, and Gamma, have one win each after three events; no one else in the field has a chance of winning three events with only two remaining, and these competitors are eliminated. The three event winners go on to compete in the race. Alpha wins the race for his second victory. Since Beta and Gamma have only one victory each, and since there is only one event remaining, neither of them has a chance of winning the two additional victories required for overall victory. Beta and Gamma are then eliminated, and Alpha wins his third event by default, as he is unopposed in the wrestling. The hypothesis is that a third event victory is required to win the pentathlon overall.

Egan's revised scheme would be consistent with the fact that three events wins in the pentathlon were possibly required. In the third scenario, though, having just three competitors in the stadion race and no wrestling contest would not be much of a spectacle for the expectant crowd.

Egan (2007) has proposed an alternative theory of how the winner in the pentathlon was decided. This theory was presented by Evangelos Pavlinis in 1927 according to Egan but was first proposed by Percy Gardner in 1880. Egan suggested that there were preliminary competitions in the pentathlon, matching pairs of competitors in elimination rounds until there were only two left. Hence, there would be a series of competitions between pairs organized by lot, each involving the five events of the pentathlon. In each preliminary competition, the person to win three events would go on to the next competition. This would continue until only one pair remained, who would compete again in the several events of the pentathlon, with the winner of three events crowned the champion. Gardner mentioned that a similar process was used in ancient Greek wrestling, boxing, and the pankration and saw no reason why this did not take place in the pentathlon. Egan illustrated this theory with a field of sixteen competitors and suggested occasional byes would have been necessary in the elimination rounds. Those athletes who competed may have been prearranged prior to the event by officials. He also stated that the one-on-one competitions in the discus, javelin, jump, and stadion races could all have been completed in a matter of minutes, and even in cases where the wrestling event was necessary, this would not have consumed much more time than it would have with the other heavy events in the games (wrestling, boxing, and pankration).

Egan (2007) suggests that in Pavlinis's specification, each one-on-one competition involved all five events but could have been relaxed to allow cases in which a winner was determined after three or four of them. If there were an odd number of competitors, there would be a bye (*ephedros*) in every round until the last one. The same athlete could be the ephedros more than once, being at a great advantage to him.

Gardner (1880) gives the example of five competitors in the pentathlon: A, B, C, D, and E. E is the ephedros. A beats B; C beats D. A, C, and E draw lots again, and perhaps A becomes the ephedros, waiting for the result of a contest between C and E to contest the winner. In my view, it is difficult to imagine these events only taking a few minutes. The preliminary competitions would not be feasible for large numbers of competitors. Christopoulos et al. (2003) suggest the competitors in the pentathlon were many. The pentathlon took place on the third day of the Olympiad after midday in the stadium. There would not be enough time for all the preliminary competitions to be completed. Even if there was a minimum field of sixteen, the eventual winner would potentially have to contest five events on four occasions. Fatigue would be a significant factor in this case, particularly as the athletes would have started to compete under the midday sun. Gardner (1880) had also considered the practical implications of his theory and the time it would take to hold these contests. He suggested that, according to accounts from antiquity, there were only a small number of competitors included in the pentathlon, and this event with his suggested format could be completed in one day. Miller (2004) remarked that it is not certain that the same procedures were followed consistently during the long history of the pentathlon at all competitions in ancient Greece. He also stated that many possible solutions have been proposed how the winner in the pentathlon was decided, but none has the advantage of ancient evidence. We may indeed never know.

2.3.3: Running
The running event used in the pentathlon was the stadion, but this was also a single event among the other various footraces. The stadion originally denoted

an ancient unit of measurement (i.e., one stadion was six hundred ancient feet). The race of that distance acquired the same name. This was essentially a sprint of the running track. This measured 192 meters at Olympia. Legend or myth says it was Heracles who determined the distance of the stadion. For his Fifth Labour, Heracles traveled to Elis with his task to muck out the stables for Augeus, the king, within a single day. This was an impossible task. Heracles diverted two rivers through the stables, and their waters did the job for him with daylight to spare. Heracles was received in the home of Dexamenus of Olympia. It was there that Heracles instituted the games at Olympia by measuring out the length of the stadium where the footraces were to be held. He took a deep breath and sprinted until he had to draw breath again (i.e., exercising anaerobically[17]), and that was the length of the stadium (Waterfield and Waterfield, 2013). The Olympic festivals up to the Thirteenth Olympiad (776–724 BC) consisted of the stadion only. In the stadion, the runners were depicted with their knees high and arms extended, as if they were sprinting down the track (Miller, 2004). The field of runners in the stadion race was probably large, so preliminary heats were held with the winner of the heats progressing to the final (Gardiner, 1930). The sprint or stadion race and wrestling were regarded as the best expressions of speed and strength, respectively. Mythologically, strength was represented by Heracles and speed by Hermes, two divinities most worshipped in the gymnasium. The stadion race like the one-hundred-meter in modern times carried the highest prestige. We have no means of estimating the performance of ancient Greek runners or comparing them with those of the modern era.

2.3.4: The Jump (Halma)

The jumping event was part of the pentathlon and not a single event. There was a takeoff board, or *balbis* (*bater*), made of wood or stone, with the final landing made in a sand pit or *skamma*. The landing pit was fifty feet long (Lenoir et al., 2005). After the jump, the athlete placed a wooden peg called a semeion in the sand to mark his performance (Patrucco, 1972). The jump, or halma (from the verb *hallomai*, "to jump"), was practiced with dumbbells or halteres. Athletes

---

17. Anaerobic exercise is any activity that breaks down glucose for energy without using oxygen. These activities are generally of short duration and high intensity such as sprinting.

carried their halteres in their hands to gain extra forward momentum and to achieve further distance. The jumping weight, according to Philostratus, was an invention of the pentathletes. Some authors claim that the halteres were dropped before landing (Kyle, 2015), while others suggest that they were swung backward but retained at the landing to gain that extra distance (Jüthner and Brein, 1968). There is no evidence that Greek jumpers dropped the halteres in midair. Vase paintings depict jumpers in midair, landing with the halteres still in their hands. Aristotle mentioned that athletes jump farther if they have the weights in their hands than if they have not (Aristotle, *Progression of Animals* 3, 705a, 17–19). These halteres varied in weight between two and five kilograms. Minetti and Ardigo (2002) used computer and experimental simulations to determine whether it was possible to extend jumping distance by using the halteres. They calculated that the halteres would increase a three-meter jump by seventeen centimeters. This study was criticized by Renson (2019), as the simulation was for a vertical and not a horizontal jump. It is not known how many attempts were allowed for each competitor in jumping or throwing events. An inscription mentioned in section 2.3.2 discovered near a stadium at Rhodes in the first century BC or AD contained regulations for the pentathlon. The term "five times" occurs in a place that suggests that it may well refer to the number of throws allowed for each competitor in the discus event. This inscription is in a very fragmentary condition, and this number may not be certain (Harris, 1964; Miller 1991).

Phayllos, a fifth-century BC champion of the pentathlon, was said to have recorded a jumping distance of over fifty feet at the Delphic games. He won at Delphi in 482 BC and 478 BC but never won at Olympia, as he was fighting against the Persians at the time of the Olympics in 480 BC (Miller, 2004). Phayllos's feats were recorded in the following epigram: "Phayllos jumped five feet more than 50 feet and threw the discus five feet less than 100 feet" (Gardiner, 1904). He jumped five feet beyond the skamma and was said to have broken his leg in the performance (Gardiner, 1930). A Delphic foot measured 29.6 centimeters, implicating that Phayllos jumped 16.28 meters and threw the discus 28.12 meters (Lenoir et al., 2005). It is agreed that this epigram is dated to the fifth century BC. The second recorded jump is one of fifty-two feet by Chionis of Sparta, mentioned by Pausanias, who was a winner of the stadion race and the Diaulos in three Olympiads between 664 and 656 BC. The Olympic foot was 0.32 meters, suggesting that Chionis jumped 16.66 meters. Both Crowther (1985) and Young (2004) suggest from their sources that Chionis's jump was twenty-two feet and not fifty-two. There is an incomplete grave inscription at Delos, which could mention a third jump of fifty feet (Ebert, 1963), cited by Lenoir et al. (2005). These are three independent accounts of jumping distances that may suggest their reliability.

The distances of jumps and throws were rarely recorded in antiquity, but jumps were measured as stated by Philostratus. He said that the laws of the jump indicate a precise landing is necessary. Unless the footprint is perfect with a precise landing, they will refuse to measure the jump (Phil, *Gym* 55). Gardiner (1930) suggests the jump was measured by rods, and the individual jumps were marked by pegs in the ground, as previously mentioned. A sixth century amphora depicts three such pegs marking the jumps of previous athletes. This is a Tyrrhenian amphora found near Rome from 540 BC showing athletes and a combat scene. It may be assumed that ancient Greek athletes could jump fifty feet using the halteres. Mike Powell's long-jump world record achieved in 1991 was 8.95 meters, or just over 29 feet. It may be unlikely, then, that Phayllos's feat or the others mentioned were single jumps but were sequences of jumps. Gardiner believed that the Greek jump was only single and assumed epigrams were wild exaggerations. Young (2004) describes the Phayllos long-jump feat as pure fiction. He also states that ancient depictions from vases show jumpers running with weights and taking off with one foot. Literary sources regarding the jump are very sparse, and we are almost exclusively dependent on iconographic sources. Vase paintings as the main source of information may be unreliable. It is not known whether the actual event is depicted accurately by the artist or is an image of a training activity. Renson (2019) provides updated comprehensive literature on the jump event and concludes that this was probably a single jump. He suggests from visual evidence that the pentathletes competing in the jump started from a spread position with the halteres in their hands.

Then followed a run-up with the halteres swung rhythmically, followed by a takeoff on the balbis with the arms swung up high. During the flight phase, the arms are first swung forward and just before landing backward and forward again to secure a stable landing with clear footmarks.

A theory formulated by Bob Spaak in the 1960s suggested that the jump included a run-up of 10.5 meters from the border of the stadion to the stone balbis (Renson, 2019). From this theory, it was implied that the overall distance achieved included a standardized 10.5-meter (34-foot) run-up, which would mean the athlete would have to jump an additional 16 feet to achieve those distances of 50 feet recorded. Renson (2019) hints that ancient Greek jumpers were capable of this distance. The discus of Phayllos's time in the fifth century BC was the same weight as the modern discus. His discus throw was poor by modern standards and not exaggerated, which could indicate his jump was a true measure. Why have a landing pit of fifty feet if it was not necessary? Themistius, a scholar from the fourth century AD, on his commentary on Aristotle's *Physics*, cites that the long jump was not a continuous movement, but that during the jump, "some amount of time and space is taken out" (Harris, 1964; Lenoir et al., 2005). As a single jump may have been unlikely, according to some scholars, several forms of multiple jumps have been proposed. A type of triple jump has been suggested. The world record of the triple jump is 18.29 meters, set by Jonathan Edwards in 1995, with standard international performances of 17 meters, which is in keeping with Phayllos's feat. The triple-jump hypothesis has not passed practical tests, with the halteres causing coordination problems. Lenoir et al. (2005) proposed a series of five standing broad jumps with a continuous movement, which would achieve the jumping distances recorded in antiquity. Sweet (1987) states there was no solid ancient evidence to support the theory of multiple jumps in this event. In my opinion, after reviewing the literature and iconography, the halma was likely a single jump, with the run-up included in the total distance achieved. Philostratus states that the rules regarding jumping are some of the most difficult, and therefore the jumper is stimulated with flute playing and lightened further by using the jumping weight (Phil, *Gym* 55).

No doubt the jumping event was more complex than it seems, with technique and rhythm aided by music, and distance increased by using the halteres.

2.3.5: Discus
The discus began as a stone platter and evolved into one of bronze and iron. Plummer (1897) suggested the discus was originally invented for athletic purposes

only and not directly associated with the feats of war. Philostratus also considered discus throwing to be a heavy event (Phil, *Gym* 3). The average weight of the discus is estimated to be around 2 kilograms, based on surviving ones from antiquity, but examples of up to 6.5 kilograms have been found (Lenoir et al., 2005). This average weight is the same weight as the modern discus. The discus throw in the Hellenic world was performed from a standing position with no run-up. There is also evidence of discus throwing in Etruscan sport seen on frescoes, painted pottery, and bronzes, which may have been inspired by the Greeks. A painted wall of the Tomba delle Olimpiadi (Tarquinia, 520 BC) shows a discus thrower moving with his left arm in front of him and his right behind, to give a greater thrust to the discus. According to Gori (1986) in Scanlon (2014a), from this position of the thighs, it seems he is running up to throw the discus. It is argued that the Etruscans may have adapted their throwing technique of the discus from the Greeks. As mentioned earlier, Phayllos threw the discus 28.12 meters. The discus-throwing distance at the London Olympic Games in 1908 was thirty-eight meters, using the ancient Greek style of throwing technique (Lenoir et al., 2005). The world record set by Jürgen Schult in 1986 was 74.08 meters.

2.3.6: Javelin
In the Olympics, the javelin event or *akon* throw was part of the pentathlon. The javelin was shaped from light elder wood and tipped with bronze (Miller, 2004). The javelin was partly bound up by a loose cord, which the thrower used to give extra pull and spin on the shaft at the time of release. As depicted on vase paintings, the javelin was held between the middle finger and forefinger, with the cord looped onto one or both fingers. The thrower took a few steps forward, extended his throwing arm, and then threw the javelin on an upward trajectory. The rotary motion imparted by the untwisting cord would keep the javelin in the air for longer and increase the distanced achieved. Measuring rods were used to determine the distance thrown, and the winner was determined by the length of the throw (Miller, 2004; Sweet, 1987).

Little is known in antiquity regarding the performance in the javelin or the distances achieved. Harris (1964) suggested that the best ancient Greek throwers could throw was well over three hundred feet. The current javelin world record of 98.48 meters, or 323 feet, was set by Jan Železný in 1996.

2.3.7: Wrestling

Wrestling was the oldest and most widespread of all sports in ancient Greece. There were two styles of Greek wrestling distinguished. This was upright wrestling or wrestling proper, used in the pentathlon. The objective was to throw one's opponent to the ground. The other type of wrestling was ground wrestling, in which the struggle was continued on the ground until one of the wrestlers acknowledged defeat. Ground wrestling was not used in competition except in the pankration (Gardiner, 1930).

Wrestling was the principal activity of the palaestra, and in my opinion, also used as a training exercise for all athletes (see chapter 5). It was perhaps the final discipline of the pentathlon but also a single event in the games. The Eleans took charge of training for the wrestling and other heavy events prior to the games. This training would be the same pre-contest and competition, which would be a test of the athlete's ability. The ancient Greeks had no classes for different weights but only for different age groups (Harris, 1964). There were no timed rounds, but a bout ended when a throw was made that left the opponent on the ground. The wrestling bouts contested were a minimum of three and a maximum of five (Beale, 2011). Philostratus stated that three falls were needed for victory (Phil, *Gym* 11).

2.3.8: Boxing

Philostratus said that boxing was a Spartan invention. The Spartans had no helmets, nor did they think it proper to fight in helmets (Miller, 2004). They practiced boxing to protect themselves from blows to the face and endure when they were struck, although, according to Philostratus, the Spartans gave up boxing and the pankration in competition, as it was disgraceful for them to admit defeat. Greeks in general never shook hands after a fight, and no Greek was ever the first to congratulate his conqueror. Boxing was introduced at the Twenty-Third Olympiad in 688 BC. There was no regular ring, so there was no opportunity of cornering an opponent or fighting on the ropes. There were no rounds, and competitors fought to the finish (Gardiner, 1930).

The training for boxing, unlike the wrestling, required the boxer only to perform a "shadow of real competition" (Phil, *Gym* 11). This may be a reference to sparring or shadowboxing. There were no weight categories in ancient boxing, which may have made the event the monopoly of the heavyweight athlete. Boxers used tightly wrapped thongs instead of padded gloves. Philostratus describes that the four fingers were wrapped in a soft band and projected beyond the band far enough to be formed into a fist when clenched together. They were then held together in a fist shape by a strap attached to the forearm as a support (Phil, *Gym* 10). Pausanias describes the boxing contest between Creugas of Epidamus and Damoxenus of Syracuse at the Nemean Games. In a famous story, Damoxenus supposedly struck Creugas under the ribs with three fingers outstretched. His sharp nails pierced Creugas's flesh, and he ripped out his guts, killing him. Damoxenus was disqualified by the judges, who awarded the wreath to Creugas (Renshaw, 2015). Pausanias, with reference to this contest, stated that boxers at that time did not wear a sharp thong on the wrist of each hand but still boxed with soft gloves. These were bound in the hollow of the hand so that their fingers might be left bare (Pausanias, 8.40.3). These "gloves" were called *himantes* and were made from oxhide.

By the middle of the fourth century BC, these soft himantes were replaced by harder himantes. A hard and protruding knuckle guard made from laminated leather strips was added. This increased protection to the knuckles and damage done to the opponent (Miller, 2004). In contrast, Philostratus suggests that in his day, a sharp, projecting boxing glove was made from cow's hide so that the thumb did not join the fingers in order to avoid excessive wounding. For this reason, gloves made from pigskin were banned to avoid blows that were painful and slow to heal (Phil, *Gym* 10). It is stated that in Roman imperial times, Greek boxing deteriorated and became more brutal, with boxers wearing a cestus, or ancient battle glove made with leather strips. It was commonly loaded with lead and glass fragments. A single punch could be fatal (Miller, 2004).

2.3.9: Pankration
The Pankration probably was the most brutal of the heavy events but was the most respected. This event was introduced at the Olympic program relatively late, in 648 BC. It was a combination of wrestling and boxing. It can be translated as "total force" and was mostly "no holds barred" (Young, 2004). Biting and gouging out the eyes were prohibited. Training for the pankration only involved practice of some techniques at a time and was not full on. There were no timed bouts but a single fight to the finish. The bout came to an end with submission or surrender, signaled by a hand gesture. The referee would thrash the fighters with sticks if they needed to be separated.

2.3.10: Other Running Events
Apart from the stade or stadion race, there were the diaulos, or "double furrow," which was up and down the stadium going around a turning point (*kampter*) at one end. The diaulos was run in lanes marked in lime, with each runner turning around their individual turning post. The length of the diaulos was two stades, or about four hundred yards (Gardiner, 1930). This race was introduced at the Fourteenth Olympiad in 724 BC. The dolichos, introduced in 720 BC, consisted of several stadium lengths ranging from twelve to twenty-four lengths (approximately two thousand to five thousand meters). In this race, runners rounded a single kampter. At the stadium in Nemea, a base has been found for this single turning post. Runners in the dolichos can be identified in paintings in which the runner's knees are low and barely bent, with the arms drawn in close to the sides (Miller, 2004). The Spartan Acanthus was the first winner of this event. According to Philostratus, the origin of the dolichos came from couriers from Elis who used to go backward and forward into the rest of Greece as messengers (Rusten and König, 2014). In fact, their role was to announce the Olympic truce, which allowed both athletes and spectators to travel to the games without military interference. Philostratus goes on to state that these messengers were forbidden to use horses and instead were made to depend on their own ability as runners (Phil, *Gym* 4).

The hippios was a race over four stades, approximately eight hundred yards. This race was not run at Olympia but at Isthmia, Nemea, Athens, Epidaurus,

Argos, and Plataea. There was no standard length of the athletic stadia, and this would have varied from every site to city-state. The stadion, as mentioned, was used by the Greeks as a routine unit of measurement. There were no timed records kept. It would have been extremely difficult to time races in antiquity. Both short- and long-distance runners used a natural standing position from the start.

Runners are depicted upon Panathenaic prize vases as having muscular thighs or quadricep muscles, large biceps, and an upper body. This may represent the muscular physique of a sprinter, particularly the images of males of the stadion race depicted on Panathenaic prize amphora from around 550 to 560 BC. In my opinion, though, some of these images appear to be distorted with exaggerated large thighs, almost like a caricature, and they do not represent the true anatomical form of the sprinter. In the text of Christopoulos et al. (2003), a runner in the stadion race is represented in scenes as running with his legs apart in a long stride, his body slightly inclined forward and his arms swinging vigorously, whereas in the dolichos, their strides are short, with hardly any arm swing held at waist level and the body completely upright. Training for the running events was harder than the Olympic contests. Those training for the dolichos event would train by running eight or ten stades. Races in the stadium were run on bare feet over a surface of sand. There was a starting line according to an order decided by lot (there were twenty starters at a time at Olympia). At the starting line, there was a stone slab with grooves or toeholds cut in. This provided an early version of a starting block for the runners and ensured equality in the lineup. At Isthma there was a wooden barrier or gate, from which runners were released at the pull of a cord. There were different races for different ages, and it is possible that the races for the boys were shorter than those for the men (Gardiner, 1930).

The hoplitodromos, or hoplite, was the race in armor. This race was a sprint over two lengths of the stadium and was introduced at the Sixty-Fifth Olympiad in 520 BC (Beale, 2011). Athletes were required run in full armor wearing helmets and metal greaves below the knees. They also had to run carrying a large shield. The shield was the main protective device of the ancient Greek infantry soldier. Philostratus agreed that the hoplite race was originally invented for military reasons and believed this race was included in the contests as a reminder of the resumption of warfare, and that the shield signified that the truce was over and weapons were necessary again (Phil, *Gym* 7).

Although the Olympic Games did not result in suspension of all fighting in the Greek world. The best of the hoplite races, according to Philostratus, was the one at Plataea. This was because of the length of the race (although not given by any ancient source) and the armor used, which stretched down to the feet, covering the athletes completely, as if they were fighting. The festival in which this race took place was the Eleutheria at Plataea. This festival was founded to commemorate the defeat of the Persians in 479 BC and was held every four years (Rusten and König, 2014). This race is mentioned by Pausanias, who stated that great prizes were offered for running. The competitors ran in armor before the altar (Pausanias, 9.2.6).

In ancient times, there were no Marathon races, but feats of running endurance were recorded. Herodotus (*Histories*, 6.105–106) mentions how Pheidippides, an Athenian herald, or hemerodrome,[18] was sent to Sparta by his generals. He ran 150 miles from Athens to Sparta in two days to ask the Spartans for help against the Persians (Miller, 2004). The Spartans were unable to help immediately due to an important festival in honor of Apollo. In another later story by Lucian, Pheidippides, a messenger, is said to have brought news to Athens regarding the victory at Marathon in 490 BC (Gardiner, 1930). He ran from Marathon to Athens, announced the victory and died. This is probably an ancient myth.

Plutarch suggests it was Eucles who took the news of the battle of Marathon to Athens. In *Moralia* 347c, he states:

> Again, the news of the battle of Marathon Thersippus of Eroeadae brought back, as Heracleides Ponticus relates; but most historians declare that it was Eucles who ran in full armour, hot from battle and, bursting in at the doors of the first men of the state, could only say, "Hail! we are victorious!" and straightway expired.

Plutarch in *Aristides* (20.5) also tells the story of Euchidas who ran from Plataea to Delphi and back after the battle of Plataea in 479 BC. He promised to bring back the sacred fire from the altar of Apollo. He arrived before sunset, covering a total of one thousand stades in the same day (approximately 114 miles)

---

18. *Hemerodrome* is translated as a day runner or courier trained to deliver messages on foot (Kyle, 2015).

but expired due to his exertions (Beale, 2011; Plummer, 1898a). The marathon race over forty kilometers, or twenty-five miles, was first introduced to the Olympics in 1896.

The official distance of the modern marathon today is 26 miles and 385 yards, which was introduced to the Olympic Games in 1908. This was the distance from Windsor Castle to the Royal box at the London Olympic Stadium,[19] not the distance between Athens and Marathon (between twenty-one and twenty-six miles).

2.4: Homer's Games

The questions as to whether Homer existed or that his poems were written by a single person are beyond the scope of this text. Scanlon (2014a) suggests that Homer's account may have come from earlier sources and that the funeral games of Patroclus (*Iliad* 23) was written by a different author using other parts of *The Iliad* as a reference. Whatever the origins of Homer, his poems provide us with descriptions of sports that may have been passed down to him from the Mycenaean age and an insight into the events that formed part of the Olympic Games. Games or sporting events are mentioned by Homer in both *The Iliad* and *The Odyssey*. In *The Iliad*, the games were part of a funeral ritual for Patroclus, whereas in *The Odyssey*, they were more for entertainment. Homer alludes to funeral games other than the one for Patroclus. For example, old Nestor recalls his prowess in the funeral games for King Amarynceus.

He described winning the boxing, wrestling, footrace, and javelin but lost in the chariot race (*Iliad* 23; Kline, 2009).[20] Homer also mentions Euryalus in the boxing match who had once come to Thebes for the funeral games of fallen Oedipus (*Iliad* 23; Johnston, 2010).

Patroclus was Achille's friend, killed by the Trojan prince Hector. Achilles took his revenge by driving a heavy bronze blade through Hector's unprotected neck and then dragged his corpse by chariot. The funeral games for Patroclus were lavish events with substantial prizes given for the competitors. Achilles sent for prizes from the ships: cauldrons, tripods, horses, mules, sturdy oxen and female

---

19. The Olympic Stadium for the summer Olympics of 1908 was located at White City, London (the White City Stadium).
20. All translations of *The Iliad* and *The Odyssey* quoted in 2.4 are available online.

slaves. Both commanders and soldiers competed in the games. The competitors were not participating for fun but wanted to win at whatever cost. A desire to be the best is a feature of classical Greek culture (Spivey, 2012). There were eight contests, starting with the chariot race, followed by the boxing, wrestling, footrace, armed combat, discus, archery, and finally the javelin. More space in Homer's *Iliad* is devoted to the chariot race than all the other events put together.

The chariot race was the first event with five competing chariots. Prizes were a female skilled in fine handiwork and a tripod with ear-shaped handles holding twenty-two measures for the winner. A six-year-old mare was the prize for the runner-up. Third place received a brand-new gleaming cauldron holding four measures, and for fourth place, two talents of gold were given. The person in fifth place received a brand-new two-handled cooking dish. Gardiner (1930) and Young (2004) suggest a two-horse war chariot was used in the race and not a four-horse chariot, as used in the Olympic Games from 680 BC. Gardiner's view is supported by the following passage from *The Iliad*: "After Diomedes came fair-haired Menelaus, royal son of Atreus, driving a yoked team, two fast creatures-his own horse Podargus and Agamemnon's mare Aethe" (*Iliad* 23; Johnston, 2010).

In the footrace there were three runners. This race was run on flat ground, as Achilles said: "Who hope the palm of swiftness to obtain, stand forth, and bear these prizes from the plain...Ranged in a line the ready racers stand; Pelides points the barrier with his hand: All start at once" (*Iliad* 23; Pope, 2016). There is the possibility that Homer is describing an early starting mechanism that was used in the running events at later sporting festivals such as at Nemea and Isthmia. This starting mechanism, called the *hysplex*, was used in the footraces at least by the fifth century BC. The earliest form of the hysplex had come from Isthmia. The system consisted of a series of hinged gates that served as barriers for the runners. Each gate was controlled by a cord that could be pulled or released by the starter, causing the gate to fall and thus allowing the runner to take off, with all runners starting at the same time (Miller, 2004). We don't know how long the race in *The Iliad* was, but the runners had to turn at the post and run back to the starting place: "as Achilles pointed out the turning post, the racecourse was the distance there and back" (*Iliad* 23; Johnston, 2010). Homer described perhaps as a short race or the just the competitors were running at a fast pace: "the youths contending in the rapid race" (*Iliad* 23; Pope, 2016). There are some similarities with the diaulos, introduced in 724 BC. In the diaulos of the Olympic Games, runners were required to up and down the stadium, going around their individual turning post or a single kampter. In Homer's version, there is a single turning post for the three runners. Ajax was winning the footrace with Odysseus close behind: "God like Odysseus ran so close his breath touched the back of Ajax's head." Unfortunately, Ajax slipped when Odysseus prayed to Athena for assistance, and Odysseus raced on to win. Young Antilochus came third. Antilochus accepted defeat and said no one could keep up with Odysseus except for Achilles (*Iliad* 23; Johnston, 2010).

The wrestling bout was between Odysseus and the towerlike Ajax: "Achilles next demands and calls the wrestlers to the level sands…The wrestlers entered the ring (or form of skamma), and came to grips, clasping each other in their mighty arms" (*Iliad*, 23; Kline, 2009). The two wrestlers were locked in combat in a form of upright wrestling rather than ground wrestling. This ancient form of wrestling starts from a standing position with the objective to throw the opponent to the ground but not pin the opponent down (Miller, 2004). Wrestling was added to the Olympic program in 708 BC as a separate discipline and as part of the pentathlon (Beale, 2011). Odysseus kicked Ajax hard in the back of the knee, so taking out his leg, toppling him backward, and he fell on his chest. The legs were used in wrestling to trip or lever the opponent off balance, as described by Homer here. Gardiner (1930) suggests that as both wrestlers fell together, the bout was inconclusive. I believe this bout was awarded to Odysseus, as he fell upon Ajax's chest, which was counted as a throw to the ground in upright wrestling. Also, afterward, "shouts of applause run rattling through the skies," further suggesting a winner of the first bout (*Iliad* 23; Pope, 2016). Harris (1964) also suggests Odysseus wins the first bout, but victory was not bought by one throw (Plummer, 1897). Odysseus in the second bout tried to lift Ajax but failed to lift him more than a fraction. Then Ajax hooked him with his leg around the knee, so the two men fell side by side on the ground, smothered in dust. The second bout would have gone to Ajax in my view, but this bout could have been inconclusive. They then prepared to wrestle again for a "third fall," but Achilles called it a draw (*Iliad* 23; Johnston, 2010).

In the boxing event, the competitors wore loincloths, which accords with boxers in earlier cultures (Kyle, 2015). The boxers in Homer's games used gloves:

"And to his wrists the gloves of death are bound" (*Iliad* 23; Pope, 2016). Euryalus buckled on his belt and bound the oxhide thongs carefully on his hand: "When the two men had laced up their hands, they strode into the middle of the group" (*Iliad* 23; Johnston, 2010). Homer is describing the himantes, which were leather straps wrapped around the wrist and knuckles. This leaves the fingers free so that the boxer could clench his fist to deliver a blow, as emphasized by Homer: "Epeius dealt a weighty blow, full on the cheek of his unwary foe" (*Iliad* 23; Pope, 2016). Epeius was the builder of the Trojan horse (*Odyssey* 8; Murray, 1919). These thongs worn by the boxers in *The Iliad* are like those worn by Greek boxers in the fifth century BC. Two events in Homer's games were not contested in Olympia. These were the armed contests after the race and archery, at which the target was a dove fastened to the ship's mast.

Plutarch suggested that armed contests did at one time take place at Olympia. There is evidence that armed combat was a feature of funeral games in the Greek world, as depicted on a Dipylon amphora or vase from the eighth century BC. Archery was part of the training of the epheboi, and there were local competitions for it, but not in the Olympic games (Gardiner, 1930).

The throwing events in *The Iliad* were the quoit and javelin. Homer indicates that only one attempt was allowed for each competitor, whereas in the Olympic Games, up to five throws may have been allowed (Harris, 1964). The quoit or discus was made from iron: "Then hurled the hero, thundering on the ground, a mass of iron, an enormous round, whose weight and size the circling Greeks admire, rude from the furnace, and but shaped by fire" (*Iliad* 23; Pope, 2016). In post-Homeric times, the discus became smaller and lighter. Homer hints at the technique of throwing the quoit: "And from his whirling arm dismiss in air. That teach the disc to sound along the sky" (*Iliad* 23; Pope, 2016) and "Godlike Epeius gripped the weight, swung it round, then threw" (*Iliad* 23; Johnston, 2010). It was Polypoetes who threw the quoit the farthest. The quoit throw was different from the other events, as there was only one victor and one prize: the rough-cast iron. Kyle (2015) suggests the single prize of iron comes from Homer's contemporary world. The javelin event was to close the games: "Then the warriors got up for the spear-throw competition" (*Iliad* 23; Johnston, 2010). There was to be no throwing. Achilles awarded the first prize to Agamemnon on the grounds of his reputation for throwing the spear better than anyone else. The spear was given to the warrior Meriones on Agamemnon's agreement.

In *The Odyssey*, Odysseus was grounded on the fictional island of Phaeacia. He is welcomed by the local people and entertained by king Alcinous at a banquet. After the banquet, the minstrel sings about the Trojan war, which makes Odysseus very sad and brings back unhappy memories. Alcinous, seeing this, invites Odysseus to the Phaeacian games, including running, wrestling, boxing, and the discus (Gardiner, 1930). The first trial was the footrace, followed by "the painful sport" of wrestling, then the jump, discus, and lastly the boxing, won by Laodamas, son of king Alcinous. In *The Odyssey*, Homer gives little detail regarding the athletic events except for the footrace.

There was no chariot race. The footrace was contested on a course laid out for them on markers. This race was a sprint on dusty ground: "They all sprinted off, moving quickly. A cloud of dust rose from the ground" (*Odyssey* 8; Kline, 2004). Again, we do not know the length of the race, but the runners had to run a distance, possibly turning and running back: "Clytoneus was by far the finest runner, so he raced ahead and got back to the crowd, leaving the others behind" (*Odyssey* 8; Johnston, 2010). A turning point is also mentioned: "A course was marked out for them from the turning point" (*Odyssey* 8; Murray, 1919). Laodamas said after the contests, "Friends let's ask the stranger whether he is practiced in any familiar sport" (*Odyssey* 8; Kline, 2004). Laodamas then challenged Odysseus to prove himself in sport. Odysseus politely refused (Waterfield and Waterfield, 2013). Euryalus then mocked Odysseus, saying that he looked like a man unused in manly sports: "Thou dost not look like an athlete" (*Odyssey* 8; Murray, 1919). This is Homer's single use of the term *athlete* (Kyle, 2015). This angered Odysseus; he leaped to his feet and seized a discus bigger than the rest, thicker and heavier, not normally used by the Phaeacians in competition. It was the goddess Athena appearing in disguise to mark the throw. Odysseus threw the discus past any other marks. Instead of being made from iron, the discus in *The Odyssey* was made from stone: "With a whirl, he sent it flying from his powerful hand; the stone made a humming sound as it flew along" (*Odyssey* 8; Johnston, 2010). Odysseus then asked anyone else to prove himself in the other events but said that they may beat him at running due his weakened legs from his long journey. King Alcinous replied, "We may not be the greatest boxers or wrestlers, but we run fast and excel in seamanship, dancing, and song." The Phaeacians then put on a show of dancers and Demodocus's ringing lyre (*Odyssey* 8; Kline, 2004).

Some scholars suggest Homer's account of the funeral games for Patroclus in *The Iliad* was part of tradition that came down to him from the twelfth century BC. This was an oral transmission, and the text was composed without writing (Wood, 2005). He may also have been giving an account of athletics in his own period of the eighth century BC, when the Olympic Games may have been founded. According to Plummer (1897) with good evidence, the portion of *The Iliad* that describes the javelin, discus and archery contests is a late interpolation. This was considered as data for an account of athletics of later times. Young (2004) suggests an approximate date of 725 BC when Homer composed his poems. Homer's account does reveal a well-organized athletic program, but the events are informal with no organized training. Homer does not describe any techniques of the events, but there are limitations in poetry for these descriptions. Homer does provide a vivid account of the athletic events, such as the wrestling and boxing. This would perhaps suggest he had observed or participated in these contests at some point and not just relied on stories past down to him. The athletics described in Homer's poems are more closely associated with the events at Olympia than those of the Bronze Age period. The prize of pig iron would give the winner "a supply of iron for five years, and neither his shepherd nor his ploughman will have to go to the city for iron but will have it already at home" (Miller, 2004).

This suggests that Homer's games are not set in a Bronze Age. Further evidence to support this is the prize for the wrestling "a great tripod for standing on the fire" (Robinson, 1955). The bronze tripod described dates from the eighth to the seventh centuries BC and not from the Bronze Age period. The chariot race is the main event in *The Iliad*, but in the Bronze Age, chariots were used mainly for hunting or warfare and not for sport, although images of chariot racing have been found from the Mycenaean period (Harris, 1964). Homer does mention a four-horse chariot in *The Iliad*: "Holy Elis owed him (Neleus of Pylos) an enormous debt—four prize-winning horses with their chariot, which had come to Elis to compete, intent on racing for a tripod" (*Iliad* 11; Johnston, 2010). The four-horse chariot, or tethrippon, otherwise not mentioned by Homer elsewhere, was introduced to the Olympic Games in 680 BC. This may imply that Homer's writings must postdate the introduction of this chariot race to the Olympic Games in 680 BC. Kyle (2015) suggests that this chariot event at Elis described by Homer had nothing to do with the Olympic Games and was likely a later interpolation. There are differences, though, between Homer's account and the events at Olympia. There are no sacred oaths, processions, or preparations for facilities (Kyle, 2015). Athletes in Homer did not compete in the nude, and prizes were given for second and even last place in *The Iliad*. In the Phaeacian Games, there were no prizes, and athletes competed for the sheer joy of the contest.

Homer's games may appear less developed, with a tree stump used for a turning post, a road filled with ruts for the chariot race, and a lump of iron or stone for the discus; a natural stone object found on the Greek landscape would be convenient to demonstrate the athlete's skill and strength in throwing. The sporting events described in both *The Iliad* and *The Odyssey* are not from the period of the Trojan War but from Homer's time in the eighth century BC (Miller, 2004). Herodotus puts the date of the Trojan War at 1250 BC. Hisarlik is the location generally agreed as the site of ancient Troy, also known as Ilion. This site is in Turkey near the modern city of Canakkale. Schliemann, a German archaeologist, began excavations at this site in 1873. Troy VII is an archaeological layer of Hisarlik that chronologically spans from 1300 BC to 950 BC. It coincides with the collapse of the Bronze Age and is thought to be the Troy mentioned by Homer as the site of the Trojan War (Wood, 2005).

In contrast to the athletic events, Homer has described artifacts from the Trojan War, which are from the Bronze Age and existed long before his time. For example, the tower-shaped body shield associated with Ajax represented on the Thera frescoes was already obsolete by the thirteenth century BC. The figure of eight shield occurs in thirteenth-century frescoes from Mycenae. An example of the wild boar's helmet described by Homer has been found from Knossos dating from the Minoan age of Crete:

> On his head he put a helmet made of leather, without a crest or plume, what people call as skull cap. It protected heads of brave young men' and 'On his head Odysseus set a hide cap, on the inside skilfully reinforced with leather thongs. Outside,

wild boar's white teeth were placed here and there. (*Iliad* 10; Johnston, 2010)

2.5: Female Exercise and the Olympic Games

Females in Greek city-states were thoroughly domesticated, spending most of their time at home. Their main duties were raising children and making clothes. Ancient Greek society in general was male dominated but did not entirely condemn females as inferior by nature. Sporting activities may have been irrelevant or improper for them. Galen never describes females as exercising and does not prescribe gymnastic exercises for them. Galen and other Greek medical writers assumed a passive lifestyle for females (Mattern, 2008). Lycurgus of Sparta (around 820 BC) established a practice of allowing girls to exercise naked with boys in running, wrestling, throwing the discus, and the javelin. The purpose of this was to give their offspring a sound start by taking root in sound bodies and grow stronger as well using their strength to withstand childbearing. This also enabled the matching of strong young males to equally strong young females (Plutarch, *Lycurgus* 14–15). Plato had used the example of Sparta to outline a theoretical ideal of females being trained in a range of athletic events: "We shall have to train the women also, then, in both kinds of skill, and train them for war as well, and treat them in the same way as men" (Plato, *Republic* 452a).

Plato also mentioned his plan for physical training for females: "I assert without fear of contradiction that gymnastics and horsemanship are as suitable to women as to me" (Plato, *Laws* VII 804). It is not known whether females attended the gymnasia in the Greek world. There is evidence of females exercising in Roman times from a mosaic in Sicily of several bikini-clad girls holding dumbbells or weights in their hands.

Participation in the Olympic Games was almost exclusively for males. Females had some involvement. There was a separate minor athletic festival for maidens in honor of Hera. The cults of Zeus and Hera were possibly both established at Olympia by the eighth century BC or even as early as the eleventh century BC. Pausanias mentions that unmarried girls or maidens were permitted to watch the boys' and mens' events. Every fourth year, the Heraia Games were held, which consisted of footraces for maidens (Pausanias, 5.16.2). According to Pausanias, at Olympia a series of running races was open to girls of various ages. These girls did not compete naked. They ran just a stadion race at the main stadium, which was shortened by one-sixth of the normal length run by the males (approximately 160 meters). Prizes for victory were olive-leaf wreaths, with a sacrificial feast for the male competitors. There were other known footraces for females in early Greece established at least by the sixth century BC with apparent similarities to the Heraia. These were the race organized for Dionysus at Sparta and the one of the Arkteia for Artemis at Brauron. The running ritual of the Brauronian Arkteia is known only from ritual vase paintings and is not mentioned at all in texts (Scanlon, 2008).

Excavations at Brauron uncovered an elaborate building with a courtyard and dining room as well as a palaestra. Miller (2004) suggests this must have been a wrestling school for females, since the sanctuary of Brauronian Artemis was a strictly female cult center where girls went through initiation ceremonies. Wrestling for females may not have spread far from Sparta, but Athenaeus[21] in about 200 AD had stated, "It is extremely pleasant to stroll to the gymnasium and running track on the island of Chios and see the young men wrestling with girls" (Sweet, 1987). Chios is a Greek island situated in the Aegean Sea seven kilometers off the Anatolian coast.

The origins of the Heraia precedes the historical institution of the sixteen females as festival organizers around 580 BC. This was possibly the date when a footrace was added to Hera's festival under the influence of contemporary athletics for girls at Sparta (Scanlon, 2014b). A bronze statuette in the British museum from the sixth century BC may represent an image of a Heraia winner. Pausanias describes the maidens running with their hair hanging down, tunics reaching a little above the knee, and baring their rights shoulder as far as the breast (Pausanias, 5.16.3). This statuette, according to Scanlon (2014b), corresponds exactly to Pausanias's description of the Heraian runners. Kyle (2007) and Langenfeld (2006) disagree that the British museum statuette is a Heraia runner. They believe this may represent a female dancer. Scanlon also suggests a sixth-century BC historical foundation date and possible Panhellenic participation.

---

21. Athenaeus of Naucratis was Greek rhetorician and grammarian in the second and third centuries AD. His work *Deipnosophistae* describes quests while discussing various topics over dinner.

Young (2008) believes that the Heraia to be a late addition to the Olympic festival calendar from the Roman period and that the girls were selected from the local population only. Scanlon argues that if the festival were only for local Eleans, it would have been held at Elis, where a track was available. Pausanias does not mention a Hera temple or shrine at Elis. Olympia was fifty-eight kilometers from Elis by road, which would have been a two-day walk, and it is likely the Hera festival was held at Olympia. Therefore, it would have made sense to stage the running events for both males and females at the same stadium. This festival was held every four years as mentioned, but according to Young (2004), it was separate from the Olympic Games and staged at a different time of the year.

A formal law of capital punishment existed among the Eleans for any females coming to the Olympics or even crossing the Alfeios River (which was the route to the Olympic sanctuary) on the days that were forbidden to them: "It is a law of Elis to cast down if any women who are caught present at the Olympic Games, or even on the other side of the Alpheius" (Pausanias, 5.6.7). It can be argued, then, why there was such strict legislation unless there was not a significant female presence at Olympia. Young (2004), though, suggests unmarried females were not prevented from watching the games. A famous violation of the ban was recorded in antiquity. Phberenice,[22] a Rhodian mother of an Olympic boxer, disguised herself as a gymnastic trainer wrapped in a cloak. Her appearance was so strong that the Eleans at first assumed she was a man (Phil, *Gym* 17). Her son Peisirodus was victorious and jumping for joy when Phrenice revealed her true self. She was let off unpunished out of respect for her father (Diagoras), her brothers, and her son, all of whom had been victorious at Olympia. This supposedly resulted in a law being passed that trainers were required to strip before entering the arena at Olympia (Pausanias, 5.6.7–8).

Females were involved in other Olympic events. In the early fourth century BC, a Spartan princess named Cynisca, daughter of Archidamus, became the first of several females especially from Lacedaemon to gain Olympic victory in the chariot racing as an owner (Pausanias, 3.8.1). Her chariot team won twice at Olympia.

---

22. Pausanias mentioned in his description of Greece the name Kallipateira, but some had called her Phrenice.

CHAPTER 2 SUMMARY

All those participating in the Olympic Games, including the trainers, athletes, and judges, were required to take an oath in the presence of the statue of Zeus before the competition commenced. The date of the Olympics was consistently the second full moon after the summer solstice. The order of events at the Olympic Games was the chariot racing, and the other equestrian contests, the pentathlon, and then the footraces, followed by the wrestling, boxing, and the pankration, known as the heavy events. Finally, there was the race in armor. The festival lasted five days. The program also included further sacred rites and processions, a grand banquet for all participants, and the prize-giving ceremony. By the fifth century BC, it was customary for victors of the games to commission Epinikion poets to compose odes in celebration of their achievements. Pindar was one of the well-known Epinikion poets.

The ancient Greek male athletes trained and competed in the nude. The origins and purpose of nudity are debated. It is suggested that nudity was associated with the warrior athlete, whose training and competition in the games was at the same time his preparation for war. There is a view that athletic culture, including training, nudism, and competition, led to the emergence of pederasty in Sparta and spread to other Greek states in the seventh and sixth centuries BC. A cultural or religious origin of Greek nudity is also suggested. Greek athletic nudity began at the Olympiad from 720 BC. Lucian suggested nudity in athletics could inspire fitness, pride, and military worthiness among the Greeks. The Romans, though, were revolted by Greek nudity.

Homer's poems, probably written in the eighth to seventh centuries BC, provide us with insights into Greek athletics that preceded the Olympic Games. In *The Iliad*, the games described were part of a funeral ritual for Patroclus, whereas in *The Odyssey*, they were more for entertainment. In the funeral games for Patroclus, there were eight contests, starting with the chariot race followed by the boxing, wrestling, footrace, armed combat, discus, archery, and finally the javelin.

Females did participate in ancient Greek athletics. It is not known whether females attended the gymnasia in the Greek world. Participation in the Olympic

Games was almost exclusively for males, but females had some involvement. There was a separate minor athletic festival for maidens in honor of Hera. Every fourth year, the Heraia Games were held, which consisted of footraces for maidens. There may have been a wrestling school for females at Brauron. Cynisca became the first of several females, especially from Lacedaemon, to gain Olympic victory in the chariot racing as an owner.

CHAPTER 3:

GYMNASIUM, EQUIPMENT, AND TRAINERS

It is not out of brutality that they strike one another and tumble each other in the mud or sprinkle each other with dust. The thing has a certain usefulness, not unattended by pleasure and it gives strength to their bodies.

—Lucian, *Anacharsis* IV

3.1: Gymnasium

According to Athenaeus,[23] the first who erected the gymnasia among the Greeks were the Lacedaemonians. Plato claims gymnasia may have existed thousands of years before his time (Blundell, 1864). Spivey (2012) suggests that the gymnasium as a formal enclosure did not exist in the age of Homer (eighth century BC), but

---

23. Athenaeus (not to be confused with Athenaeus of Naucratis) was a physician in the first century AD who subscribed to Galen's continuum theory of the four elements/qualities, a theory also embraced by Hippocrates, Plato, and Aristotle. According to this theory, matter is composed of the four elements—fire, water, air, and earth—and the four elemental qualities associated with them are hotness, wetness, coldness, and dryness.

such dedicated sites and buildings for exercise were in use by the middle of the sixth century BC. According to W. C. Decker, the gymnasium originally was nothing more than the place and structure for military exercise for the youth of the Greek polis. It developed over time to focus on sport and finally served for the purposes of intellectual education (Scanlon, 2014b). Delphi provides the earliest extensive remains of a gymnasium around 330BC. This complex includes running tracks, a palaestra, a dressing room, and a large pool (Kyle, 2015). Decker suggests the development and spread of gymnasia culture in the ancient world were due to the change in military style (hoplite) and the need for the city to train more soldiers (Scanlon, 2014b).

Delorme (1960), cited by Crowther (1985), also believed that the gymnasium was a creation of archaic Greece brought about by the rise of the hoplites. The development of the hoplite phalanx in addition to conventional fighting techniques required continued military training to enable maximum effectiveness. In the hoplite phalanx of the archaic and classical periods of Greece, soldiers would form in close order with their shields close together. They would project their spears over the first rank, allowing more soldiers to be engaged in combat. Thus, this military training showed there was a close connection between sport and war. The development of the gymnasium was attributed to the prominence of pederasty, the increasing popularity of athletic nudity, and the proliferation of games and festivals in the late seventh and sixth centuries BC (Scanlon, 2014b). The gymnasium was generally considered a public amenity, but the palaestra could be privately established and operated. Certain categories of persons were not allowed in the gymnasium premises. Those barred included slaves, prostitutes, market traders, drunkards, and the mentally deranged.

Vitruvius's textbook on architecture was written in 27 BC (Robinson, 1955). This work described architecturally what a gymnasium should look like. The gymnasium included all facilities for athletic disciplines. The key sporting facilities in the gymnasium were an indoor running or sprinting track (approximately two hundred yards), which was kept soft but firm. Vitruvius suggested also a stadium should be designed for the viewing of athletic contests. Spaces for jumping and throwing were also provided, as well as shaded areas for walking or strolling. There was a plunge bath, showers, and washbasins. There was also a palaestra or wrestling school consisting of a shallow rectangular recess known as the skamma.

This was possibly a sandpit, which was a place for lessons, drills, sparring for boxing, wrestling, and the pankration (i.e., heavy events). The ground of the skamma was loosened up by athletes themselves using pickaxes. Lucian mentions the area for wrestling consisting of mud and dust. He suggests the reason for this surface is so that the athlete tumbles on a soft surface rather than a hard one (Lucian, *Anacharsis* 46). Lucian also refers to the continual somersaults in the mud (referring to wrestling) and the open-air struggles in the sand (Lucian, *Anacharsis* 46). There may have been separate areas for wrestling and boxing or pankration but in the same vicinity of the palaestra. Philostratus mentions those who have toiled in the mud in the palaestra and those who have toiled in the dust (Phil, *Gym* 53). Philostratus is referring to wrestling in the palaestra, but what was he referring to with "those having toiled in the dust"? This could be boxing or a surface for other athletes to perform different exercises (see chapter 5).

The gymnasium had many separate rooms of varying sizes described by Vitruvius. This included a spacious hall, or exedrae, with seats on which philosophers, rhetoricians, and other folk would sit for their intellectual pursuits and discussions. The gymnasium was a place for both physical and intellectual culture.

The training of the body and mind went hand in hand. Some recited poetry, and others recited Homer or delivered lectures on philosophy, whereas others were performing or criticizing the performances of various exercises designed to develop the physical body and/or qualify them for arms (Taylor, 1880).

A club room or ephebeum was where the epheboi could gather and socialize. There were changing and storage rooms. The apodyterium was the undressing room and a standard feature of the palaestra. There was a room for preparation for oiling, as described in the section on athlete's equipment (3.2) as well as area for applying powders (*conisterium*). The oil storeroom was called the elaeothesium. A separate room was also provided for training drills where punching bags were suspended. The punching bag area was called the *coryceum*. Philostratus mentions different types of punching bags. A lighter punching bag was hung up for boxers to train their hands, whereas heavier bags were used by the pankration athletes so that they could develop their shoulder muscles and keep their footing by standing up to the impact of the bag (Phil, *Gym* 57). A good example of a gymnasium is found at the complex at Olympia built in the Hellenistic period. This closely matches Vitruvius's conception. This was a square layout of 66.5

meters along each side, featuring an open inner courtyard. An inner peripheral corridor passed nineteen different spacious areas. These included three lecture halls, the ephebeum, three equipment rooms, a washroom, well house, and various practice spaces (Miller, 2004).

Pausanias in his travels noted an old gymnasium in the city of Elis. There he suggested the athletes would go through all the customary training before they went to Olympia. The site consisted of tall plane trees growing between the running paths inside a wall. This running path was named by the locals as the sacred running path. The whole enclosure Pausanias said was called Xystos ("scraped") because Hercules, the son of Amphitryo, exercised himself every day by scraping up the thistles that grew there. The running path for the trees was separate from two that were used by the runners and pentathletes for practice. In the gymnasium Pausanias described a place called the *plethrium*. In this area the umpires would match competitors in wrestling according to age and proficiency (see chapter 2). Another enclosure in the gymnasium was of a smaller size and adjoined the larger. This was named "the square," due to its shape, which may be as the skamma described by Vitruvius. This was where athletes first practiced wrestling and then boxing after. There was a third enclosed area of the gymnasium called the *maltho* because of the softness (*malakotes*) of the ground. This was used by boys for the whole time of the Olympic festival (Pausanias, 6.23.5).

After the Lacedaemonians, the Athenians also created their gymnasia, of which Pausanias testifies that there existed three in the city but there may have been more: the Alcademia, or Academy, where Plato orated; the Lyceum, where Aristotle taught (according to Lucian, the Lyceum was called after the temple of Apollo); and the third was Cynosarges and was connected to the Greek philosopher Antisthenes (445–365 BC), who was regarded as the founder of Cynic philosophy. It was also where the ill-bred (Athenians born of foreign mothers) and the illegitimate exercised, but they were held in contempt among the Greeks, for those who were legitimate and noble, according to their custom, refused to exercise in the same place as these people. There was another gymnasium called Canopus, but little was known about this place. Corinth also had its gymnasium called Craneum. In antiquity there was scarcely any walled town of the Greeks that did not have its gymnasium (Blundell, 1864).

There was a significant cost and organization to running a gymnasium. Large quantities of olive oil were required daily, as well as fuel for heating the baths and a continuous water supply. The leadership of a gymnasium, or *gymnasiarchy*, could only be performed by someone with access to funds who was prepared to put them to general use. This was a voluntary service for the public good, which was expected from members of the local aristocracy. The running of the gymnasium provided a living for a many people who were needed to provide the various services, such as guards, oil stewards, cloakroom attendants, and trainers. The gymnasium retained such prestige in the Hellenistic period that the duties and rights pertaining to the leadership were regulated by law. The gymnasiarch was required to pay a fine if he knowingly contravened any of the rules, such as allowing the entry or slaves or prostitutes, which was not permitted (Scanlon, 2014b).

3.2: The Athlete's Equipment

Oil was an important part of Greek training, especially for wrestlers. It was standard practice to rub oneself with olive oil before athletic activity or competition. The term "boy rubber" or *aleiptes* indicates the importance of oil and massage in Greek athletics. The phase "those who anoint themselves" was regularly used to describe those engaged in athletic activity (Gardiner, 1930). By the fifth century BC, the athlete would carry with him a jar of olive oil. At the times of competition, oil would be free, and a free supply was also provided to the epheboi in training. The standard oil jar was the aryballos, which was a small spherical or globular flask. This aryballos would vary in size, with the most common being the size of a tennis ball. A cord was threaded through the handles for carrying or hanging from a peg. Athletes would anoint themselves with oil before entering the sandpit. There is some debate as to the purpose of the oil, but this may have been used to keep the skin moist or protection against the weather or make the body more aesthetically pleasing. Protection against the weather may be partly the reason, as indicated by Lucian: "Best to begin by habituating them to the weather…Then we rub them with olive-oil." Lucian goes on to say that the skin is softened by the oil, made more durable and in a better condition (Lucian, *Anacharsis* 38–39). Miller (2004) suggested that the coating of oil prevented the loss of body fluids during exercise and was a protection against dehydration. The oil was also used for a training stimulus as well. Lucian suggests the combination of sweat, mud, and oil added to the athlete's slipperiness, like an eel. This, according to Lucian, improved muscle strength, as one needed to grip firmly and hold fast to prevent the other wrestler from slipping away. Lucian says that picking up a man who is muddy, sweaty, and oily while he does his best to break away is no easy task and may be useful in war for picking up a wounded friend. Lucian goes on to say, "So we train them beyond measure, setting them hard tasks that they may manage smaller ones with far greater ease" (*Anacharsis* 46).

After exercise, the athlete scraped his body with a strigil or *stlengis* (Harris, 1964). The strigil for scraping was applied with water and would be used to clean the skin. This was a curved tool, concave in section and usually made of bronze. Philostratus stated that the trainer would carry a strigil at Olympia. He stated that it was necessary for the athlete to dust his body with sand of the palaestra and then to be covered with mud. To keep good condition of the skin, the strigil reminds the athlete that he must apply the oil abundantly and scrape once he has oiled himself (Phil, *Gym* 18). The athlete also carried a sponge that was used to wash up after the scraping was completed. Dust or powder was used by the athlete before exercise and in cleaning up.

There was a special room in the gymnasium called the *conisterion*, which was used by athletes to "dust up" or powder themselves before exercise (Miller, 2004). Gardiner (1930) suggested the powder may have helped close the pores of the skin, prevent excessive sweating, and keep the body cool, but this is different from Philostratus's description. He described different types of powder and their uses. Dust made from clay was suitable for cleansing, brick dust was good for opening pores and bringing out sweat, and asphalt was used for warming chilled parts of the body. Black and yellow dust were good for softening and nourishing the body. Yellow dust made the body gleam and made it more pleasant to look at (Phil, *Gym* 56). Hence, athletes leaving the sand pit or training area would be routinely coated in a mixture of dust, oil, sweat, and possibly blood.

Another piece of athletic equipment was a cap. This may have been used to hold the athlete's hair down, as it did not cover the ears. This cap was not worn in competitions, only in practice. It may have been a type of hairnet used by pentathletes as a way of preventing their hair from becoming entangled with the throwing strap of the javelin.

3.3: Ancient Greek Trainers

Athletes preparing for competition used the services of paedotribes, who offered formal and systematic training. They would be responsible for the daily practical implementation of the athletic training program. In Plato's *Gorgias*, Socrates states that if a trainer or paedotribe were to identify himself, he would say, "My work is making men's bodies beautiful and strong" (Plato, *Gorgias* 452b). Plato speaks of a paedotribe working with a person in training (Lehmann, 2009). Taylor (1880) describes him as the director of movements. In the Hellenistic and Roman periods, the cities regularly hired paedotribes and sometimes elected annual officers to oversee training in the gymnasium (Lehmann, 2009). Plato used the term paedotribe for a trainer in an educational context. He usually pairs *gymnastai* with physicians as experts whom people consulted concerning their bodies. They were the principal officers in carrying out the exercises and possessed the knowledge regarding their capacity for health. Galen noted that the appearance of the term *gymnastes* at the end of the fifth century BC coincided with the rise of professional athletes and increased sporting specialization. As Galen had mentioned in *Thrasybulus*, in ancient times when a man was in truly excellent condition, he would excel in all athletic activities, such as wrestling, running, javelin, discus throwing, and racing war chariots. Later, though, like Homer's Epeius, the boxer from *The Odyssey*, they would only excel in one thing (i.e., be specialists in their own sports) and be of no use in other activities, to perform well in battle (Galen, *Thrasybulus* 33). Hence, the word *gymnastes* came to mean a specialized trainer who possessed medical knowledge relating to anatomy, athletic experience, understood the laws of heredity, and could affect sport performance (Gardiner, 1930; Robinson, 1955). The paedotribe became more of a preliminary trainer, whereas the gymnastes was the coach or athletic expert.

Philostratus confirmed this fact, as he said that the paedotribe demonstrated different types of wrestling moves, as well as giving instruction on the degree of force to be used and how one can defend oneself or defeat an opponent, whereas the gymnastes teaches the athlete things he does not know. Philostratus goes on to say that the gymnastes knows all the skills of the paedotribes (Phil, *Gym* 14). Pindar, in his *Eleventh Ode*, had ascribed the success in the heavy events to the excellence of the trainer: "Now let Agesidamos, winner in the boxing, so render thanks to Ilas [his trainer], as Patroklos of old to Achilles. If one be born with excellent gifts, then may another who sharpeneth his natural edge speed him, God helping, to an exceeding weight of glory. Without toil there have triumphed a very few" (*Olympic Ode 11*). Plato mentions Iccus of Taras and Herodicus of Selymbria (in his day) as physical trainers (Plato, *Protagoras* 316d–e). Herodicus, in the mid–fifth century BC, wrote the first manual of theoretical gymnastics according to Lehmann (2009). His teachings emphasized the care and training of the body to enhance life. Plato criticized Herodicus, whose own health had failed (he was described as a chronic invalid), for combining medicine and physical training. He suggested that his methods kept treating a disease without curing it and so extended suffering for others (Plato, *Republic* 406a–b). Aristotle considered the work of the gymnastes and the paedotribe to be complementary components of physical training. Isocrates, the Greek orator in the fourth century BC, said that gymnastics constituted part of the paedotribic art (Isocrates, *Antidosis* 15.181).

Galen approached training as an aspect of health, not of education. Health in Galen's *Hygiene* was defined and identified as either a constitution of the body that allows the bodily functions to be carried out faultlessly and naturally, or the bodily functions themselves all being normal (Johnson, 2018). Galen suggested that someone skilled in the whole art of health be called a hygienist. Hygiene was defined as that "department of knowledge or practice which relates to the maintenance of health: a system of principles or rules for preserving or promoting health" (Johnson, 2018). Gymnastics, in Galen's view, were part of hygiene and has health as its telos (end) unless it shades over into the excesses of the wrestling schools and gymnastic trainers when the end is an abnormal bodily state, achieved in the presence of mass and strength aimed at overcoming opponents in contests (Johnson, 2018). Galen found fault with the *euexia* (good state or health) of these athletes and similarly with the gymnastic master in charge. Galen mentioned that those gymnastic bodies are trained in activities for actual strength to throw their opponents in a contest and are not natural in keeping with Hippocrates's views (Galen, *Thrasybulus* 6–9). This condition that athletes strive for is particularly dangerous to health. This was also known to both Hippocrates and Plato. Galen suggested athletes could still have euexia as long this remained in this stable state. According to Galen, someone who is perfectly healthy also needs exercises and a regimen. Therefore, the gymnastic art was part of the hygienic art. Galen suggested in Homer's time that there was not yet a name for the gymnastic art, nor was anyone at all called a gymnastic trainer, as they were considered doctors. Plato had called the gymnastic trainer a "physical trainer." The art of gymnastics, according to Galen, had started earlier than Plato's times, when they were involved in the practice of athletics (Galen, *Thrasybulus* 33). One who is concerned with exercises alone should be called a gymnastic trainer, and one who is concerned with treatment a doctor. Galen argued that paedotribes or physical trainers did not have the physiological knowledge necessary to care for the body. He said the paedotribes were more knowledgeable pertaining to exercises in the wrestling school, but they were more of a servant to the gymnastic trainer. He did not like the idea of failed athletes becoming trainers. In the Hellenistic period, medical writers tended to assign the term gymnastes to the more theoretical aspects of training, while paedotribes designated someone who offered practical instruction and followed the guidance of the gymnastes. Hellenistic cities regularly employed paedotribes in their public gymnasia. Philostratus considered gymnastics part of medicine and a more complete form of training. He suggested the gymnastes knew how to condition the body and train athletes for competition, just as the paedotribe could. The gymnastes were also able to determine the bodily response to exercise, judge the satisfactory progression of training, and detect signs of overwork by assessing the color and quality of the athlete's skin (Bourne, 2008). In addition, the gymnastes knew enough physiology to use diet and massage to purify the humors, moderate excess, smooth wrinkles, and fatten, warm up, or change any part of the body. The gymnastes could address certain problems of health, as could the physician, but only the physician could heal breaks, wounds, and dislocations (Phil, *Gym* 14).

Philostratus states that the gymnastes did not know about all sports. He suggested in his time there were specialist trainers for runners, wrestlers, or pankration athletes (Phil, *Gym* 15). The term *aleiptes* or *aleipteior* came into use by the fourth century BC. This means someone who anoints with oil and could be referred to as a masseur, but its first use was associated to the athlete's diet. Celsus, in his second book of medicine in the first century AD, provides reference to a rubber and an anointer. He described there being a distinct difference between the two. It was the Greek physician Asclepiades who, according to Celsus, taught when and how rubbing should be practiced with a wider application (see chapter 5). Harris (1964) suggested that massage was an important part of the aleipteior's duties. Christopoulos et al. (2003) stated that massage became an integral part of effective training in ancient Greece and assisted in the recovery of an athlete after a long training session. Blundell (1864) mentions the *spheristici* who was the teacher of ball play. There was part of the gymnasium called the *sphairisterion*, which was the area for playing ball. Miller (2004) suggests this area may have resembled a handball court or could have been used for storage. There were many games of ball played in this area. In addition to the gymnastes and paedotribe was the *xystarches*, who was master of the athlete as well as fencing and wrestling. Galen mentions that the xystarches was the manager of most of the exercises, judge of victories, and regulator of prizes. Hippocrates called him *palaistrophulus*, or prefect of the palaestra (Blundell, 1864).

CHAPTER 3 SUMMARY

The gymnasium as a dedicated site and building for exercise was in use by the middle of the sixth century BC. The development of the gymnasium was associated with military training, the growth of pederasty, the increasing popularity of athletic nudity, and the proliferation of games and festivals in the late seventh and sixth centuries BC. Virtually all towns in ancient Greece had gymnasia. Vitruvius's textbook on architecture described architecturally what a gymnasium should look like. It had many separate rooms of varying sizes for sporting activities.

Athletes' equipment included an aryballos containing oil. It was standard practice for athletes to rub themselves with olive oil before sporting activity or competition. A strigil was used by the athlete to scrape the body after exercise and clean the skin. A sponge was used to wash up after the scraping was completed. There were several different types of powder used that may have helped close the pores of the skin, prevent excessive sweating, and keep the body cool. Finally, a cap was used to hold the athletes' hair down during throwing events like the javelin.

The paedotribe was a preliminary trainer who assisted athletes in their preparation for competition. The appearance of the term gymnastes at the end of the fifth century BC coincided with the rise of professional athletes and increased sporting specialization. The word *gymnastes* came to mean a specialized trainer or athletic expert who possessed medical knowledge relating to anatomy and athletic experience, understood the laws of heredity, and could affect sport performance. The aleipteior was a masseur and anointer, becoming more prominent by the fourth century BC. The spheristici was the teacher of ball play, and the xystarches was a master of the athlete as well as fencing and wrestling.

CHAPTER 4:

MODERN PRINCIPLES OF EXERCISE TRAINING

And so in gymnastics, if a man takes violent exercise and is a great feeder, and the reverse of a great student of music and philosophy, at first the high condition of his body fills him with pride and spirit, and he becomes twice the man that he was.

—Plato, *Republic* III

This chapter outlines some of the basic principles of modern training and historical aspects from sports science. This will then be related and compared to what we know about ancient Greek exercise and the training methods in chapter 5.

4.1: Strengthening

Strength is the ability of muscle to exert force or torque at a specified or determined velocity (Lorenz et al., 2010). Strengthening leads to neuromuscular adaptations, with the increase in recruitment and synchronization of motor units leading to more efficient muscle contraction. Weight or resistance training is a term for training with resistance equipment (barbells, et cetera), exercise machines, or body weight that provides the working muscles with a resistance overload to increase muscular strength.

Strengthening exercises also leads to an increase in the size of muscle fibers (i.e., hypertrophy; Baar et al., 2006). Strength training will also increase the strength of tendons and ligaments and improve bone density. Load is the amount of weight assigned to an exercise set. The load of an exercise program has often been characterized as the most critical aspect of a resistance-training program. An inverse relationship exists between the amount of weight lifted and the number of repetitions performed. There are different loading schemes. Increasing the load can be based on the 1 RM (the maximum amount of weight that can be successfully lifted at one time), by increasing the absolute load based on a targeted repetition number, and/or increasing loading within a prescribed zone (e.g., 8–12 RM). Specified loads are required for specific training effects. High-intensity training involves few repetitions, whereas low-intensity endurance training requires much higher repetitions (e.g., 15–25 RM). DeLorme and Watkins in the 1940s showed that muscle strength returns more quickly to atrophied muscles if relatively few repetitions are performed at high levels of resistance. They hypothesized that the rate of muscle hypertrophy is proportional to the resistance overcome by the muscle and suggested that twenty to thirty repetitions per set was satisfactory, but fewer repetitions permit exercise with heavier muscle loads and yield greater, more rapid results. Their training regimen determined the ten-repetition maximum (10 RM). The 10 RM is the weight the individual could lift only ten times before temporary failure of the muscle occurred. Once the 10 RM is determined, the subject begins three sets of training by performing the first set at 50 percent 10 RM, the second at 75 percent 10 RM, and the third, final set at 10 RM. More recently, it has been shown that for novice trainers, loads of 45 to 50 percent of 1 RM or lower have been shown to increase dynamic muscular strength, whereas more advanced trainers should train with loads of 60 to 70 percent of 1 RM for eight to twelve repetitions (Lorenz et al., 2010). The 1950s saw more research into the effects of weight training on speed, power, and endurance that did not produce detrimental effects associated with "muscle boundness" or muscle tightness. The development of strength through a systematic program of weight training would be accompanied by increased coordination and speed of movement (Mastley et al., 1953). We see today that weight training is integral for all professional sports people, including swimmers and track athletes. Designing a resistance-training program requires knowledge of acute training variables including frequency, intensity, and volume (sets and repetitions) and the manipulation of these acute training variables. Krieger (2010) found that two to three sets of resistance exercises compared with a single set was associated with approximately 40 percent greater muscular hypertrophy and strength increases.

The current recommendations for strength training for healthy adults are as follows:[24] one to three sets of resistance exercises per muscle group for novice to intermediate individuals at 60 to 70 percent of 1 RM (eight to ten exercises to train all the major muscle groups—e.g., pectorals, latissimus dorsi, deltoids, abdominals, gluteal, quadriceps, hamstrings, and calves). Performing too many sets (more than six per exercise) may lead to regression and overtraining. Multiple-joint exercises, as opposed to single-joint, performed in a pain-free range of motion with controlled joint movements are recommended for maximizing overall muscle strength, but single-joint (unilateral and bilateral) exercises such as knee extensions or hamstring curls should also be included. Eight to twelve repetitions per set induce muscle fatigue but not exhaustion. It has been established from previous research that a minimum intensity of greater or equal to 65 percent of 1 RM is required to optimize gains in muscular hypertrophy and strength (Kraemer and Ratamess, 2004). Schoenfeld et al. (2016) have suggested that training with loads less than or equal to 60 percent of 1 RM can also promote substantial increases in muscle strength, but greater loads may be required if an individual attains a more advanced level of training status to see further improvements, as suggested by Lorenz et al. (2010). A shorter recovery period between sets (less than sixty seconds) is suggested to induce greater metabolic stress (e.g., buildup of metabolites such as lactate acid).

Metabolic stress is thought to be an important factor implicated in the promotion of exercise-induced muscle hypertrophy (Amirthalingam et al., 2017). For muscle endurance training, it is recommended that light to moderate loads (40–60 percent 1 RM) be performed for high repetitions (more than fifteen to twenty-five repetitions) per set using shorter rest periods (less than ninety seconds) with multiple sets depending on the individual's target goals. For core strengthening exercises using heavier loads such as the squat, a two- to three-minute rest interval between sets is recommended. Optimal gains in muscle

---

24. Recommendations for resistance or strength training taken from the American College of Sports Medicine (2009).

function and size can occur with training two to three times per week by whole-body training for novice individuals or by split-body routines (four times a week to train each muscle group twice). A split routine involves performing different exercises targeting specific muscle groups in each training session during the week—for example, chest and upper back, legs, shoulders, and arms. A rest period of forty-eight to seventy-two hours between sessions is needed to optimally promote cellular as well as molecular adaptations that stimulate muscle hypertrophy and associated gains in strength (Pollock et al., 2000; Ratamess et al., 2009).

4.2: Training Volume

Training volume is a summation of the total number of repetitions performed during a training session multiplied by the resistance used in kilograms or pounds. This reflects altering the duration of which muscles are being stressed. Altering training volume can be accomplished by either a combination of changing the number of repetitions performed per set, the number of sets per exercise, or the number of exercises per session. Lifting heavy loads with low repetitions using a moderate to high number of sets used for strength training to produce muscle hypertrophy would be considered as a low-volume program. Volume can be increased by either increasing the number of sets and/or exercises performed or by increasing training frequency. Exercise intensity and training volume are inversely related. Intensity in weight training relative to the individual refers to the load lifted and, increasing the load this increases intensity. Intensity could also refer to the percentage of 1 RM lifted.

Thus, increasing 65 percent 1 RM for five repetitions to 75 percent 1 RM for the same number of repetitions would increase the individual's exercise intensity. It has been found that two to six sets per exercise produce significant increases in muscular strength in both trained and nontrained individuals. For novices, an initial one to three sets per session is recommended. Intermediate or advanced trainers require progression to multiple sets with variation of volume and load over time. Not all body parts or exercises need to be performed with the same volume (Kraemer and Ratamess, 2004).

4.3: Power and Exercise Intensity

Power is defined as a product of force and velocity or the rate of doing work. Muscle power is the rate at which a muscle does work or transfers energy to complete a movement task (van der Kruk et al., 2018). Increasing power can improve sports performance. Explosive power output is the main determinant of performance in activities requiring one movement sequence to produce a high velocity at release or impact, such as throwing or jumping. Sudden bursts of power are needed when rapidly changing direction or accelerating during various sports or athletic events (for example, in sprinting). Athletes cannot be powerful without being relatively strong.

Strength training using high resistance and slow velocities of muscle action leads primarily to improvements in maximal strength, but the improvements are reduced at higher velocities. Thus, this may reduce the ability to develop force rapidly. Power training, which utilizes lighter resistances and higher velocities of muscle action performed in a ballistic fashion, results in increases in force output at the higher velocities and in the rate of force development. The rate of force development or explosive muscle strength describes the rate at which force is expressed during a sporting movement. The optimization of the rate of force development and subsequent power development is better achieved with the incorporation of explosive or ballistic exercises (Haff and Nimphius, 2012). In untrained individuals, a variety of training interventions will produce increases in strength and power. If an athlete already has an adequate level of strength, then increases in explosive power performance in response to traditional strength training will be poor, and more specific training programs will be needed to improve power. Thus, the improvement of power performance in trained athletes requires more complex or mixed-training strategies. To improve power performance, both the force and velocity components must be trained (Newton and Kraemer, 1994). One example of a mixed-training approach is to use a variety of training loads, such as the back squat. The back squat is one of the most effective exercises for enhancing athletic performance and is used to strengthen the lower-body musculature (Myer et al., 2014). Power development can occur in the back squat between loads of 30 to 70 percent of 1 RM as a submaximal load performed explosively, whereas higher loads (greater than 75 percent of 1 RM) would typically be employed for strength development (Haff and Nimphius,

2012). Another example of power development is using a combination of strength training with loads of 75 to 100 percent of 1 RM and plyometric training, such as an unloaded jump squat (see 4.7). This combination has been found to be the most effective method for improving leg muscle power measured by vertical jumping ability (Adams et al., 1992). Power training ideally should be performed at the beginning of a training session or on separate days as not to pre-fatigue the athlete with strength or endurance training.

Exercise intensity can be defined as the rate of energy expenditure ranging from low levels of sedentary activities, such as sitting or lying down, to high-intensity exercise like running, which cannot be sustained for longer than ten minutes. Exercise intensity can be expressed as an absolute measure such as metabolic equivalent (MET). One MET, equal to 3.5 $mLO_2/kg/min$, is considered as the average resting expenditure of an individual. Intensity of exercise can be expressed as multiples of resting energy expenditure such that high-intensity exercise for conditioned athletes can range from 9 METs to over 20 METs. Peak power output in watts is a common measure of exercise intensity. The Wingate anaerobic test using a cycle ergometer to measures anaerobic power and capacity. This requires the participant to cycle at maximum effort for thirty seconds against a resistance set as a percentage of their body weight.

Peak power is recorded as the maximum power output achieved in the first five seconds of the test (Norton et al., 2010; Zupan et al., 2009).

4.4: Endurance

Endurance can be defined as the capacity to sustain a given velocity or power output for the longest possible time. There are four key parameters of aerobic (endurance) that have been previously identified. These are $VO2_{max}$, anaerobic threshold (AT), exercise or work economy and oxygen-uptake kinetics (Whipp et al., 1982). $VO2_{max}$ is the measure of maximal oxygen uptake and an indicator of aerobic capacity (Neufer, 1989). $VO2_{max}$ has been considered the gold standard for assessing cardiovascular fitness. Anaerobic threshold is the physiological point during exercise at which lactic acid starts to accumulate in the muscles. This occurs during increased exercise intensity when anaerobic processes become more dominant. This is a regarded as a determinant of physiological fitness. Trained athletes accumulate less lactate than untrained athletes at a given submaximal workload.

Running economy (RE) reflects the energy demand of running at a constant submaximal speed. Runners with good economy use less oxygen than runners with a poor economy at the same steady-state speed. RE is also a useful predictor of running performance. Oxygen-uptake kinetics refers to the processes involved in taking oxygen from the lungs and delivering it to the mitochondrion, where it is consumed by the working muscle. The final phase in the process is the "steady state" in which oxygen delivery equals oxygen utilization. This steady state is reached in about three minutes (Diamond et al., 1977).

Trained individuals will reach a steady state faster than nontrained individuals. Biochemical adaptations that occur in the muscle with training such as increased mitochondrion size and number may contribute to increased oxygen-uptake kinetics.

4.5: Progressive Overload

To continue making gains in an exercise program, stress to the muscle must be progressively increased as it becomes capable of producing greater force, power, or endurance. Once the muscles adapt to an exercise program workload, they will not continue to progress in the desired training goal unless the workload is increased in some way. Therefore, to continue improving strength and function, progressive increases in load must be applied, to which adaptations will again occur. If the athlete does not continue to adapt, they will reach a plateau, and regression may occur. Progressively overloading the muscle can be achieved in the following ways: by increasing the resistance, by increasing the training volume (achieved by increasing either number of repetitions, sets or exercises performed), by altering rest periods, or by increasing the repetition velocity during submaximal resistances. Progressive overloading should be gradually introduced to the training program, with the athlete having time to adapt before making significant changes (Lorenz et al., 2010). The specificity of the training stimulus is also important in terms of the type of training practiced (endurance, strength, or speed), and the exercise modality used. Appropriate recovery periods are required to allow adaptation to the training load. An insufficient training stimulus and/or too much recovery can lead to a lack of progress or detraining. A training load too great with insufficient recovery can lead to overtraining (Jones and Carter, 2000).

4.6: Interval Training

Continuous training consists of aerobic exercise bouts performed at low to moderate intensity without rest periods, whereas interval training consists of alternating high-intensity periods of exercise with active or passive periods (Khammassi et al., 2018). Hence interval training permits variations in exercise intensity during the training session by alternating more intensive and less intensive periods. This low-intensity period could be classified as the recovery period (Bertani et al., 2018). Interval training was first used by Hannes Kolehmainen, a Finnish gold medalist at the five-thousand-meter and ten-thousand-meter running events in the 1912 Olympic Games. The technique was popularized in the 1950s by Emil Zátopek, a middle-distance runner and gold medalist from the Czech Republic.

A typical interval training program was used by Siegfried Herrmann, a German runner in the 1950s, for the fifteen-hundred-meter race. This consisted of four times (6 x 200 m) with a rest of fifty to sixty seconds between runs and of eight minutes between each series but aiming to run faster in the last series (Billat, 2001). Interval training should not be confused with Fartlek runs. Fartlek training was developed in the 1930s in Sweden. This training combines continuous and interval training. The system allows the athlete to run whatever distance and speed they wish, varying the intensity and occasionally running at high-intensity levels, aiming to stress both aerobic and anaerobic energy pathways (Elekuvan, 2014). High-intensity interval training (HIIT) is a relatively recent concept used to improve sport performance. Acevedo and Goldfarb (1989) showed that increased training intensity improved athletic performance in previously trained runners. HIIT is broadly defined as repeated bouts of short- to moderate-duration exercise (i.e., ten seconds to five minutes) completed at an intensity that is greater than the anaerobic threshold. Exercise bouts of "all-out" effort are then separated by brief periods of low-intensity work or inactivity that allow a partial but not full recovery.

HIIT is associated with activities such as cycling or running. A common mode of HIIT used in research is the Wingate test mentioned in 4.3, which involves thirty seconds of all-out maximal cycling against a high resistance on a specialized ergometer. The Wingate Test is repeated four to six times. This is separated by a four-minute recovery period providing a total of two-three minutes of very intense exercise.

Three training sessions are advocated per week (Gibala and McGee, 2008). The objective of HIIT is to repeatedly stress the physiological systems that will be used during a specific endurance-type exercise more than that which is usually required during the activity. HIIT has been shown to improve performance in trained runners and team athletes such as football players and cyclists (Laursen and Jenkins, 2002). For example, Jakeman et al. (2016) found that following a four-week HIIT intervention for speed involving inclined sprinting in semiprofessional female field hockey players, there were significant changes to straight-line sprint speed compared with a normal training program.

4.7: Plyometrics

Most athletic competition involves lower-body performance, whether in the stance or active phase. Athletes use a variety of training methods. Plyometric and resistance training are two of the primary non-sport-specific methods utilized in strength and conditioning programs to improve lower-body performance. Lower-body performance can be separated into high- and low-speed muscular strength, speed, and agility. High-speed muscular strength, also known as anaerobic, is the ability of the muscle to exert high force while performing at a fast rate of contraction. This can be evaluated by testing the broad and/or vertical-jump distances. Low-speed muscular strength is the force a muscle or muscle group can exert in one maximal effort. This can be evaluated by repetition maximal tests (i.e., repeated single-heel raises until fatigued to evaluate the calf-muscle strength; Whitehead et al., 2018). Plyometrics is a popular training method based on the stretch-reflex properties of the muscle to produce power.

Professor Rodolfo Margaria in the 1960s was the first to identify the value of the prestretch in producing a strong muscular contraction. It was the Soviet researcher V. M. Zaciorskiji in 1966 who used the work done by Margaria to devise training programs involving the stretch reflex. He coined the term *plyometrics*, which is Greek in origin, coming for two words meaning greater, longer, or wider and to measure, appraise, or compare. Zaciorskiji used the term plyometrics to describe the greater tension that could be developed in muscles when a quick stretching phase is followed by a fast contraction (Zanon, 1989). Plyometrics has become a valuable element of training toward the enhancement of performance in athletes and professional sport. For example, plyometrics is used by elite rugby union players to improve the rate of force development and for injury prevention (Jones et al., 2017).

Lower-body plyometric training consists of three phases: eccentric muscle action, amortization, and concentric. The amortization phase in plyometric training is the transition phase and the time between the concentric and eccentric phases. This is the phase of the stretch-shortening cycle and should be kept to a minimum. If this phase is too long, the energy stored during the eccentric phase dissipates and negates the plyometric effect, hence just becoming a standard exercise. Plyometric training involves performing body-weight jumping-type exercises using the stretch-shortening cycle of the muscle action. The objective is to increase power of subsequent movements using both natural elastic components of the muscle and tendon as well as the stretch reflex (Jarvis et al., 2016). Eccentric muscular activity is the key feature of plyometric exercise. The load during plyometric exercise is a product of the athlete's mass, falling height, and ability to resist yielding (flexion of the ankle, knee, and hip) and apply force, whereas the volume of the exercise can be measured by counting the number of repetitions and sets. The intensity of the exercise may be more difficult to measure objectively (see 5.4.1). Examples of plyometric exercise include depth jumps, drop jumps (falling from a height), vertical jumps, pike and tuck jumps, single leg jump, countermovement jump with arm swing, and jump squat while holding dumbbells (Jarvis et al., 2016). Isotonic resistance training typically uses alternating cycles of eccentric and concentric muscle actions, aiming to cause joint motion and move loads as a training stimulus. Both plyometric and resistance-training modes of exercise follow the principles of progression in which frequency, volume, and intensity are manipulated to gain the desired training effect. Plyometric training may be important for enhancing the rate of force development during jumping and sprinting, whereas resistance training is needed to enhance muscular strength and acceleration (Fleck and Kraemer, 2014). Whitehead et al. (2018) investigated the effects of short-term plyometric and resistance training on lower-body muscular performance. They found that after eight weeks of training, the plyometric exercise group showed significantly better vertical-jump distances compared to the resistance-training group. There were no differences observed between the two training regimens for the twenty-meter sprint.

4.8: Periodization

This is the planned manipulation of training variables (load, sets, and repetitions) to maximize training adaptations and prevent overtraining. All types of training, whether aerobic, strengthening, or sport specific, can be periodized. Periodization is widely regarded as a principal method of developing an athlete's peak performance. Some form of periodization is usually needed for maximum strength gains to occur. Periodization is related to Selye's general adaptation syndrome (GAS), which states that systems will adapt to any changes they might experience attempting to meet the demand of the stressor—in this case, the training regimen. Stress is defined as a "real or interpreted threat to the physiological or psychological integrity (i.e. homeostasis) of an individual that results in physiological and/or behavioural responses" (McEwan, 2005). Any activity, event, or stimulus including exercise that causes stress can be referred as a stressor. Selye (1976) defined stress as a nonspecific response of the body to any demand. He classified a stressor as an agent that produces stress at any time. Physical exercise has been known to provoke large and diverse stress responses within the neuroendocrine system. For example, the major stress-related hormones typically affected substantially by acute exercise training include cortisol, epinephrine, testosterone, and b-endorphins (Hackney, 2006). The GAS describes how biological organisms react to physiological stress. The GAS has three distinct chronological phases: alarm, resistance, and exhaustion phases (Selye, 1976). The alarm phase represents an initial reaction to stress, which initiates defensive mechanisms in the organism. The alarm phase often results in the overall decrease in general function of the body. After this initial alarm response, a continued exposure to the stressor allows the resistance phase to be activated. In the resistance phase, the body ceases to react negatively but instead positively to the perceived or actual stress. This aims to achieve a biological state equal to or exceeding the state prior to the alarm phase. If the stress continues to be applied, the adaptation response from the resistance phase is eventually lost, leading to the exhaustion phase.

If the application of stress continues, according to Selye, the organism will remain in the alarm or exhaustion phase, eventually leading to death. It the stress stimulus is controlled, decreased, or removed, the earlier experience of stress will allow for the biological organism to adapt and then become capable of responding to more stress in a positive way. According to the GAS theory, both disease and exercise are forms of stress that elicit physiological responses in the body. Exercise prescription, applied correctly, can manipulate the GAS. By actively controlling physiological stress through exercise prescription, the athlete is able to progress through the alarm and resistance phases. Once the athlete has gone through the first two phases in the GAS, the stress must be removed during or before the exhaustion phase. This allows for what is known as the supercompensation effect to occur (Issurin, 2010). This is defined as the athlete's peak or improved performance. There are four phases involved in supercompensation. The first phase of the training cycle with initial loading causes fatigue and an acute reduction in the athlete's work capability. The second phase is characterized by marked fatigue and a pronounced process of recovery. Consequently, toward the end of this phase, the athlete's work capability increases and reaches preload levels. During the third phase, work capability continues to increase, producing higher fitness levels in anticipation of the next training session—thus surpassing the previous level of fitness and achieving a peak that corresponds to the supercompensation phase. In the fourth phase, work capability returns to the preload levels. If there are no further workouts, the fitness level will slowly decline back toward the initial fitness level. The supercompensation effect is induced following a specific training cycle but not a single workout.

Prescribing exercise based on the GAS is a method to control when an athlete would reach their maximum potential. The objective of a periodized program is to optimize the principle of overload, the process by which the neuromuscular systems adapt to the unaccustomed load or stressors. The training program specifies the intensity, volume, and frequency, and the interactions of these variables result in the overload. There is an inverse relationship between training volume and intensity, as mentioned in 4.2. Training volume and alterations of intensity are necessary for the neuromuscular system to maximally adapt to the stress or training load. Hence, the neuromuscular system adapts to the increasing demands, which leads to an increase in muscular performance. If the system adapts to stressors without concomitant changes in overload, no further adaptations are needed, and increases in the desired outcome will eventually stop. Periodization constantly changes the load on the neuromuscular system to avoid this problem. It also varies the workouts and avoids plateaus or boredom.

The linear or classic model of periodization was developed by a Russian scientist, Lev Matveev, and applied by the Soviet Union from the late 1950s to the 1980s (Bartolomei et al., 2014). This was originally based on a twelve-month period. The program is referred to as a macrocycle with two subdivisions: the mesocycle (three to four months) and the microcycle (one to four weeks). Another model of periodization first proposed by Poliquin in 1988 is undulating or nonlinear. Nonlinear periodization is based on the concept that training volume and load are altered more frequently, either on a daily, weekly, or biweekly basis, to allow the neuromuscular system more frequent periods of recovery. Phases are much shorter, providing more frequent changes in stimuli, which may be highly conductive to strength gains. Traditional periodization consists of increasing intensities and decreasing volumes throughout the training period, whereas nonlinear periodization is characterized by alternating high-volume, low-intensity with low-volume, high-intensity training sessions within the same week (e.g., by performing strength-training sets of 12–15 RM on a Monday, 8–10 RM on a Wednesday, and sets of 3–5 RM on a Friday; Rhea et al., 2002).

Kraemar and Fleck (2007) proposed planned versus flexible nonlinear periodization. The planned model follows predicted loading schemes. The flexible plan allows the trainer to adjust the plan based on the status of the athlete. Reverse linear periodization follows modifications in load and volume but in a reverse order, increasing volume and decreasing load. There are numerous periodization programs possible. Training adaptations using periodization can be achieved by manipulating sets, repetitions, exercise order or type, type of contractions, training frequency, and rest periods.

Periodized strengthening programs have been found to elicit greater strength gains than non-periodized programs, but no significant differences in strength gains have been found when training volume and intensity have been equated between linear periodization and nonlinear in untrained or trained individuals, whether male or female. A study by De Sousa et al. (2018) investigated the effects of non-periodized, traditionally periodized, and daily undulating periodized regimens on muscle strength and hypertrophy in thirty-three untrained males after a twelve-week program. They assessed muscle strength by the squat and measured the quadriceps cross-sectional area (QCSA). All training groups increased QCSA after twelve weeks. Similar training-induced adaptations were seen after twelve weeks in both the non-periodized and periodized regimens, but after the initial six weeks of training, the periodized regimens elicited greater rates of muscular adaptations. The authors concluded that exercise intensity is the most important variable for stimulating muscle growth. An earlier study compared two different periodized regimens to improve muscular strength. Alvar et al. (2010) compared the effects of a linear periodization (LP) program with a daily undulating periodization (DUP) program on maximal strength gains in athletes. This was a six-week training program equating intensity and load in both groups. The LP group followed a training program that decreased volume of repetitions while increasing intensity (percentage of 1 RM), whereas the DUP group performed a high-volume, low-intensity; a medium volume and medium intensity; and a low-volume, high-intensity workout each week. Both training programs showed significant strength gains in the bench press after six weeks, but there was no statistical difference between the groups.

When an athlete is training for an endurance event, the commonly used method of periodized training is linear. This usually begins with a period of high-volume, low-intensity training to improve aerobic capacity before increasing the proportion of high-intensity training. This ensures a level of aerobic capacity so that the athlete can tolerate high-intensity exercise in later training. Reverse linear periodization is used in short- to middle-distance runners and begins with a period of high-intensity training. Continuous training, or long-interval training, is gradually introduced to further develop aerobic capacity and fatigue tolerance. High-intensity work early on aims to enhance an aerobic threshold and innervate more muscle fibers to improve running economy (defined as the steady-state oxygen consumption; see 4.4). Bradbury et al. (2018) compared a linear and reverse linear periodized program with equated volume and intensity for endurance training. The study found no superior benefit of either program but showed that periodized training elicited greater improvements in endurance performance[25] than non-periodized training, which acted as the control. This study emphasized the importance of a planned training structure for endurance training.

---

25. The periodized training group in the Bradbury et al. (2018) study showed greater increases in $VO2_{max}$, AT, and RE, which are measures of endurance performance.

CHAPTER 4 SUMMARY

This chapter outlines some of the basic principles of modern training. Strength is the ability of the muscle to exert force or torque at a specified or determined velocity. Optimal gains in muscle function and size can occur with training two to three times per week by whole-body training or by split-body routines. The training volume is a summation of the total number of repetitions performed during a training session multiplied by the resistance used in kilograms or pounds. The training volume can be altered by changing the number of repetitions performed per set, the number of sets per exercise, or the number of exercises per session.

Power is defined as the product of force and velocity. Muscle power is the rate at which a muscle does work or transfers energy to complete a movement task. Increasing power can improve sports performance. Exercise intensity can be defined as the rate of energy expenditure ranging from low levels of sedentary activities, such as sitting or lying, to high-intensity exercise like running, which cannot be sustained for longer than ten minutes. Exercise intensity can be expressed as an absolute measure such as the metabolic equivalent (MET).

Endurance is the capacity to sustain a given velocity or power output for the longest possible time. The four key parameters of aerobic endurance are $VO2_{max}$, anaerobic threshold, exercise or work economy, and oxygen-uptake kinetics. $VO2_{max}$ is the measure of maximal oxygen uptake and an indicator of aerobic capacity.

Progressive overload is required to continue to make gains in an exercise program and adapt to the training stimulus, or a plateau will be reached. In strength training this can be achieved by increasing the resistance, by increasing the training volume (achieved by increasing either number of repetitions, sets, or exercises performed), by altering rest periods, or by increasing the repetition velocity during submaximal resistances. Interval training involves alternating high-intensity periods of exercise with active or passive periods. Fartlek training combines continuous and interval training. Continuous training consists of aerobic exercise bouts performed at low to moderate intensity without rest periods.

High-intensity interval training (HIIT) involves repeated bouts of short- to moderate-duration exercise (i.e., ten seconds to five minutes), completed at an intensity that is greater than the anaerobic threshold. HIIT has been shown to improve performance in previously trained runners, cyclists, and team athletes such as football players. Plyometrics is a training method based on the stretch-reflex properties of the muscle to produce power. Examples of plyometric exercise include the vertical jump, the single leg jump, and jump squat while holding dumbbells. Plyometrics has become a valuable element of training toward the enhancement of performance in athletes and professional sport.

Periodization is the planned manipulation of training variables (load, sets, and repetitions) to maximize training adaptations and prevent overtraining. Periodization is related to Selye's general adaptation syndrome (GAS). The GAS has three distinct chronological phases: alarm, resistance, and exhaustion phases. Once the athlete has gone through the first two phases, the stress must be removed during or before the exhaustion phase. This allows for the supercompensation effect to occur. Supercompensation enables the athlete to surpass their previous level of fitness.

There are two main types of periodization training: linear and nonlinear. Linear periodization was originally based on a twelve-month period and consists of increasing intensities and decreasing volumes throughout the training period, whereas in nonlinear periodization, the training volume and load are more frequently characterized by alternating high-volume, low-intensity with low-volume, high-intensity training sessions during the workout. Periodized strengthening programs have been found to elicit greater strength gains than non-periodized programs, but there is no difference between linear periodization and nonlinear regimens when training volume and intensity have been equated.

CHAPTER 5:

GYMNASTICS, EXERCISE, AND TRAINING IN ANCIENT GREECE

Moreover, indolence and present enjoyment can never bring the body into good condition, as trainers say, neither do they put into the soul knowledge of any value, but strenuous effort leads up to good and noble deeds.

—Xenophon, *Symposium* 2.19–20

5.1: Gymnastics and General Exercise

The ancient Greeks held physical fitness in high regard. Obtaining an athletic physique was important to them, as to look good was to be good. The ancient Greeks were the first physical culturists, as they developed a regimen of exercise and diet to achieve the ideal body. Sculptures of their muscular physiques with broad shoulders, narrow waists, and prominent buttocks exemplify this fact (see chapter 6). Greek athletic trainers in theory aimed not only at success in competition but for beauty, strength, agility, and grace in the body (Lehmann, 2009). Gymnastic exercises along with exposure to the arts and music were all considered vital in the education of the Greek citizen. The mind and body were educated together to achieve "individual completeness and harmony of parts" (Leonard, 1915).

There is limited evidence regarding the methods of training in ancient Greece. The works of early theorists from antiquity do not survive, and what we do have only exists in fragmentary form. The likes of Iccus of Tarentum (fifth century BC), Herodicus of Selymbria (fifth century BC), Diotimus (before the third century BC), Theon of Alexandria (AD 130–160), and Tryphon (15 BC–AD 20) all laid out not practical exercise but theories about training. Herodicus (also see chapter 3) was a paedotribe and was reputedly a teacher of Hippocrates. He is described by Robinson (1955) as a gymnastic trainer who started the era of medical gymnastics. Harris (1964) also mentioned that Herodicus was a doctor and the greatest of all trainers, who recommended maintaining health by a combination of strict diet and regular physical activity. He believed that illness resulted from an imbalance between food intake and physical activity (Shephard, 2012). Galen, in *Hygiene*, cites Theon's[26] lost *Gymnastrion*. Galen mentions that Theon wrote four books about individual exercises and many other exercises common to all actions. According to Galen, he created a work chiefly for training athletes. Robinson (1955) suggested several training manuals pertaining to physical training existed in antiquity but only that of Philostratus's *Gymnasticus* has survived.

Numerous studies have used Hellenistic and later sources of training practices because of the paucity of sources for early athletics. Kyle (2015) has warned against relying heavily on the literary works of Philostratus, Galen, and Lucian on athletics. He suggests these sources are of limited value because of their lateness, technical approach, and imaginative content. I disagree, as Galen mentioned previously, and likely Philostratus had access to earlier sources on athletics and thus provided important insights into the type of exercises used and training regimens.

In the opinion of Galen, before the time of Plato, gymnastics became an art, but it was at the time of Trojan War that it began to fully develop. It may have existed before that period but was not named, cultivated, or formed into a regular art form.

---

26. Theon was an ex-athlete who wrote a work on exercise and a longer work, *Gymnastrion*, both only known to Galen.

According to Galen, those knowledgeable in the gymnastic art were the physicians Hippocrates, Diocles,[27] Praxagoras,[28] Philotimus,[29] Erasistratus,[30] and Herophilus[31] (Galen, Thrasybulus 38). It is strange that Galen regarded Erasistratus as being knowledgeable on gymnastics, as Erasistratus had suggested exercise was not necessary for the health of the animal frame.

There was nothing clearly explained in ancient literature as to the manner or order these exercises arrived to form the art itself (Blundell, 1864). Plutarch considered that exercises were, in the first instance, simple contests in which men engaged with the sole object of victory with its rewards. From this, these contests were afterward translated into a sort of sacrifice or dedication to the gods and became sacred festivals attracting the people of Greece. Aristotle agreed that when the celebration of these sacrifices to the gods increased in number, these exercises were permanently instituted in their honor. In *The Iliad*, the games and exercises were instituted by Achilles for the improvement of his army. In the early ages, great delight was taken in these exercises to reap rewards, combining agility and strength to enable the Greeks to conquer in the wars (Blundell, 1864).

Taylor (1880) suggests the ancients defined exercise as movements that had different physiological effects and were determined by specific rules. These effects were modified according to the position of the body and were sometimes slow, quick, or moderate but always regular. Movements were precise in their quantity, quality, duration, and rhythm. These movements were divided into three kinds according to their effects.[32] The first kind of movement proceeded within, having its origin in the depths of the body. These were active movements, such as raising a weight and holding it at arm's length, walking up a steep ascent,

---

27. Diocles of Carystus was a physician referred to by Galen on several topics. He held the Hippocratic view on the importance of opposites. His treatment methods included diet, exercise, and bathing.

28. Praxagoras of Cos was a follower of Diocles. He expanded the concept of the humors, subdividing the basic four on the grounds of color, taste, and other aspects to make ten.

29. Philotimus was a pupil of Praxagoras and was regarded by Celsus as one of the eminent physicians of antiquity.

30. Erasistratus made a significant contribution to the anatomy of the cardiovascular system. He was strongly criticized by Galen for his corpuscular theory.

31. Herophilus subscribed to the same physiology based on the four elemental qualities as Galen. He also played a major role in establishing the pulse theory, which Galen had taken up.

32. Taylor (1880) in his work used Galen's exercise description for the three type of movements used by the ancients (see 5.2).

climbing a rope, or resisting the efforts of one trying to lower the extended arms. These movements required the exertion of power and were performed in the palaestra directed by the paedotribe. The second kind of movements were rapid, but neither intense nor violent. Examples of these movements include a mock combat, play with a small ball, running in a circle that constantly diminished till a point has been reached, walking on tiptoes, raising the arms and causing them to move rapidly, alternately forward or backward, finally rolling, either alone or together in the palaestra. The third kind of movements were violent, consisting of exercise with force and rapid exertion. These included using the spade, leaping constantly without resting, throwing heavy projectiles, walking up or down an artificial hill, or working rapidly in heavy armor.

Plato explains that gymnastic training combined dance and wrestling to result in strength, grace, and good health (Plato, *Laws* 7.795e–796a). In accordance with Galen's view, Plato condemned the body type the resulted from training in what Greeks called the heavy events. These were wrestling, boxing, and the pankration (see chapter 2). This training resulted in fleshy, overmuscled bodies, gracelessness, and ill health. In the fourth century BC art, Hermes represented grace and agility, whereas Heracles represented the overly muscled type. As the number of games and stakes (in terms of glory and prizes) increased, specialization followed. This specialization reached a point that a runner knew nothing of wrestling (Galen, *Thrasybulus* 33; Phil, *Gym* 15). This contradicts Young's view (1996) that in this period, there was increased diversity in Greek athletics rather than specialization (see chapter 1).

John Blundell's 1864 work included a translation of *De Arte Gymnastica*, by Mercuriale. Girolamo Mercuriale (1530–1606) was one of the most famous physicians of the Renaissance. He was the personal physician to the emperor Maximilian II. Mercuriale classified exercise into two main types: preventive and therapeutic. He believed that the quantity and duration of exercise should be individualized according to a person's constitution and level of fitness (Todd, 1995). *De Arte Gymnastica* revived an interest in Galen and the training methods of the ancient Greeks.

Blundell's work contained a great body of ancient knowledge gathered from older sources comprising nearly two hundred ancient writers (as it is claimed by the author). Blundell included the Mercuriale text in his work but interspersed this with other material. He mentions that Oribasius had stated there were six hundred exercises conducted in the palaestra. Oribasius, also mentioned by Taylor (1880), was a Greek physician in the fourth century AD. Galen's *Art of Medicine* was quoted or utilized by Oribasius, who was a major medical encyclopedist of his time. He may have had access to Galen's writings on exercise. It was suggested the "ancient" movements of exercise were derived from Oribasius, but he probably also had access to the ancient sources on this subject. Blundell describes three kinds of ancient gymnastics taken from Mercuriale: the medical, the warlike, and the athletic.

All these exercises were similar in character, as they aimed to train the body but differed in their objectives and were separately instituted. Simple gymnastics were moderate and part of medical science. By the fourth century BC, the science of gymnastics was closely connected with the emerging field of medicine. The warlike exercises were classified as military gymnastics. These required more exertion and not only prepared the subject for war but also allowed them to acquire military skills. The third and most common form of gymnastics was the athletic, for which Galen called by making men stronger than they were by nature. Those who trained for war were not necessarily athletes. The medical and warlike exercises gave strength and health, whereas the athletic gymnastics gave strength but not health. Mercuriale coined athletic gymnastics as "the vicious art." As mentioned previously, some ancient writers criticized athletes and athletic training. Galen mentioned that these athletes had too much heaviness of the body and comparative robustness, but heaviness of mind and dull senses. Plato called the athlete slothful, and Hippocrates detested them in every respect. Plutarch had compared them to the stones and columns of the gymnasium (Blundell, 1864).

Bourne (2008) suggests that preparation for an athletic event primarily involved practice of the event, rather than any specialized exercises. This may be partly true, but the ancient Greeks were aware of many training methods to develop different parts of the body for the athletic events or activities. Athletes later found it necessary to specialize in one event, as different events required different methods of application and training. Galen defined exercise to be a strong motion and a change of breathing, alternate or varied. He also demonstrated that exercise, motion, and labor were aspects that differed from each other. Galen had observed there were numerous kinds of exercise practiced in the gymnasium. A form of training called Kabaskevi included a wide variety of exercises and could last several hours (Paleologos, 1961).

5.2: Galen on Health and Exercise

Galen defined hygiene as the therapeutic art concerning the body. He stated, "We call health that state in which we neither feel pain nor are impeded in the functions pertaining to life" (Johnson, 2018). Galen suggested that both Asclepiades and Erasistratus opposed exercises, but almost all other doctors praised them, not only in regard for achieving a good bodily condition but also for improving health. Asclepiades is mentioned along with Erasistratus by Galen more often than he is with any other doctor. Galen mentions them together when he is attacking them with their shared doctrine. According to Asclepiades and Erasistratus, there was just one cause of all disease. Erasistratus said it is the transference of blood into the arteries, whereas Asclepiades it was the impaction of corpuscles in pores. They both rejected the theory of the humors as a cause of disease, in which Galen strongly believed (Vallance, 1990). Galen probably criticized Asclepiades, as his therapeutic practice had an emphasis on nonviolent exercise advocating the benefits of "passive exercise," which was contrary to Galen's exercise beliefs. In *Thrasybulus*, Galen lists three groups of people to whom hygienic measures may properly be applied: those who are in a good state already, those who are recovering from illness, and those who are in a state intermediate between health and disease. The gymnastic trainer, according to Galen, knows the effects of all exercises and can select those that are moderate and midway between the excesses of each. For the best constitution of the body the individual requires, moderate exercise is best for the preservation of health. Galen goes on to suggest that those exercising for health alone should not lead themselves to excessive exertions as to be overcome by fatigue. Galen was highly critical of athletes in general. Galen quotes from Hippocrates that "the athletic disposition is not natural, better the healthy condition or state (hexis)" (Johnson, 2018).

According to Galen, it is necessary for someone who practices the art of hygiene to know about all the kinds of exercises. The one who is concerned with exercises alone should be called the gymnastic trainer. The one concerned with treatment is a doctor (see chapter 3). The exercises Galen described were comparable to the ones used by athletes like Milo in the sixth century BC and were perhaps in vogue in Galen's time (Robinson, 1955). Galen defined three categories of exercise. His first category was called vigorous exercises, performed with strength but without speed (Galen, *Hygiene II*, 9). These were essentially a type of exercise to improve muscular strength—for example, having to lift a great weight remaining on the spot, or to step forward a little and then walk uphill (with the weight). Controlling four horses with reins was a very vigorous exercise, according to Galen. He also mentioned that a vigorous exercise is when someone takes hold of a rope or a high piece of wood and remains hanging from it as long as he can (Green, 1951). In this instance he is practicing a robust and strong exercise but not, in fact, one that is rapid. Galen mentions there are countless vigorous exercises in the wrestling school to prepare for strength that involve two people performing various wrestling maneuvers. The gymnastic trainer is experienced as well as practiced in all these exercises, according to Galen (*Hygiene II*, 9). As mentioned in chapter 4, strength development is an integral part for all professional sports training regimens. Modern wrestling bouts frequently require the ability to push and pull while stabilizing with the upper body and torso as well as performing lifts with the body weight of a competitor by using the legs (Kraemer et al., 2004). This requires total body strength to improve these skills, and development of this strength should include a variety of exercises, not dissimilar to those described by Galen above. Unfortunately, we have no details from Galen regarding the training variables such as the frequency, intensity, and volume (sets and repetitions) required to design a resistance exercise program.

The second category of exercises he classified as rapid without being vigorous and violent—for example, running or shadowboxing, and the exercise with the punching bag or small ball. An exercise with a leather bag is described by Oribasius. This bag was filled with flour or sand and suspended from a height. It was then pushed forward with the hands to the extremity of the rope, and as it recoiled, the person performing the exercise would retreat backward to escape from it. This exercise was also mentioned by Hippocrates. This was different from the follis, or leather ball inflated with air used by the Romans (Adams, 1844). Martial, a Roman poet born in approximately AD 41, also describes the follis, or bladder ball, as a variety of Roman ball. This ball, he claimed, was invented for Pompey the Great[33] by his trainer, Atticus of Naples, possibly when he was recovering from a serious illness in Campania in the spring of 50 BC. There were several kinds of balls, both large and small, used and played with in different ways. The three most common types of ball were the *harpastum* (see 5.3), *paganica*, and the follis. The harpastum was small and hard stuffed with hair like a golf ball. The paganica was a ball stuffed with feathers, and the follis was the largest, comparable to the modern basketball (Morindin, 1890; Sweet, 1987). This second category was classed as speed exercises developed to improve speed mostly but not strength. Reaction speed and punch force are two important qualities in boxing.

The precompetition training period for boxers includes tempo training with a boxing bag, sparing at high intensity, speed endurance runs and maximal strength training (Hukkanen and Häkkinen, 2017). The second category of exercise described by Galen could have been used for boxing training in antiquity. Galen gives a further example of *pitylisma*, which is when someone stands on tiptoe, stretches his arms up, and, moving very quickly, carries them backward and forward (Robinson, 1955). Again, he describes this exercise as rapid but not violent.

Galen also suggested it was possible to practice rapid exercise with the legs alone by repeatedly springing backward only and sometimes also advancing each of the legs forward in turn (Galen, *Hygiene* II, 10). Is Galen describing an early form of plyometric training, which could have been used for improving performance in the jumping and sprinting events? As mentioned in chapter 4, plyometric training involves performing body-weight jumping, hopping, or skipping type exercises using the stretch-shortening cycle of the muscle action. During the stretch-shortening cycle (SSC), the preactivated muscles experience a rapid elongation (eccentric phase), followed by an immediate shortening action (concentric), thus utilizing the elastic energy stored during the eccentric phase. This eccentric/concentric coupling (SSC) produces a more powerful contraction than concentric actions alone (Komi, 1984).

Plyometric training is generally accepted to be part of an athlete's training program and is usually combined with other training modalities, such as weight training. It has positive effects on the development of jumping power, speed,

---

33. Pompey the Great, born in 106 BC, was a Roman general and statesman. He was a rival to Julius Caesar. His illness was a recurring fever, possibly due to malaria (Goldsworthy, 2007).

and even running economy (Lievens et al., 2020). Galen is describing a type of bounding horizontal jump but backward. The transfer of plyometric training (PYT) to athletic performance depends on the specificity of plyometric exercises performed. Therefore, athletes who require power for moving in the horizontal plane (e.g., sprinters or long jumpers) mainly engage in bounding plyometric exercise. Sprinting requires an explosive concentric and SSC force production of the lower-limb muscles. It has been suggested that the greatest effects of PYT on sprinting performance occur in the acceleration phase, since the velocity of muscle action in bounding plyometric exercises most closely approximates the velocities of muscle action in the acceleration phase of the sprint (Markovic and Mikulic, 2010). PYT has the potential to improve sprint performance but has not been found superior to traditional sprint training (Rimmer and Sleivert, 2000). PYT has smaller effects on horizontal jumping performance (i.e., the long jump), compared to the effects on vertical jumping performance (Markovic and Mikulic, 2010). Therefore, Galen's second category of exercise may have used a form of PYT to improve speed for the running event such as the stadion race.

Lucian also mentions possibly an earlier form of plyometric training: "Others in other places are all exerting themselves; They jump up and down as if they were running but stay in the same place; and they spring high up and kick the air" (Lucian, *Anacharsis* 4). Lucian could be describing a type of countermovement jump (CMJ). For the CMJ, athletes start from an upright starting position and then perform a fast downward movement by flexing the knees and hips, which is immediately followed by a rapid leg extension resulting in a vertical jump (Bouguezzi et al., 2018). The CMJ is a popular training exercise and assessment for anaerobic leg power. It is also a critical skill for sports such as basketball and high jumping (Rugg and Sternlicht, 2013). Typical plyometric exercises include the CMJ, as well as drop and squat jumps, which should be combined to improve jump performance rather than using only one form alone (de Villarreal et al., 2009). PYT can be combined with other training modalities as mentioned previously and can be performed at various intensity levels.

Previous research has shown that PYT significantly improves strength performance independent of fitness level or sex of the subject (Markovic and Mikulic, 2010). When PYT is combined with weight training, there have been found to be greater relative changes in muscle strength and power compared to PYT alone

(Adams et al., 1987). Montero (2020), though, in his article suggests Lucian's description is an example of a runner's warm-up routine. The conversation between Solon and Anacharsis is supposed to have taken place in the Lyceum at Athens. Anacharsis describes the activities taking place at the gymnasium, including wrestling and the pankration. I suggest this activity described by Anacharsis is more than just a warm-up, as the athletes are exerting themselves, indicating a more intense form of exercise.

The third category of exercises comprises violent exercises, which were described as a combination of vigor and rapidity. This exercise combined strength and speed, which equals power. The exercises that were classified as strong or vigorous became violent by accelerating their speed (Galen, *Hygiene* II, 10). For example, digging or throwing a quoit (see 5.4), moving and jumping continuously without a rest, or hurling any one of the heavy weapons. Galen suggests these power exercises are brought into use intermittently. Muscle power is the product of force and velocity; thus, using either of these components, or combining them, needs to be addressed in a training program to develop power (Zaras et al., 2013). An individual cannot possess a high level of power without first being relatively strong.

Previous research has demonstrated that heavy strength-training programs involving untrained to moderately trained subjects resulted not only in improved maximal strength but also increased maximal power output, but this diminishes as strength levels increase. Traditional resistance-training exercises, such as the squat or bench press, can be used to increase maximal power output in the early phases of training or with endurance athletes who only need to maintain a relatively low level of strength. Further improvement in maximal muscular power and performance enhancement in well-trained athletes requires a multifaceted approach incorporating a variety of training strategies (Cormie et al., 2011). Heavy resistance training using high resistance increases power output at low velocities, whereas light resistance training (30 percent of MVC) at higher velocities of muscle action increases power output for those higher velocities. Thus, increases in power are specific to the training resistance and velocity used (Newton and Kraemer, 1994). To maximize the transfer of training to performance, power training must involve the use of movement patterns, loads, and velocities that are specific to the demands of the individual's sport.

Ballistic or explosive resistance training to improve power, such as jumping or throwing activities, utilizes lighter resistances and higher velocities of muscle action performed in a ballistic fashion. Due to the continued acceleration throughout the range of motion, force, power, and muscle activation are higher during a ballistic movement in comparison to a similar traditional resistance-training exercise. As a result, coaches recommend the inclusion of ballistic exercises rather than traditional resistance training exercises in power-training programs (Cormie et al., 2011). Several studies have shown that explosive lifting of light loads (30–50 percent of 1 RM) to be effective for increasing dynamic athletic performance. The closer the movement pattern and velocity of the training exercise is to the actual sporting movement, the greater the transfer of training gains to athletic performance (McEvoy and Newton, 1998). Hence, Galen's power exercise of throwing the quoit could be used to improve performance in the discus event. Plummer (1898a) stated that in the local gymnasium, the size and weight of the discus varied in order so that the athlete might select one in accord with his strength in preparation for the discus event. But in the pentathlon competition, a standard weight and size of discus was used so that the competitors might be impartially tested.

Plyometric exercises are also ballistic in nature but are performed with little or no resistance, such as body mass. Overload in plyometric training is achieved by increasing the stretch rate either by minimizing the duration of the SSC and/or the stretch load—for example, increasing the height of the drop in drop jumps. Plyometrics is specific to a variety of movements typically encountered in sport and have been used to significantly improve maximal power output during sports-specific movements. Ballistic, plyometric, and resistance training can be used effectively within a power-training program to enhance maximal power in dynamic and multijoint movements common to many sports (Cormie et al., 2011).

The categorization of these three main types of exercise (strength, speed, and a combination of speed and strength = power) may demonstrate the ancient Greeks' awareness of basic exercise principles. Issurin (2010) suggests Galen's category of exercise description may qualify as a precursor of contemporary periodization for strength training but said this could be questionable based on current knowledge. Traditional periodization consists of increasing exercise intensities and decreasing volumes throughout the training period. Training adaptations using periodization can be achieved by manipulating the exercise type and other training variables such as load, sets and repetitions. I do not think Galen's exercise categories can be equated with periodization. I believe Galen's category of exercise may indicate knowledge of sports-specific training. The first category trains for strength required in the heavy events such as wrestling; the second category for speed required in the stadion race (sprinting) or boxing; and the third category for power necessary for the throwing events such as the discus. Galen saw the importance of exercising at the right intensity for health benefits. He wrote, "To me, it does not mean that all movement is exercise, but only when it is vigorous. The criterion of vigorousness is change of respiration. Those movements that do not alter respiration are not called exercise" (Callaghan, 2004). Galen also mentions exercises for specific parts of the body. He suggested exercises for the upper parts included shadowboxing, discus throwing, the use of handheld weights when jumping (exercise for the upper limbs, in this instance), and all those exercises done on the ground when in the wrestling school. For those thin (with a lack of flesh) in the legs, Galen recommended running more than any other exercise (Galen, *Hygiene* V, 3). Galen claimed that it was accepted by all gymnastic trainers that rapid exercise thin the athlete, while slow exercises enflesh him (Galen, *Hygiene* VI, 3). He gave an example for someone who was very fat became moderately well-fleshed in a short time by fast running (Galen, *Hygiene* VI, 8).

5.3: Galen: On Exercise with the Small Ball

Galen believed that exercises with the ball were the best of all exercises, as one can exercise vigorously and enjoy the activity at the same time, exercises that "delight the soul." There was no need for equipment or any associated expense with this activity. As mentioned previously in chapter 3, there was a trainer and specific area in the gymnasium for ball games. Galen does not describe the type of balls used. He suggests the exercises with the ball can exercise all parts of the body. As well as being vigorous, these exercises can also be gentle. One of the ball games Galen describes is one in which men place themselves across from each other and prevent another in the middle from intercepting the ball. The ball game of interception was called Harpastum, according to Harris (1972). This game was a Roman adaptation of the Greek game Episkyros, in which a player, standing between two lines of opponents, tries to intercept the catches as they throw to one another. Players are entitled to fight each other, using wrestling holds to incapacitate the opposing team. This is reflected in Galen's description of the game when he suggests it involves much seizing of the neck and many wrestling holds all mixed together. This activity, according to Galen, strengthened the abdomen, back, and lower legs. Marindin (1890) also believed Galen was describing the game Harpastum in his treatise.

In this short treatise, Galen mentions his disapproval of running and other such exercises that thin the body. He also mentioned exercises worked in the wrestling school that brought excess flesh. He found fault with disproportion and advocated exercise, or the practice of the art in moderation. He suggested that those who exercise the body unequally are unhealthy. Galen believed that the exercise with the small ball was beneficial to health because it creates a proper balance to the body, training both speed and strength. Galen said that the exercises with the small ball were free of external dangers (significant injury), unlike running swiftly, jumping, or discus throwing which can lead to twisting of the limbs. The ball game of Harpastum was surely not free of potential serious injury, as Galen describes wrestling holds and the aim to incapacitate opponents. The Trigon was another Roman ball game described by Martial. This involved three players who stood in a triangle throwing several balls at each other. Each player would feint, dummy, and deflect, trying to mislead the others. The winner of the game was the one who dropped the fewest catches. This was a fast and vigorous game (Marindin, 1890).

5.4: Specific Aspects of Exercise Training in Ancient Greece
5.4.1: Strengthening
The ancient Egyptians practiced lifting heavy bags for strengthening, and there is evidence of the Greeks using weighted implements in the sixth century BC, which continued through to the Roman imperial period (Crowther, 1977). Dumbbells have been depicted in Roman mosaics. An Etruscan relief on a marble chair in the Lateran dated probably in the fourth century BC shows two athletes holding weights that resemble modern dumbbells. Gardiner (1930) suggests that these

are Greek jumping weights and not dumbbells. The two athletes holding the weights in the Etruscan relief are described as boxers. These weights, whether dumbbells or not, were probably used for strengthening the upper limbs. A later Roman mosaic in the baths of Porta Marina in Ostia[34] depicts an athlete holding cylindrical objects in his hands with one raised high and the other lowered like the boxers depicted on the Etruscan relief. This may suggest the use of weights for training rather than for jumping by the way he is holding them (Newby, 2005). Crowther (1977) mentioned that Antyllus, a second-century AD Greek surgeon, had described three types of exercises with halteres or weights, perhaps used for strengthening. The first exercise consists in bending and straightening the arms, an exercise that strengthens the arms and shoulders. This exercise is equivalent to the biceps curl using dumbbells. For the second exercise, the athlete with arms extended lunges, and the third alternately bends and straightens the trunk with arms extended. These exercises strengthen the legs and trunk, respectively, and again are familiar exercises using dumbbells in modern weight training.

Christopoulos et al. (2003) describe the term "*halterobolia*," or weight training for developing the muscles of the body. The halterobolia was an exercise with weights mentioned by Oribasius, but Mercuriale believed this referred to throwing of the weights rather than involving exercises with weight in hand. It was most likely these weights described were used for strengthening well before the time of Antyllus. Pausanias reported halteres being of an oval form and made with holes, or else covered with thongs, through which one could put their fingers. Mercuriale described them as masses or weights of different materials and of such a size that ropes could be fastened to them for holding. The heaviest haltere discovered was only approximately five kilograms, which was too light for strength improvement but useful for flexibility and calisthenic exercises. Heavier spherical weights have been found at Olympia varying from five to twenty-four kilograms. An inscription on a gravestone from antiquity found in Dalmatia may refer to the deceased weight training with a graduating set of weights from 13.5 kg, 17 kg, and 34 kg (Crowther, 1977). The bodily ideal of the ancient Greeks could only be achieved through resistance training. Philostratus mentioned that the trainers of old only trained their athletes for strength and by any means

---

34. The baths of Porta Marina in Ostia were built during the reign of the Roman emperor Trajan, who reigned from AD 98–117.

possible. He said that some trained perhaps metaphorically by carrying weights that were hard to lift, some by competing for speed with horses and hares, and others by bending a thick piece of wrought iron. Others yoked themselves with powerful wagon-drawing oxen, and still others wrestled bulls or even lions by the throat (Phil, *Gym* 43). There were a variety of weight-training type exercises designed by the Greeks to develop and strengthen the muscles. This emphasis upon the use of specific strength training suggested a rudimentary understanding of the progressive overload principle.

Milo of Croton in the sixth century BC was a wrestler, strongman, and famous Olympian. He won six wrestling titles at the Olympiad. A classic fable tells how Milo would do his morning exercises every day with a calf draped across his shoulders. As the calf grew, so did Milo's strength. By the time of the Olympiad, he would be carrying a full-grown bull on his shoulders. This is the first example of the progressive overload principle used in muscle strengthening (increasing training load gradually to continually challenge adaptations in strength), which the Greeks would have understood. Muscle hypertrophy occurs with progressive exercise overload, consisting of the correct load, frequency, intensity, and duration, causing adaptation (Baar et al., 2006). Without overload, there is no adaptation. Neuromuscular adaptation occurs first, followed by increases in muscle and connective tissue strength, and bone mass (Kavanaugh, 2007). A clear minimum level of training is required to induce adaptations, which is highly related to the characteristics of the individual who is training. Milo's story is an early example of progressive overload representing a linear model of exercise progression. The very heavy training load used by Milo may lead to a paradoxical and persistent decrease in performance or overtraining (Foster et al., 2007). The human body's reaction to a training stimulus can be described by Selye's GAS. In the resistance phase, the body is adapting to the stimulus, but the exhaustion phase may result if the training persists for too long and does not allow for adequate recovery. The exhaustion phase in GAS would prevent Milo's type of progressive overload training from occurring. The exercise stress must be removed during or before the exhaustion phase to allow the supercompensation effect to occur (see chapter 4). A periodized training regimen alternating between hard and easy training sessions is required to reduce the risk of developing overtraining syndrome. With the use of periodization, the athlete can continuously challenge the body with progressive overload while avoiding plateaus or detriments to training (Kavanaugh, 2007).

An awareness that speed and strength need to be combined to produce violence or power is required to succeed in athletic events indicates the concept of specificity. This specific speed-strength training was exhibited with the use of specialized jump training, such as scissor jumps or *aphalmos*. The objective was to increase leg strength and power used in the power events such as the jump or throwing (mentioned by Galen). This may be viewed as the first use of plyometric training described in section 5.2 (Yallouris, 1979).

Plyometric training with a progressive overload has been used in young football players as a sport-specific and easy-to-implement training strategy. Ramírez-Campillo et al. (2015) found that a progressive overload plyometric training program was more effective than a constant volume-based overload plyometric program for improving ten-meter sprint and jump performance in young football players. The progressive overload principle in this instance consists of progressively increasing the training loads in time by modifying mainly the training volume and intensity. Plyometric volume is usually defined as foot contacts or time spent doing the exercise (Sankey et al., 2008).

Plyometric intensity is much more difficult to define but requires consideration of both the mass of the mode of resistance or athlete and the acceleration of that mass (Jensen and Ebben, 2007). Plyometric intensity has been defined as the amount of stress placed on involved muscles, connective tissue, and joints being dictated by the type of exercise that is performed (Potach and Chu, 2000). The drop jump used as a plyometric exercise involves jumping off a box (usually 0.3 to 0.6 meters high) and making a two-legged landing with impact absorption (eccentric phase) followed by a powerful concentric movement. Exercise intensity in the drop jump may be defined by parameters such as ground reaction forces and the rate of force production. Altering the drop height makes it possible to manipulate the intensity of this exercise, as increases in drop height from 0.2 m to 0.6 m leads to an increase in ground reaction forces (Makaruk and Sacewicz, 2011). Ramírez-Campillo et al. (2015) concluded that the adaptations induced by progressive overload plyometric training can potentially increase performance and reduce the risk of injury.

A strengthening type of exercise in antiquity was ascending a rope or funambulation by means of the hands and other parts of the body. Rope climbing prepares the muscles for strength even more, according to Galen. Rope climbing has been shown to be a valid a test for upper body power in special forces soldiers (Dhahbi et al., 2015). The *petaurum* was a seat suspended by ropes, and the individual in the seat would be tossed about by assistants. This was presumably an exercise for strengthening the body, especially the stomach (Adams, 1844). Antyllus had described the effects of equitation on the human frame, which the petaurum would mimic. Another substantial strengthening exercise described by Galen was to hold a weight with each outstretched the hands apart (weights from the wrestling school) and then direct someone to draw them down or bend forcibly, while keeping himself immobile and rigid, using the legs and spine. An exercise was also described for strengthening the whole spine. This was to approach another from the side when the other has bent forward, throwing his arms around the flanks to encircle them, lifting him up, holding him for a while, and at the same time carrying him forward. He would then continue to carry the person while bending forward and backward, aiming to exercise the whole back (Robinson, 1955). Lucian quotes that an implement in the gymnasium was made of bronze, circular and resembling a little shield without a handle or straps. This was probably the quoit described later. The athletes threw this shield or quoit high into the air and aimed for a distance to see who could go the farthest and throw beyond the rest (see 5.4.4). This exercise strengthened their shoulders and put muscle into their arms and legs (Harmon, 1961).

We have seen particularly from Galen's description of exercise related to strength training that the ancient Greeks understood the concepts of improving muscular strength, particularly for competition and achieving the Greek ideal. There is evidence that boulders, blocks of stone, metal balls, and cattle were used by the Greeks as tests of strength (Crowther, 1977), whereas ancient resistance training involved the use of rocks, rounded stones, clubs, or large tablets, which were readily available from the gymnasium. These items used for strength training by the Greeks are like those used by strongman competitors in the twenty-first century. The farmer's walk, log press, and stones are the mostly commonly performed strengthening exercises used in strongman training. This type of exercise represents functional movements in multiple planes and challenges the whole musculoskeletal system, in contrast to traditional gym-based training exercise in which the load is moved in a vertical plane (Winwood et al., 2011).

In antiquity there were examples of incredible feats of strength. Homer describes Diomedes lifting a rock heavier than two men of his time easily on his own, and Hector who seized a rock that lay before the gate and handled it alone, which two of the strongest men could barely have levered from the ground onto a cart (*The Iliad*, 5 and 12; Kline, 2009).

The two brothers Kleobis and Biton[35] were famous for their strength. They carried their mother several miles in a cart to the Sanctuary of Hera when their oxen were late returning from the field (Miller, 2004). Polydamas, an Olympic champion of the pankration, in 408 BC was known for his strength, like Milo. He was credited with the ability to grab a speeding chariot with one hand and stop it (Pausanias, 6.5.6).

At Olympia, a block of red sandstone was found weighing 143 kilograms (315 pounds) with a sixth-century BC inscription, which Bybon with one hand threw over his head. The feat claimed of Bybon is probably a myth, but Crowther (1977) suggested a lift of 140 kilograms, and then throwing with one arm is possible. A larger block weighing 480 kilograms was found at the island of Thera (Santorini) bearing the following inscription, also from the sixth century BC: "Eumastas, the son of Kritobolos, lifted me from the ground" (Sweet, 1987). The strongman Eddie Hall in 2016 became the first man to deadlift five hundred kilograms. It is possible Eumastas's feat could have been a type of dead lift, but it would have been difficult to grip such a boulder and lift it to groin height required in this event. Crowther (1977) suggests this feat could be achieved if the weight was only lifted a few centimeters off the ground.

Strengthening exercises were not for all Greeks. The Theban general Epaminondas (420–362 BC) rejected gymnastic exercises that aimed at strength as rendering men unfit for military service, and he suggested his soldiers should focus on developing agility. He warned his fellow Thebans that if they wanted the sovereignty of Greece, they must make more use of the camp and less of the wrestling school (Robinson, 1955).

---

35. The stone statues of Kleobis and Biton date from 590 BC.

5.4.2: Running and Walking

Running was part of training for athletes and was invaluable, particularly for health. The ancients realized that running was especially useful to the lower extremities. Galen described long-distance running and walking as gentler exercises but without intervals. There were several kinds described. These may have been used to train for specific running events and show evidence of specificity. Lucian mentioned training athletes to be good runners, habituating them for long-distance running as well as training others to be light-footed and to increase speed over short distances (Lucian, *Anacharsis* 44). Philostratus suggested runners in the stadion should have moderate muscle development and not excessive as to hinder speed, whereas competitors in the diaulos should be more powerful than those in the stadion (Phil, *Gym*, 33). Examples of types of running include running forward, backward (*anatrochasmos*), in circles (*peritrochasmos*), or ever-decreasing circles until the center point of the circle was reached, running repeatedly back and forth the length of a plethron approximately one hundred feet, decreasing the length each time until a single step was reached (*ecplethrisma* or *ekplethrism*) and running to the right or obliquely on a flat (Gardiner, 1930). Ekplethrism was described by Galen as running back and forth within the length of a plethron, turning to either side, shortening the distance a little each time and ending by coming to stand at one pace (Green, 1951). There is no modern equivalent of the ekplethrism. This could be classified as a form of moderate-intensity continuous training. These training programs consisted of exercise intensity at 50 to 60 percent maximum aerobic capacity, designed to improve endurance (Rognmo et al., 2004). The pace of running is not described by Galen, but a repeated distance of approximately thirty meters is.

Short-duration sprints interspersed with brief recoveries are common in most modern team sports. The ability to produce the best possible average sprint performance over a series of sprints (less than ten seconds), separated by short recovery periods (less than sixty seconds) has been termed *repeated-sprint ability* (RSA). This is an important fitness requirement of team and racquet sports. RSA been shown to improve $VO2_{max}$ by 5 to 6 percent and mean sprint time (Bishop et al., 2011). Is the ekplethrism a form of shuttle run? The twenty-meter multistage shuttle run (SR) test was originally developed by Leger and Lambert (1982) and has been widely used as a predictive test for $VO2_{max}$ by sport scientists, coaches, and fitness advisers (Stickland et al., 2003). The maximal rate of oxygen consumption or $VO2_{max}$ is considered the gold standard for measurement of aerobic fitness (see chapter 4). The SR involves graded exercise to exhaustion with a typical duration of eight to twelve minutes. Subjects run back and forth on a twenty-meter course (usually indoors) and must touch the twenty-meter line at the same time a sound signal is emitted from a prerecorded tape. The frequency of the sound signals is increased 0.5kmh-1 every two minutes from a starting speed of 8.5kmh-1, when the subject can no longer follow the pace (Leger et al., 1988). The increase in running speed is described as a change in test level (Ramsbottom et al., 1988). The last stage number announced is used to predict $VO2_{max}$ from speed corresponding to that stage and age. In theory, the SR could be used to improve aerobic fitness, as the ekplethrism was.

Running in antiquity was performed also outside the gymnasium. Several places were chosen according to the objective of the exercise or trial of physical endurance. Flat ground for running was often sought, or rough, which was even or uneven, either of a meadow or mountain. Running on sand increased the level of work, difficulty, and resistance. Lucian suggested running was not done on hard, resisting ground but in deep sand. This made the exercise harder, as "it is not easy to plant one's foot solidly or to get a purchase with it" (Lucian, *Anacharsis* 44). Galen placed running as among the exercises that were swift without force or violence. There were great differences in the way running was performed, and they had varying effects, perhaps more specific to the athletic event. One form of running was swifter and stronger (sprinting), which necessitated holding and retention of the breath. Other types relating more to an endurance type were slacker and more placid (Blundell, 1864).

Greek doctors after Hippocrates believed that exercise particularly walking was important for good health and could cure health problems. For example, Diocles, a physician and nephew of Hippocrates who lived in Athens around the fourth century BC, said, "A young or middle-aged man should take a walk of about ten stadia just before sunrise. Long walks before meals clear out the body, prepare it for receiving food, and give it more power for digesting" (Dawson, 2005). Celsus also suggested walking as a good exercise for health. He recommended walking up and down hills, which would vary the movement of the body. Walking was not used as a training regimen by athletes but only following heavy exercise (as a cooldown). It was practiced by many nonathletes in the Xysta of the gymnasium (Blundell, 1864).

5.4.3: Jumping

Jumping was described as one of the more warlike exercises, to enable soldiers to overleap ditches or to surmount without effort any high structures of the enemy during battles or sieges. A moderate form of jumping occurred when the subject held plummets (*lialteres*) of lead. These plummets (*tabula plumb*) were heavy sheets of rock or lead described by Galen (Mercuriale, 1569). It was said they jumped better if they carried a stone or plummet in the hands than if they jumped with empty hands (see chapter 2). Galen defined jumping as being among the strong exercises, being robust and of a quick nature. In the gymnasium, there were many different methods of leaping practiced, as through a hoop or over a rope. A high jump was also practiced whereby athletes leaped over pointed poles fixed in the ground, or over one another's heads (Plummer, 1898a). Jumpers also leaped from a low to a high place, requiring greater force and effort. They not only used small weights in the hands but sometimes bore heavier weights on their head or shoulders and even on the feet. These weights aimed to increase strength but were not used to maintain health; rather, they were to allow the athlete to demonstrate his power to jump long and high, laden with these heavy weights. Blundell's sources also mention these jumps were performed only with one foot on the ground (a one leg take-up, as seen in modern-day long jumpers). The jump, as mentioned in chapter 2, was an Olympic event performed in the stadium, where the greatest feat of all was to leap the trench (Blundell, 1864). This is mentioned by Lucian in the *Anacharsis*; he said that athletes are trained to jump a ditch or any other obstacle, sometimes carrying weights as large as they could grasp (Harmon, 1961). Apart from using the halteres and plummets in jumping, they were also used as strengthening exercises (see 5.4.1). In the palaestra, the halteres were sprinkled with particles of lead to make them heavier. Galen suggested the back was strengthened by tossing the plummets (Blundell, 1864).

5.4.4: Throwing

Throwing the quoit or discus was an exercise in the gymnasium. It was considered a very ancient exercise, having been mentioned in *The Iliad*. Apollo was said to be a master of throwing the quoit. Galen and others strongly approved of this as a heavy exercise. Galen stated that throwing the quoit yielded a moderate degree of strength to the inferior extremities and lumbar region. This exercise must have developed to a remarkable degree the muscles of the upper part of the body, shoulders, arms, and hands (Plummer, 1898a). Absolute strength of the upper body plays an important role in discus throwers with the significance for implementation of strength training.

Karampatsos et al. (2011) found that resistance exercises—specifically the inclined bench press—were significantly correlated with discus-throwing performance. In antiquity, it required considerable effort to throw the quoit any significant distance. It was equally used by athletes and nonathletes in the gymnasium. The quoit was sometimes round and very heavy, requiring the strength of one man to raise it. A form of haltere was in the shape of a sling also for throwing. In another example, perhaps as part of the military gymnastics previously described in 5.1, the quoit was a smooth globe of brass or bronze, which was thrown into the air with the arm, protected by a small shield bound with a leather thong or belt. In another instance this quoit was lozenge-shaped and round and was called the discus because of its resemblance to the sun. It was considered by some to have been a plate, with a thickness of three to four fingers and a little more than a foot long. This was either in stone or iron, would have been difficult to throw in the air, and may have been used as a strengthening exercise to improve the throw of the standard discus. The discus depicted in the *Discobolus* statue (see chapter 6) differed entirely from the lozenge-shaped one, which was perforated in the middle and allowed us to understand the mode of throwing the discus. The discus was not as severe an exercise as throwing the iron bar or javelin (Blundell, 1864). Mercuriale described men holding a set of weights curved to fit on the shoulders from a Roman illustration. This may have been used for throwing or a strengthening exercise for the shoulders (Hugh, 2004).

5.5: Diet in Ancient Greece and of the Athlete
5.5.1: Greek Diet
The ancient Greeks recognized the importance of diet for health and treating illness. Knowledge of diet in antiquity is based on archaeological evidence from remains of food, skeletal remains, surviving artifacts, and painted or sculptured representations of activities such as baking or cooking. Many physicians such as Hippocrates (in his work *On Diet*), Erasistratus, and Herophilus emphasized the importance of diet for maintaining health. *Diet* in Greek medicine did not refer just to food but to the whole lifestyle, including nutrition and exercise. Their regimens differed in accordance with the physique of the individual (Simopoulos, 1989). They believed different physiques required special diets. Hippocrates was one of the first physicians to note the association of obesity with reduced life expectancy. He said, "Persons who are naturally very fat are apt to die earlier than those who are slender" (Hippocrates, *Aphorisms* II 44). Plato claimed the physician knew which food was healthy and which was harmful to health. Celsus and Galen also wrote extensively on diet. Galen commented that one should eat in moderation so as not to take too much or too little (Galen, *Hygiene* V, 2). Athenaeus of Naucratis (second and third centuries AD) was a Greek rhetorician and grammarian who recorded nutritional habits of the Greek classical era in his work *Deipnosophistae*.[36] According to Philemon of Syracuse, during the classical period, Greeks had four meals a day: a light breakfast, midday meal, early evening meal, and late dinner.

Olive oil, cereals, legumes, pulses, dairy products, honey, fish, and moderate amounts of meat were the basis of the ancient Greeks' nutrition (Skiaolas and Lascaratos, 2001). This basic diet was generally vegetarian. Meat was not part of everyday meals and may have only been eaten at religious festivals. Their usual diet consisted of thick soup made chiefly from vegetables, fresh and dried bread, as well as cakes made from honey (Harris, 1964). It was Plato who described the diet of the ancient Greeks and how citizens should live. According to Plato, for food, they should prepare wheat or barley meal for baking or kneading. Barley was a major staple of the peasant diet in antiquity, as it was much easier to grow

---

36. The *Deipnosophistae* was written by Athenaeus in the third century AD. This work, split into fifteen books, presents a series of discussions over dinner pertaining to Greek life. Food and drink are the most common topics of conversation throughout.

than wheat. Galen mentions that bread can be made from barley, but the Roman army believed barley did not provide enough strength for the body. Thucydides's account of Athenian rowers during the Peloponnesian war in 431 BC suggested otherwise. During an emergency mission from Piraeus to Mytilene on Lesbos, the rowers consumed a mixture of barley flour, honey, and oil as they rowed to provide them with enough energy. Barley was a less successful cereal for bread but was better suited to barley cakes and flatbreads. Wheat, according to Galen, was superior to barley in strength and nutrients. Barley water was a gentle food for those who would not take solids and could not tolerate the thick humors that wheat produced in the body (Wilkins and Hill, 2006). Wheat was preferred to barley, particularly for making bread. The purest bread, according to Galen, was called *silignis*, which was the most nourishing. Galen went on to say that pure loaves like silignis had a tenacious substance (dough). They required more leaven. The best breads, like the pure loaves, were those that had been most leavened, very well kneaded, and baked in an oven with a moderate heat. These were more suitable for ordinary individuals or older people (Powell and Wilkins, 2003). Salt, olive oil, and cheese were also consumed.

There were several different kinds of vegetables to make country dishes, such as beans and chickpeas (Plato, *Republic* 372c). Galen believed vegetables and legumes as well as fish and birds were not very nutritious (Galen, *Hygiene* VI, 6). Beans were made into soup. Fruit was consumed after the main meal. The most popular fruits included figs, pears, apples, and pomegranates. Plato went on to say it was Homer who stated that ruling kings ensured, with the fear of god, that the land would yield wheat and barley, the trees would be laden with fruit, the sheep would never fail to bring forth their lambs, nor the sea to provide fish (Plato, *Republic* 363c). The support of the gods in ancient Greece was important to ensure a good harvest. There was a diversity of meats in ancient Greece, including beef, pork, goat, mutton, wild boar, deer, and hare, in addition to wild fowl, like pigeon, partridge, peacock, swan, dove, duck, goose, and pelican (Plato, *Laws* 849d). Galen suggested that pork was nutritious and those eating it gained in excess very quickly and had to exercise vigorously (Galen, *Hygiene* VI, 6). Plutarch[37] (AD 46–120) was opposed to the current thinking of his time

---

37. Plutarch, as mentioned previously, was a Greek biographer and essayist known for *Parallel Lives* and *Moralia*.

and advocated a low-fat diet (Simopoulos, 1989). Plutarch suggested one should make the quantity of food less burdensome but also nourishing (e.g., meat and cheese, dried figs, and boiled eggs).

He advised sticking to light things such as vegetables, birds, and fish, which did not have much fat but still should gratify the appetite. One should be careful of meat that could cause indigestion (Plutarch, *De tuenda Sanitate* Vol. 2, 18). The most common way of preparing meat was boiling it while adding salt and other spices to the broth. Meat was preferred roasted. Most of the milk produced was converted to cheese and rarely drunk. Galen recommended consuming milk in moderation. He felt it better to use goats' and asses' milk. Goat's milk was thicker and nourished more (Galen, *Hygiene* V, 7). There were both saltwater and freshwater fish available, such as tuna, mackerel, mullet, anchovy, sole, and eels, as well as octopus, mussels, and oysters. Honey was the only sweetener, as sugar was not available in ancient Greece at the time. Wine was very common and often mixed with water (Simopoulos, 1989). Plato believed in moderation of the diet. He said that the regulation of the diet should be done by physicians or the trainers in gymnastics.

5.5.2: Athlete's Diet

An athlete's daily nutrition should meet the fuel requirements of training to support high-intensity workouts, facilitate muscle growth and repair, as a well as provide essential micronutrients for general health. In addition to a food diet, athletes use supplements to reach a macronutrient[38] target and reverse any nutritional deficiency. Supplements taken by elite rugby players, for example, include whey protein concentrate (a mixture of globular proteins isolated from whey[39]), creatine, omega-3 fish oils, multivitamins, and electrolyte tablets (Bradley et al., 2015). The ancient Greeks knew much about diet for the athlete to achieve strength and body composition. Specific texts that describe the diet of ancient athletes are rare. Diet was regulated in a quadruple sense: quality, quantity, order,

---

38. Macronutrients are what the body requires in large amounts for normal growth and development, namely carbohydrates, fats, and proteins.
39. Whey is a liquid material created as a by-product of cheese production. It is produced as a powder, which is quickly absorbed by the body and a useful protein supplement.

and time. They consumed various kinds of food at intervals of time. Pliny stated that the pupils under Pythagoras the philosopher, when exercising, first ate meat (flesh) and figs. Meat was chiefly pork and often goat and sometimes wild boar. Galen suggested that athletes ate both beef and pork, adding unfermented bread and cheese. Athletes' foods were seasoned with sweet herbs (Blundell, 1864).

Philostratus mentioned that Olympic athletes like Amesinas[40] had a diet of barley cake. They also ate unleavened bread as well as meat from cows, bulls, goats, and deer (Phil, *Gym* 43). Leavened bread contains a raising agent such as yeast, as opposed to unleavened bread, which are flatbreads. Galen suggested that breads that do not have much leaven and have not been baked very well are suitable for the athlete. Galen also suggested athletes take very wholesome foods, but the heavyweights among them should especially take foods that are fatty and glutinous. Eating bran, in contrast, has a more cleansing property and is used for the elimination of any residues. Galen was referring to wrestlers, pankration fighters, and boxers. He suggested that as these athletes exercise all day long, they require food "which is both difficult to corrupt and not easily dispersed" (Powell and Wilkins, 2003). He said that these heavy athletes eat pigs' flesh and bread. These foods would consist of complex carbohydrates, which are digested slowly and converted into glucose for energy. There would be a more gradual rise in blood sugar levels. Galen commented that nutriment from pork and bread consisted of thick, glutinous humors, which athletes consume extensively. A diet of just vegetables and barley water would not be suitable for the athlete, as such a diet would soon wear out the whole body (Powell and Wilkins, 2003). Galen mentioned that bread with honey was prepared for athletes (Galen, *Hygiene* V, 7). He also mentioned that athletes eat food beyond what is necessary. Meats were described in some ancient medical writings as being hard to digest, except pork, which was viewed as easily digestible and good for the humors. Therefore, it was good for the athletes, which is a similar principle for using whey protein as a supplement in modern athletic diets because it is easily digestible. According to Masterson (1976), trainers supervised a diet of porridge, cheese, figs, and meal cakes, whereas meat was only eaten occasionally as a relish with wine. This was a diet also consumed by Greek country folk.

---

40. Amesinas was a victor in the Olympic wrestling in 460 BC but was named as Alesias in Philostratus's *Gymnasticus*.

Pausanias had said that the first athlete to conceive the idea of a meat diet was Dromeus of Stymphalus, twice winner of the Dolichos at Olympia in 480 BC. Cheese was the basic element of an athlete's diet up to the time of Dromeus (Pausanias, 6.7.10). Another story attributes Pythagoras (mentioned by Pliny on page 108) as the instigator of a meat diet for Eurymenes of Samos. He was an athlete of the heavy events, who is said to have won at Olympia some forty years before Dromeus (Harris, 1964). This latter story may be untrue, as Pythagorean philosophy had an insistence on vegetarianism. Africanus, a historian of the second and third centuries AD, recorded that Charmis of Sparta, an Olympic champion in the seventh century BC, trained on a diet of figs. Xenophon suggested that a man in training should avoid bread (Harris, 1964).

This may suggest the ancient Greeks knew the disadvantages of eating excessive carbohydrates, which would affect lean body mass. Bradley et al. (2015) found the elite rugby players self-selected a low-carbohydrate diet and a high-protein diet to increase fat-free mass. The aim was to optimize body composition. They also found peak losses of body fat were correlated with substantial strength improvements preseason from 8 to 11 percent. Interestingly, in contrast with Greek athletes, the gladiators in ancient Rome depicted in Hollywood as muscular men were bulky men fattened on a special high-carbohydrate vegetarian diet. The fat that the gladiators accumulated offered insulation from serious injuries.

The quantity of food consumed was greater in proportion than that of other men or nonathletes. Two pounds of meat was one of their smallest meals (Blundell, 1864). Milo is reported to have consumed twenty pounds of meat, twenty pounds of bread, and eighteen pints of wine every day. Theogenes of Thasos was said to have eaten an ox all by himself (Athenaeus, *Deipnosophists* Book 10 412 d-e). Theogenes, a boxer and competitor of the pankration, was inspired by the story of Milo and displayed his strength at the age of nine by shouldering a bronze statue in the marketplace and carrying it off. He had made athletics a career (Harris, 1964). Theogenes was a successful athlete with a grand total of some fourteen hundred victories, according to Pausanias, in all the festivals he entered (Newby, 2005). The objective of the meat diet was to produce the bulk and strength supposedly necessary for the boxer or the wrestler. Therefore, to produce bulk, the trainer prescribed large quantities of meat, which had to be counteracted by excessive exercise, eating, and sleeping such that this regimen occupied the athlete's entire time. Philostratus also mentioned that the situation of athletic diet had changed, that athletes had become more sluggish rather than energetic, soft rather than hardened, when Sicilian gastronomy become popular. The athletes had pleasure-bringing cooks providing pastry making them gluttonous and greedy. They were given bread and an unnatural diet of fish (Phil, *Gym* 44).

5.6: The Tetrad System

The tetrad system described by Philostratus in *Gymnasticus* was a four-day cycle training regimen. *Gymnasticus* was written in the third century AD. There is no evidence as to when the tetrad training cycle was first implemented. Christopoulos et al. (2003) suggest this training method was devised after the Roman conquest of Greece. The Roman conquest of Greece started after the battle of Corinth in 146 BC. Gardiner (1930) suggests that wrestlers, boxers, and pankration competitors formed the majority athletes at that time of the Roman imperial period after 31 BC, when the tetrad system was perhaps used. This system, according to Lehmann (2009), involved building up and reducing effort: a day of preparation with short intense movements, a day of all-out effort, a day of relaxation, and a day of moderate exercise. Spivey (2012) mentions Philostratus's structuring of training around a "four-day cycle" of varying intensities. Christopoulos et al. (2003) describe the tetrad as a four-part cycle or training system, which lasted four days and was continually repeated without a break. Montero (2020) also describes the tetrads as rigid cycles of four days, alternating with hard workouts and gentler exercise. Harris (1964) suggests that the tetrad was a form of interval training. The tetrad system is not a type of interval training. Interval training permits variations in exercise intensity during the actual training session, whereas the tetrad alters exercise intensity with subsequent training days, as traditionally defined.

Harris (1964) describes the tetrad as a routine of four days: preparation, concentration, relaxation, and moderation. Stocking (2016) mentions in his review that the tetrad presents a specific sequence of training days: preparatory day, intense day, recovery day, and mediating day. This method of training described is different from the standard linear model of exercise progression. In the linear model, stress to the muscle must be progressively increased as it becomes capable of producing greater force, power, or endurance. To continue to improve strength and function, progressive increases in load must be applied, to which adaptations will again occur. An example of the linear model is the progressive overload principle, which the story of Milo of Croton (described in 5.4.1) represents an early instance of this training. The disadvantage of progressive overload training is that it produces diminishing returns over time. Linear and uniform increases in strength and performance can quickly plateau. The nonlinear model presented by the tetrad system can be viewed as a method to organize training better and reduce diminishing returns, as well as avoiding plateauing, which can result from a standard linear progression of exercise. The tetrad system does demonstrate a knowledge to vary intensity levels of exercise to produce a training effect, but at the same time avoid overtraining by varying the intensity and provide a relative rest period for the athlete (Bourne, 2008).

This nonlinear, cyclic model of training represented by the tetrad may be reviewed as an early form of periodization (see chapter 4). The traditional or linear model of modern periodization was proposed by the Russian professor Lev Matveev at the end of the 1950s and has been used by both elite and amateur-level athletes. Periodization is the preplanned systematic variation in training specificity, intensity, volume, and rest organized in periods or cycles within an overall program. Periodization manipulates training variables such as load, sets, and repetitions to maximize training adaptations and prevent overtraining, although Philostratus's account of the tetrad system does not provide any information regarding the volume of the training load, which is one of the key variables related to periodization. This principle of periodicity is also found in ancient medical theory. A four-day cycle of disease was described by Hippocrates and later by Galen. Galen stated that all stages of disease come in fours: the beginning, the increase, the acme, and the decline. He suggested that by observing the patient's symptoms carefully according the four-day cycle, one will be able to predict the peak of the disease. According to Galen, Hippocrates stated, "It is necessary to consider from the first day and to observe according to the additional four-day cycles and you will not miss when the disease will turn" (Stocking, 2016).[41]

---

41. Stocking quotes Galen from his treatise *On Crises*. The term *crises* was understood by the ancients as a sudden and rapid change in disease, tending to recovery or death.

This concept of physiological cycles was applied to athletes by medical practitioners. Hippocrates stated:

> In the athlete, embonpoint [this term refers to the fleshy part of the body (muscle) or heaviness, pertaining in this case to the athlete exercising to increase muscle bulk], if carried to its utmost limit, is dangerous, if they cannot remain in the same state nor be stationary nor improve; and since they can neither remain stationary nor improve, it only remains for them to get worse; for these reasons the embonpoint should be reduced without delay, that the body may again have a commencement of reparation. (*Aphorisms* 1.3)

In Stocking's opinion, Hippocrates is suggesting here that an athlete's peak or limit of performance can't be maintained and must be intentionally lowered to start the process of improvement or renewal again from the beginning. In my opinion, Hippocrates is also referring to the dangers of athletes training to excess and such a condition of "heaviness" adversely affects health. This is further supported in Galen's *Thrasybulus*, in which he quotes Hippocrates as saying it is dangerous for those who exercise at their peak and the athletic condition is not natural (Galen, *Thrasybulus* 9).

Galen suggests the *hexis*, or state of the athlete, is a good condition at its peak but is unstable and likely to fall (Stocking, 2016).[42] Peak performance is a behavior that goes beyond the level at which an individual normally functions. It is the best or superior performance that the individual can achieve. In this context, peak performance is achieved by following a specific training regimen (McInman and Grove, 1991). The athlete's peak performance is achieved due to the supercompensation effect. There are four stages experienced by athletes training at high intensities: initial fitness, training, recovery, and finally supercompensation.

---

42. Stocking's source is from Galen's *Protrepticus ad artes addiscendas* (*Exhortation to study the arts*). In this treatise, Galen criticizes athletic training, as its product is useless for life beyond sport other than helping them to perform agricultural activities and interferes with the care of the soul. He accuses athletes of neglecting the old rule of health, which prescribes moderation.

The athlete, due to supercompensation, experiences higher levels of performance capabilities in comparison to their previous cycle of training. Supercompensation is based on the interaction between load and recovery. It is not possible to maintain the peak level of performance (Issurin, 2010). If the training overload stimulus is too much or without adequate rest, then the athlete may not be able to adapt. If their training is continued to be progressed at higher levels, or continued periods of inadequate rest, the athlete moves into overtraining and may develop the characteristics of overtraining syndrome. Overtraining syndrome can lead to decreased performance, reduced muscular strength, increased muscle soreness, and fatigue. The overtraining syndrome reflects Selye's exhaustion phase in the general adaptation syndrome (GAS). The exhaustion phase occurs when the accumulation of stress reaches a peak and is too great. Hence, this peak should be lowered to prevent overload, which could lead to overtraining and a decline in performance or injury.

According to Stocking (2016), the unique sequence of training days in the tetrad could be an example where the athletic trainers are attempting to actively control naturally occurring cycles in the athlete's development. This is supported by Montero (2020), who suggests the ancient Greeks realized the concept of periodization with the establishment of a microcycle training structure to maintain the athlete's fitness and peak condition. Stocking believes the GAS theory can help explain the specific sequence of training days in the tetrad described by Philostratus. The first day of the tetrad is termed the preparatory day. This is described in part as "a fast movement which arouses the athlete" (Phil, *Gym* 47). This initial regimen of exercises would put the athlete into Selye's alarm phase. This is stated by Philostratus as follows: "And makes him ready (the athlete) for the toil which is to follow" (Phil, *Gym* 47) or preparing the athlete's body for the coming hardship. This first day of training is interpreted as being of moderate intensity and of short duration (Stocking, 2016), thus, allowing the athlete to enter the resistance phase but not the exhaustion phase.

The second day of the tetrad is characterized by greater intensity and duration of exercise. The body has been "prepared" with the initial stimulus on the first day and is now able to exercise at a higher intensity or take part in more difficult activities. Philostratus refers to this day as a "test" for the athlete and describes it as intensive exercise. According to Selye's theory, physiologically the athlete would enter the exhaustion phase on this day. The third day of training is termed "relaxation" or a rest day but does suggest some moderate exercise. This day of relative rest removes the stress, and the athlete leaves the exhaustion phase, but this allows physiological adaptations to occur. The Greeks had recognized the importance of rest in athletic training. Galen suggested that those who had exerted themselves in vigorous exercise to manage their fatigue should stop the exercise, undertake soft massage, and rest (Berryman, 2012).

The fourth day of training in the tetrad cycle has been interpreted as a day of moderate exercise and technical aspects of training. The athlete has had time to recover from the exhaustion phase and able to perform better in the technical aspects of exercise (Issurin, 2010). Philostratus focuses specifically on wrestling on day four (Stocking, 2016). Since the last day of the cycle teaches "the athlete to flee from his opponent, and not to relax when his opponent is fleeing" (Phil, *Gym* 47). As previously mentioned, the heavy events including wrestling were prominent at the time the tetrad was devised and may suggest an example of sport-specific training.

The tetrad system was criticized by Philostratus, who stated that its rigidity prevented due consideration to the psychology of the individual. Philostratus mentioned the old system of training that produced athletes like Milo and Hipposthenes from Sparta (a five-time Olympic victor in wrestling from 624–608 BC). The training of his time has changed the nature of athletes, making them more inferior to those of former times (Phil, *Gym* 1–2). He indicated this was due to a lack of healthy training and vigorous exercise, hence suggesting that athletes should return to an earlier method of training (Harris, 1964). Philostratus said the system was too strict and was responsible for the death of the wrester Gerenus. Gerenus celebrated his victory at Olympia by a feast with his friends. Eating more than he used to, he was deprived of sleep. He attended the gymnasium the next day, admitting to the trainer he was unwell with indigestion.

The trainer became angry, as Gerenus was relaxing his training and interrupting the tetrads. Gerenus was killed through his training and the ignorance of the trainer. The trainer should have been more perceptive regarding Gerenus's condition and prescribed the correct exercises. According to Philostratus, the tetrad system was to blame as well as the trainer, who was uneducated (Phil, *Gym* 54).

He also argued the regimen was useless when it came to the thirty-day training period conducted at Elis prior to the Olympic Games. According to Philostratus, athletes during that period do not train by prescription but provide exercises all improvised for the right time. Although the tetrad system was accepted by some, according to Philostratus, "and for those who welcome the tetrad system" (Phil, *Gym* 54), it was abandoned by the Hellanodikai during the month preparation at Elis. The Hellanodikai at Elis opposed the tetrad system during the one months' preliminary training and judging prior to the Olympic Games. They used more traditional exercises as they believed that training should not be based on a fixed program of exercises advocated in the tetrad, but a program based on the circumstances of the athlete (Yallouris, 1979). There is no evidence as to when the thirty-day training period at Elis was introduced. This training could only have taken place in Elis from 472 BC onward since it was this year when the city was founded (Drees, 1968). Pausanias (6.23.1) mentions that athletes go through training in the gymnasium, which they must pass before going to Olympia. Miller in Philips and Pritchard (2003) suggested that at the Olympic Games of 300 BC, and the games thereafter, there could have been up to two hundred athletes. In addition to these, there were large numbers of trainers and family members. Young (2004) doubts whether the city of Elis could accommodate large numbers of people for such a long period of time. It is also questionable whether athletes could cover the expenses of board and lodging during this period.

The traditional interpretation of the tetrad from the literature indicates that the ancient Greeks had some basic knowledge of modern sports science. The tetrad was organized around modern theories of periodization, as mentioned. Periodized training typically uses periods of higher intensity with lower-volume training alternated with periods of lower intensity and higher volumes of training. Periodization aims to manipulate training variables such as load and intensity to maximize training adaptations, leading to supercompensation, as well as to incorporate rest periods to prevent overtraining. Periodization can be defined by programmed variation in the training stimuli with the use of planned rest periods to augment recovery and restoration of the athlete's potential (Jiménez, 2009). The ancient Greeks realized the concepts of varying the daily training intensity and the inclusion of recovery sessions to control the physical condition of the athlete (Montero, 2020). The tetrad training cycle may be further defined as an undulating form of periodization. As mentioned in chapter 4, undulating periodization (UP) is characterized by more frequent alterations in the intensity and volume. Rather than making changes over a period of months, the undulating model makes these same changes on a weekly or even daily basis as in the tetrads (Rhea et al., 2002). Daily modifications in intensity are effective stimuli to increase muscle strength and reduce training monotony. When training variables are altered daily, the undulating model seems to demonstrate significantly more strength gains than linear models or schedules—for example, daily changes in exercise volume, intensity, or other variables. Pitta et al. (2019) found in their review for trained individual's superior results in strength using undulating periodized programs versus linear, suggesting UP would produce a higher stress to the neuromuscular system. In the studies reviewed, there was no standardization in repetitions used for UP, which would make comparisons with linear programs more difficult. Although the tetrad mentions training days of varying intensities, there is no mention of exercise volume or mode apart from perhaps a combat sport such as wrestling on day four.

Rating of perceived exertion (RPE) is a simple measure that is associated with exercise intensity and has been suggested as an alternative marker for controlling the intensity of exercise. RPE, or exercise intensity, is measured by Borg's rating of perceived exertion scale (Borg, 1982). The scale was based upon a positive correlation between perceived exertion and heart rate (Marriott and Lamb, 1996). The fifteen-point scale has become the most frequently used rating scale for adults. The scale range is from 6–20, with 6 defined as no exertion and 20 as maximal exertion.

Periodization can include any type of exercise mode such as weight-training to improve strength or cardiovascular training to improve endurance. There are four conditioning concepts used in endurance sports training (e.g. running, cycling, or cross-country skiing) to maximize performance. These are firstly prolonged high-volume, low-intensity exercises. This is the fundamental training concept in preparing for endurance events. Secondly, training at or near lactate threshold. At rest and under steady-state exercise conditions, there is a balance between blood lactate production and blood lactate removal (Brooks, 2000). The lactate threshold refers to the intensity of exercise at which there is an abrupt increase in blood lactate levels (Robergs and Roberts, 1997). The lactate threshold occurs at 80 to 90 percent of heart rate reserve in trained individuals and is the most important determinant of success in endurance-related activities or events (Weltman, 1995). The best way to improve lactate threshold is to increase training volume, regardless of the cardiovascular mode of exercise. The RPE can be used to prescribe cardiorespiratory exercise intensity. An RPE of 11–12 on the fifteen-point scale for high-volume training would be classed as light exercise intensity.

Increasing the training volume increases the capacity for mitochondrial respiration, which is important for improving lactate threshold. In previous studies, endurance athletes perform approximately 75 percent of their yearly training program below the lactate threshold (Stöggl and Sperlich, 2014). Maximal steady-state exercise refers to training at the lactate threshold. Lactate threshold occurs between 13 and 15 on the RPE scale, which corresponds to feelings of "somewhat hard" and "hard" (Weltman, 1995). Foran (2001) recommends the training at the maximal steady state should consist of no more than 10 percent of the total weekly volume to prevent overtraining and injury. The third conditioning concept in endurance training is low-volume, high-intensity interval training (HIIT). HIIT is above the lactate threshold, with an exercise intensity above 15 RPE (hard or very hard) but below all-out effort (19 or 20 RPE).

At exercise intensities above the lactate threshold, there is a mismatch between production and uptake, with the rate of lactate removal apparently less than the rate of lactate production (Broberg et al., 1988). Again, the total interval training workout time should not exceed 10 percent of weekly training volume. The fourth training concept is polarized training (POL), which is the combination of the first three endurance regimens. This regimen is used by elite marathon runners and can be defined as a periodized training program (Stellingwerff, 2012). Research has indicated that training programs that are a combination of high-volume, maximal steady-state and interval workouts have the most pronounced effect on lactate threshold improvement (Robergs and Roberts, 1997). Hence, POL has shown the greatest improvements in most key variables of endurance performance (Stöggl and Sperlich, 2014). The tetrad was a four-part cycle of training, which lasted four days and was continually repeated without a break. One of the four days was a day of all-out effort, or high-intensity exercise. Therefore, with this training system, there would be two days each week of high-intensity exercise or all-out effort, perhaps exercising above the lactate threshold. This would equate to approximately 28 percent of the total training program, which is in line with modern endurance exercise programs (training at approximately 25 percent of their yearly training regimen above the lactate threshold).

Several studies have shown increases in endurance performance resulting from the addition of various types of strength training to endurance training regimens. Taipale et al. (2010) found that periodized maximal or explosive strength training performed concurrently with endurance training was more effective in improving strength, $VO2_{max}$ and running economy than concurrent circuit and endurance training in recreational runners. Unfortunately, it is not known whether the tetrad consisted of strength or endurance training or both. Apart from Philostratus, there is no other text in antiquity that mentions the tetrad. There are limited details of this training system to make accurate modern comparisons or apply the tetrad to current modern exercise regimens.

There is a suggestion that the tetrad incorporated sport-specific training involving practicing the technical aspects of a sporting event (i.e., wrestling on day four). Sport-specific training, such as on-court tennis training, is time efficient and involves physical fitness, technical skill, and tactical awareness. This form of training is effective for improving aerobic fitness without the negative effects on sprinting and jumping performance. Kilit and Arslan (2019) showed in their study that on-court tennis training was effective at improving aerobic and anaerobic fitness variables, such as sprinting and jumping in young tennis players. Combat sports, such as wrestling, boxing, and judo, require highly developed technical and tactical skills as well as high levels of fitness. HIIT sessions are used to prepare the athlete for the high-intensity intermittent activity patterns and physiological demands required in these combat sports (Franchini et al., 2019). HIIT training sessions can vary in terms of exercise mode from general such as running or rowing to sport specific. Typical judo training sessions, for example, may last two hours, with forty minutes of general exercise, such as strength and conditioning programs, forty minutes of judo-specific exercises, such as repetitive throwing training and forty minutes of combat or fight practice (Franchini et al., 2014). It is possible that the tetrad was centered around combat sport training, which included varying exercise intensity daily and sport-specific training sessions.

5.7: An Alternative Interpretation or Theory of the Tetrad System

As mentioned in section 5.6, Philostratus in his *Gymnasticus* described a specific sequence of training days for athletes: these were a preparatory day, intense day, recovery day, and middling day. Philostratus said, "We take the tetrad system to be a circle of four days, where the athlete does different things on different days" (Phil, *Gym* 47). A cycle of training days is described with varying exercise intensities, a rest day, and technical skills day in wrestling. This seems to be from my sources the accepted interpretation of the tetrad in the literature. It can be argued that Philostratus was not an athlete or had any experience of training, but he had most likely, as is the case of Galen access to ancient writings on athletic training now lost. I suggest that there is an alternative interpretation of the tetrad, which I will outline in the following section.

Galen in *Hygiene* mentions the followers of Theon[43] and Tryphon,[44] who both practiced the base art concerning athletes. They used the terms *preparatory* and *bodily exercise*, something partial and something complete, and *apotherapy* (meaning restoration therapy), and inquire into whether the athlete must be trained and exercised according to such a course or in another way (Galen, *Thrasybulus*, 47). Stocking (2016) suggests that the four stages of training mentioned in the *Thrasybulus* seem to correspond at least normally to the four days of training in the tetrad described by Philostratus. This is assuming that the "intense day" in the *Gymnasticus* corresponds to the "complete" stage of training described in the *Thrasybulus*. Apotherapy, or restoration therapy, does not correspond to any of the training days in the tetrad.

Galen in *Hygiene* mentions it is necessary for athletes to prepare themselves for their labors in competition to practice sometimes all day at a complete level their objective exercise, which they call training (Green, 1951). The terms from

---

43. According to Galen, Theon wrote four books about individual exercises chiefly or training athletes (Galen, *Hygiene* III, 3).
44. Tryphon was sometimes called a surgeon, who worked with gladiators.

Hygiene "complete" and "preparation" do correspond to the technical terms for exercise described by Theon and Tryphon in the *Thrasybulus*. Galen mentions in this extract that the athlete should prepare their body for the competition by exercising at the most complete level. If this relates to the tetrad, by this definition, the athlete would go through two intense days of exercise, a preparatory day of mostly completing exercise, followed by an intense day, which is a test for the athlete. It is unlikely the tetrad would advocate two consecutive days of intense training. The third day of the tetrad is described by Philostratus as "the day of relaxation is a time for starting up his activity again in a moderate way" (Phil, *Gym* 47). This day correlates with something partial described by Theon and Tryphon. There is no mention of wrestling or any other sporting activity.

Theon and Tryphon describe a system of training that has similarities to the tetrad, as they describe a form of preparation for training and varying levels of exercise intensities, but apotherapy, or restoration therapy, is not part of the tetrad. It has been suggested that the tetrad training method was devised after the Roman conquest of Greece, from 146 BC. Montero's view is that the tetrad emerged not long before the criticisms expressed by Philostratus of this training system in the third century AD (Montero, 2020). Theon of Alexandria is dated from AD 130–160 (Johnston, 2018); if he was referring to the tetrad in his writings, then it must at least be before AD 160.

The training for the tetrad is assumed to have taken place in the gymnasium. In the case of the unfortunate wrestler Gerenus, Philostratus states that he came to the gymnasium the next day to continue the tetrad cycle with his trainer. There is no indication from Philostratus as to what the preparatory day consisted of. Blundell (1864) provides from his sources a description of preparatory exercise provided by Galen. According to Galen, preparatory exercise was a motion done in a manner proportionate to what is to follow. It is performed briskly or otherwise, not only by the motion of the body but by frictions, anointings, and similar measures, though at times it was used after heavier exercises, as Galen speaks of it being proper for the athlete. This description from Galen of preparatory exercise partially corresponds to Philostratus's description: "quick movements to arouse the athlete with those performed briskly or otherwise." The term *frictions* are used, which refers to a type of massage. Galen suggests there are many different forms of massage (Galen, *Hygiene* III, 1).

Massage was used in the medical context to increase muscle tone and reduce pain. There is evidence that physicians like Hippocrates in ancient Greece applied their principles or techniques to athletics. This concept of massage to assist with stiffness, soreness, and muscle strength existed before ancient Greece. In ancient Egypt, methods of medical examination, principles of diagnosis, and treatment techniques, including massage for the management of disease, were apparent long before Hippocrates. Medical papyri provide important sources of information for the insight into ancient Egyptian medicine, with the most significant ones discovered in the nineteenth and twentieth centuries (Sullivan, 1995). There is evidence from these papyri that the ancient Egyptians had discovered the beneficial effects of massage and other treatments. In the Ebers papyrus, written about 1500 BC, a mixture of oil and honey was recommended as a remedy for pain and stiffness of the limbs or joints. The limbs could also be made supple by smearing them with a liniment consisting of asses' dung mixed with honey and sea salt (Bryan, 1930). Remedies were listed in the Ebers papyrus to strengthen the *met* of the backbone, shoulder, and the thighs. For the met that runs to every limb, rubbing with a paste of sour milk was recommended. The met or *metu* has multiple meanings but may refer to tendons or muscles, as well as the vascular system and nerves (Nunn, 1997). Ghalioungui (1963), though, interprets the term metu or *metou* to mean *vessel*, and Bryan (1930) suggests it refers to the nerves of the body but could also apply to the blood vessels. The Hearst medical papyrus dated from the eighteenth dynasty of Egypt within the New Kingdom (1550–1292 BC) is more of a practicing physician's formulary. It does not deal with examination of patients or with diagnosis, but prescriptions are offered for diseases that are named and indicated. There are lists of prescriptions to deal with expelling pains within the body and limbs using applications of bandages and ointments. Ointments were perhaps applied to relieve painful and aching muscles in the hope of strengthening them. For example, there are prescriptions for removing pain and swelling from the limbs. The metu is also mentioned in the Hearst papyrus, but this relates to vessels (Reisner, 1905).

In *De Medicina Book II*, by Celsus, the term *rubbings* is used, but this probably also refers to frictions. Galen states that it makes no difference whether we say *massage* or *rubbings*; he goes on to say that the term *rubbing* was more customary among the ancients and *massage* was a term used in his time (Galen, *Hygiene* II,

3). Celsus goes on to state that it was Asclepiades who taught when and how rubbings or frictions should be used in the context of mild therapeutic methods, including the regulation of diet and wine, bathing, body-massage, walking, and rocking.[45] Celsus does stress that Asclepiades's claims of innovation, such as his discovery of the therapeutic effects of frictions, were not always justified, and these practices had already been established in Greek medicine. The rules for the application of friction were attributed to Hippocrates. Hippocrates in Celsus's account said that rubbing, if strenuous, hardens the body; if gentle, it relaxes. If it is too much, it diminishes, and if it is moderate, it fills out. Paulus Aegineta[46] quotes Galen, Celsus, and Pliny on the rules of friction and states that hard friction contracts, whereas soft friction relaxes, so that those persons who are relaxed should be rubbed hard, and those who are immoderately constricted rubbed softly. Moderate rubbing would be between the two extremes. Hard friction diminishes the bulk of the body, while soft distends it. If the three different kinds of friction as to quantity are joined to the same number as to quality, this will produce nine combinations (Adams, 1844).

Oribasius also made many observations on the practice of frictions. Celsus suggested that rubbing should be employed when either a feeble body needs to be toned up, to disperse harmful superfluity, or a thin body needs to be nourished, although nourishment is not achieved by rubbing itself but by diet. Celsus recommended rubbing should be applied to the body all over or to a part that needs strengthening, such as a partially paralyzed limb. Rubbing can also be used for pain and headaches. The rubbing technique involves stroking and is regulated by the individual's strength. If the individual is more robust, up to two hundred strokes are required but with an intermediate number, according to his strength. Limbs require many strokes and forceable rubbing.

For general bodily weakness, the rubbing should be applied all over but should be shorter and gentle, just to the extent of softening the skin. This is to ensure the body may be more easily capable of forming new material (muscle) from food recently consumed (Spencer, 1935).

---

45. Rocking, according to Pliny the Elder in his *Naturalis Historia* (26, 12–15) involved suspending patients from couches and rocking them to alleviate diseases or induce sleep.
46. Paulus Aegineta was a seventh-century AD Byzantine Greek physician best known for his seven-book medical encyclopedia.

Theon and Tryphon used the term apotherapy with reference to athletic training. Apotherapy was defined by Galen as both part of exercise and a kind of exercise (restoration therapy including massage and bindings). It is possible that the concept of rubbings or frictions described by Celsus had already been applied to apotherapy and used postexercise. In the preservation of health, Galen suggested the sequence of exercise followed by apotherapy, then bathing, food, and rest. Galen gives an example of a thirteen-year-old boy he treated for having thin legs. After the boy finished his run, Galen applied what he termed *apotherapeutic massage* (Galen, *Hygiene* V, 10).

Apotherapy was called the final part of all completed exercise with the aim of evacuating the superfluities (excesses) and to keep the body free of fatigue, particularly in the athlete undertaking immoderate exercise. To completely evacuate the excesses following exercise, Galen recommends that massage by others (masseurs) should be undertaken, along with stretching of the massaged parts. Oil is used, which helps to soften and reduce tension. Apotherapy also consists of holding the breath to strain the muscles of the thorax and relax the diaphragm, aiming to expel the superfluities downward. Bindings are applied to the abdomen and loins to aid this process. Galen also mentions that gymnastic trainers use apotherapeutic massage in the middle of exertions and in those who practice strong contests (Galen, *Hygiene* III, 2). Galen uses the term *fatigue*, describing seven in total: three simple and four-compound.

The concept of fatigue relates to tension, pain (distressing sensations), and inflammation caused by activity or exercise. The first type of fatigue is woundlike and occurs in those who exercise too rashly, causing pain. This fatigue is managed with gentle massage and combined with apotherapeutic exercise consisting of moderate movements. The second is a type of fatigue that effects the muscles following violent exercise, which is associated with stretching or even tearing of the muscle fibers. This is related to tension, and according to Hippocrates, it is managed with relaxation and softening. The third fatigue relates to inflammation involving the muscles and tendons beyond an accord with nature. This occurs with very violent movements but rarely occurs in those accustomed to this type of exercise (i.e., athletes). This is managed by cold treatments and massage. A fourth fatigue is described, which occurs in immoderate exercise without proper apotherapy. It occurs in well-trained athletes with no superfluities and relaxed structures. Apotherapeutic exercise is required in this case, which is brief, slow, and soft in movements and massages (Galen, *Hygiene* III, 5-7).

In my view, preparatory exercises including frictions and other measures were used as techniques to prepare the athlete for exercise (i.e., to relax, soften, or harden muscle), whereas apotherapy was used after strenuous exercise to relieve soreness or inflammation. Galen stated that continuous and vigorous massages were specific to the preparatory exercises but were not fitting for apotherapy. Galen had further mentioned that preparatory exercises involved less than moderate movement but quite vigorous and rapid in quality (Galen, *Hygiene* III, 11). Lucian also mentions this preparation for wrestlers: "Then we rub them with olive-oil and supple them in order that they may be more elastic" (Lucian, *Anacharsis* 38). Then their muscles were first heated and managed by frictions and gentle motion to prevent injuries and dislocations (Blundell, 1864).

D. Graham (1890) from his sources suggested that preparatory massage or frictions were used prior to severe tests of strength (the second day of the tetrad has been described a severe test for the athlete), so that strains and ruptures would be less likely. By a combination of appropriate massage, passive and resistive movements, atrophied muscles, tendons, and ligaments would have their circulation increased. This would consequently improve their nutrition and innervations so that they would become larger and firmer. Galen also suggests that the individual prior to exercise should be rolled, thrust away, and turned quickly. These movements were used to warm and prepare the body before the application of oil. Specific stretches and movements were then applied to clear out the superfluities (Galen, *Hygiene* III, 2).

Philostratus suggests that both light and heavy athletes should be softened by the trainer with massages that use a moderate amount of oil, especially to the upper body (Phil, *Gym* 50). These maneuvers described could all refer to soft-tissue techniques, joint mobilizations, and/or muscle stretches that are used by physical therapists in the modern era. This idea of someone applying these techniques is supported by Taylor (1880), who describes from his sources that frictions may also be classed among the exercises that come from exterior sources. Taylor suggested athletes are prepared for exercise by special frictions. He goes on to describe massage techniques such as kneading, pinching, and using pressure points as well as many other movements that belong to the same class. Galen had also mentioned that there are nine kinds or varieties of friction but was probably quoting from Hippocrates. These varieties of friction in terms of quality were hard, soft, and moderate, and each with quantities of little, much, and moderate (Galen, *Hygiene* II, 4). He said that frictions are employed as a remedy or to preserve the body in a healthy state or as a preparatory to gymnastic exercises.

Therefore, these frictions are capable of much modification, and they will depend also on different circumstances, as to the region, locality of the gymnasium, period of the year, and time of day in which they are employed (Coxe, 1846). Paulus Aegineta describes preparatory frictions in this medical encyclopedia. He states that before gymnastic exercises, the body ought to be rubbed moderately first with towels, and then with oil in the hollows of the hands, until it is properly warmed and softened. According to Alexander Aphrodisias,[47] the objective of this was to soften the parts so that they might not be ruptured (Adams, 1844). Galen describes these frictions or rubbings as among the extrinsic movements (i.e., not performed by the athlete; *Hygiene* II, 11). He later mentions that Theon had stated that preparatory exercises are only suitable for athlete and these preparatory techniques may have been applied by a trainer on the first day of the tetrad. Walter Johnson (1866) from his sources suggests that frictions with oil were used to prepare the athlete before their exercises. They were first rubbed by the paedotribes, and then they proceeded with lighter exercises. Athletes preparing for competition used the services of a paedotribes, or trainer who offered formal and systematic training. Therefore, I believe the preparatory day of the tetrad mostly involved massage techniques and perhaps gentle exercise or no exercise at all. The athlete had already exercised for three consecutive days: intense, moderate, and activity based (wrestling). As previously mentioned, the ancient Greeks understood the basic principles of training, and it is unlikely their trainers would put their athletes through a continuous cycle of exercise without rest periods. Philostratus states that these tetrad cycles are constantly repeated (Phil, *Gym* 47). They considered rest to be an important aspect of training.

Hence, this was a day in which the athlete had his restoration therapy to prepare him for the next day in the cycle, which was the intense day. This restoration therapy involved a type of massage (frictions) for the muscle or soft tissue

---

47. Alexander Aphrodisias was a philosopher born in AD 200 who is known for his commentaries on Aristotle's work.

to reduce the soreness from the previous days of exercise and passive movements to the limbs for relieving stiff joints. The frictions and/or passive movements were applied externally according to Taylor (1880), probably by someone skilled in the art, such as the paedotribe or aleipteior.

There are similarities with the preparatory exercises and apotherapy to techniques applied to modern sports professionals either preexercise, postexercise, or in competition. Massage has been defined as "a mechanical manipulation of body tissues with rhythmical pressure and stroking for the purpose of promoting health and wellbeing" (Galloway et al., 2004). There are five basic techniques of classical massage described in the current literature: effleurage, petrissage, frictions, tapotement, and vibrations. Effleurage is a gliding or sliding movement over the skin with a smooth and continuous motion used to enhance venous return. Petrissage is a deeper technique than effleurage and is directed toward the muscles. This involves the lifting, wringing, or squeezing of soft tissues or between the hands. This increases local circulation and assists in venous return. Friction, or rubbing, is an accurately delivered penetrating pressure applied through the fingertips. This is used to treat muscle spasm or break up adhesions from old injuries. Tapotement, or hacking, is a series of gentle blows with the ulnar border of each hand. The tissues are struck rapidly and used to stimulate either by direct mechanical force or by reflex action. Finally, vibration or shaking is used on the extremities and is said to lower muscle tone (Callaghan, 1993; Gasibut and Suwehli, 2017). Classical Western or Swedish massage is the most common form of massage used for athletes (Weerapong et al., 2005). This includes a combination of effleurage, petrissage, friction, percussion, and vibration (Best et al., 2008).

Apotherapy in ancient Greece was possibly used after strenuous exercise to relieve soreness or inflammation. High-intensity exercise, as performed on day two of the tetrad, results in metabolic and mechanical stress to muscle fibers, leading to delayed onset muscle soreness (DOMS) and/or increased fatigue, which can be associated with performance decrements. DOMS, which can follow unaccustomed physical activity, is a sensation of discomfort, predominately within the skeletal muscle. It may be experienced in the elite or novice athlete. The intensity of discomfort increases within the first twenty-four hours following cessation of exercise, peaks between twenty-four and seventy-two hours, subsides, and eventually disappears by five to seven days postexercise (Cheung et al., 2003). High-intensity exercise is thought to disrupt muscle microstructure, leading to an inflammatory response. The inflammatory response is important for recovery and repair of stressed or damaged muscle tissue. Prolonged inflammation can lead to edema, local hypoxia, accumulation of noxious substances, and phagocytosis of healthy tissue by inflammatory cells, resulting in soreness and tissue disruption (White et al., 2020). This may have parallels to the third fatigue described by Galen and the use of apotherapy to manage it. Galen recommended this fatigue should be managed by cold treatments and massage. Massage therapy is one of the postexercise techniques used anecdotally to enhance the recovery of athletes by improving DOMS, reducing perceived fatigue, and enhancing performance recovery. White et al. (2020) in their study found that massage therapy did not reduce measures of pain or soreness compared to a nonmassage control group in subjects who completed a high-intensity intermittent sprint exercise protocol. Other studies have found massage administered postexercise does reduce the effects of DOMS (Zainuddin et al., 2005; Hilbert et al., 2003), but this remains inconclusive due to small sample sizes and study limitations.

These limitations may include a lack of sham massage, no specific exercise protocol to induce DOMS, and differences in amount of preseason resistive training between athletes (Mancinelli et al., 2006). White et al. (2020) also did not observe any significant effects of massage therapy on muscle performance, indicated by the squat jump and drop-jump heights. This finding is consistent with previous research. Poppendieck et al. (2016) in their review found the effects of massage on performance recovery postexercise to be small and partly unclear. White et al. (2020) did find that inflammatory marker concentration returned to baseline levels earlier, following the massage therapy group compared with the control. Massage therapy may have enhanced the clearance of inflammatory markers by stimulation of the lymphatic circulation.

Monedero and Donne (2000) investigated different recovery interventions on subsequent performance. Eighteen trained male cyclists performed two simulated five-kilometer maximal effort cycling tests separated by a twenty-minute recovery. Four recovery interventions were investigated: passive (doing nothing), active (submaximal cycling at a load equivalent to 50 percent of individual $VO2_{max}$), massage, and combined (massage and active). Combined recovery was found to be the most efficient intervention for maintaining performance time during the second five-kilometer cycling test. These findings were explained by the high rate of blood lactate removal during the active portion of the intervention. This combined recovery intervention may be compared to apotherapy, which was defined as both part exercise and restoration therapy including massage.

Therapeutic massage in modern sport is used for the preparation precompetition or training. The effects of preexercise therapeutic massage on performance is not yet proven with conflicting evidence (Arabaci, 2008). There is also limited evidence of the effects of preexercise massage on injury prevention (Gasibut and Suwehli, 2017). Preparatory exercise, or frictions as described in the tetrad, may have consisted of a combination of techniques including massage and passive movements. Passive movement therapy is a therapeutic intervention designed to increase the passive extensibility of muscles, ligaments, and collagen aimed at achieving maximal joint range of motion (Hobbelen et al., 2012). Passive movements are assessment and/or treatment techniques performed by another person or machine and may provide positive effects in the rehabilitation process. There is no modern equivalent to preparatory exercise/frictions. Lomilomi massage is a technique that combines passive movements and massage. This treatment, which may have some similarities with preparatory exercise, originates from an ancient Maori massage technique. Lomilomi massage is used to improve joint range, tissue elasticity, and flexibility (Posadzki et al., 2009). In a survey of intercollegiate athletes in Hawaii representing twenty sports teams, Lomilomi massage was used by 10 percent of the athletes to improve general health, enhance performance, and treat injuries (Forman et al., 2006).

Theon and Tryphon had used the terms *preparatory* and *bodily exercise*, but this does not suggest that these components were applied together particularly in the tetrad cycle. In the modern era, a preparatory period of training for high-performance athletes in endurance, combat sports, or ball games usually contains a program for the development of general aerobic ability, muscle strength, technical preparation, and treatment of previous injuries. This is a multitargeted mixed-training program aimed at improving the athlete's performance. For example, rugby union is a highly demanding physical, tactical, and skill-based team sport. Elite players aim to fine-tune physical qualities, such as strength, power, speed, and endurance within an annual plan. Within this annual plan, the season is divided into preseason, in-season, and off-season phases, with weekly training microcycles involving the manipulation of training loads through the variables of intensity, duration, and frequency (Duthie, 2006). The tetrad cycle has parallels with such a modern athletic preparatory period because in its entirety, in my view, it was preparatory in relation to the Olympic Games and/or other competitions. This may be supported by Philostratus, who said when referring to the tetrad, "What will those who are so enthusiastic over the tetrad do with it when they come to Olympia" (Robinson, 1955). Alternatively, though Philostratus could be implying that the tetrad was of little use in preparation for the Olympic Games, as it was abandoned by the Hellanodikai, who did not exercise athletes to previous instructions (Robinson, 1955).

Philostratus describes the second day of the tetrad as "the next makes him exert himself" (Phil, *Gym* 47). There is no dispute that this day consists of intense exercise and is the most strenuous part of the tetrad cycle. The third day, as agreed, relaxes the athlete but does involve a moderate intensity of exercise. It has been suggested in the literature that the third day is a rest or relaxation day, which is misleading. Relaxation gives the athlete a chance to recover from the previous day of all-out effort concentration (Harris, 1964). Philostratus does not advocate complete rest for the athlete: "For complete rest after exercising in dust is a poor doctor for tiredness, since it slackens one's strength rather than maintaining it" (Phil, *Gym* 53). Therefore, the third day of the tetrad, in my opinion, consists of low- to moderate-intensity exercise. This may not be dissimilar to professional rugby union players in the 2000s who would perform light to moderate exercise such as swimming or light jogging the day after match day. Active recovery modalities consisting of low-intensity exercise have been advocated for recovery after rugby matches. Suzuki et al. (2004) found that performing low-intensity exercise during the rest period after a rugby match did not impair physiological recovery but actually promoted psychological recovery.

The evidence regarding the effect of different recovery modalities following rugby competition and/or training is limited. Some studies, though, have investigated the effect on acute recovery postmatch or posttraining. Cold modalities, including cold baths, contrast baths, and cryotherapy are the most common recovery strategies used in rugby. Other modalities used include compression garments and electromyostimulation (EMS). EMS consists of a series of electrical stimuli being delivered superficially using electrodes on the skin to initiate a muscle pump, thus increasing venous blood flow. This can promote the clearance of creatine kinase (CK), which is elevated after exercise-induced muscle damage due to the high-intensity and collision-based activities in rugby. Cold-water modalities seem to be the most effective strategy to recover from rugby training or matches in terms of CK clearance and decreased DOMS (Tavares et al., 2017). It is possible the third day of the tetrad was a recovery day following the second day of intense exercise, but this is unlikely, in my opinion. This day was probably allotted to a different mode of lower-intensity exercise.

The fourth day of the tetrad is the "middling day." This is a day of moderation according to Harris (1964). He suggests this day is devoted to technical exercises in the athlete's individual event. The quote from Philostratus that the athlete is to flee from his opponent has been suggested as a reference to wrestling, but this is not for certain, although Philostratus goes on to state, "it is enough for those who have toiled in mud in the palaestra to relax" (Phil, *Gym* 53). The palaestra was part of the ancient gymnasium. According to Vitruvius, the ideal palaestra had a large central courtyard, open to the sky and surrounded by roofed colonnades. There were areas within the courtyard for training in wrestling, boxing, jumping, and so forth, usually covered with dust or sand (Christopoulos et al., 2003; Miller, 2004). There is also evidence for separate rooms with floors covered with mud or earth used for practicing parts of wrestling that took place on the ground. The mud in this instance rendered the body slippery and difficult to hold (Gardiner, 1930). It has been suggested that wrestling as a sport was central for Greeks in the Roman imperial period and at the time of Philostratus.

Thus, the tetrad training cycle was specified to the wrestler (Stocking, 2016). In the *Gymnasticus*, Philostratus does refer to all types of athletic events that took part in the Olympic Games: running, pentathlon, wrestling, boxing, and the pankration. I believe that the fourth day in the tetrad cycle consisted of wrestling used as an exercise for general athletic conditioning. Lucian quoted that with wrestling the athlete's body becomes less susceptible and more vigorous through being exercised thoroughly (Lucian, *Anacharsis* 40). As quoted in part previously, Philostratus says, "In cases it is enough for those who have toiled in the mud in the palaestra to relax in a general fashion, in the way I have indicated, while those who have toiled in the dust should be trained again on the next day in mud, and with a small increase of intensity" (Phil, *Gym* 53).

The first part of the quote is a reference to the tetrad on the fourth day, which is allotted to wrestling as proposed. Gardiner (1930) suggests that ground wrestling was practiced under cover on ground that had been watered until it became muddy. This type of wrestling was used in the pankration (see chapter 2). This was an event requiring power, endurance, and high skill. This could be classed as high-intensity exercise, perhaps requiring a rest day afterward. Thus, the athlete the following day relaxes, which corresponds to the first day of the tetrad, a day that I suggested was used for preparing the athlete by means of massage, et cetera, for the next day of training but no exercise. The last part of the quote in my opinion may refer to upright wrestling or wrestling proper, which took place on sandy ground or the skamma, hence in the dust. This could also refer to other training activities, such as jumping, which were also performed on the sandy service within the palaestra. Lucian mentions that wrestling is performed in the mud and in the sand (Sweet, 1987).

The third day of the tetrad consisted of moderate-intensity exercises but not a rest day, followed by the fourth day of wrestling or the pankration, with slightly greater exercise intensity. In Philostratus's quote, it is possible he was referring to the third day of wrestling in the sand or other training activity, followed by higher-intensity exercise in the mud on the fourth day. The third and fourth days of the tetrad may have been allotted to any of the heavy events such as wrestling, boxing, or pankration. This would be in line with Gardiner's theory that the majority athletes at that time of the tetrad were trained in the heavy events. Philostratus could also just be giving an example of athletes using wrestling as a training activity in the fourth day of the tetrad. In support of this view, Lucian gives the example of the heavy events, such as the pankration, which not only accustoms the athlete to hardship but produces strong and healthy bodies (Harmon, 1961). According to Blundell (1864), the ancients contended wrestling to be the oldest of all exercises. Galen had mentioned that wrestling was carefully studied. It was added by the trainers of athletes to prepare them for all contests. Both men and boys played at it and acquired excellent body conditioning from it (Blundell, 1864).

Wrestling and other gymnastic exercises were part of Galen's daily regimen. Galen considered wrestling to be a normal activity for men of his class (Mattern, 2008). For example, Galen mentions his autocrat friend Antoninus Pius coming to the wrestling school to take care of his body (Galen, *Hygiene* VI, 5). Plato had stated that upright wrestling develops the upper parts of the body, the arms, shoulders, chest, and neck (Plummer, 1898b). Several physical-fitness parameters are related to high-level wrestling performance. Maximum dynamic strength (1 RM) is required in wrestling with elite male wrestlers able to squat between 87 and 150 kg and bench press 74 to 130 kg. Both upper- and lower-limb strength development is required, particularly when lifting an opponent. Isometric strength is important, such as hand-grip strength for wrestling holds. Muscular power is also required for sudden explosive attacks and counterattacks to lift the opponent powerfully. To maintain a high intensity of competitive actions for an extended period of the match, strength endurance is required. Finally, a high level of aerobic capacity is required to sustain effort throughout the wrestling match (Chaabene et al., 2017). Hence, wrestling as an exercise itself can improve muscular strength, power, and aerobic endurance. There is evidence that wrestling has been used as conditioning exercise in modern professional sports. Duthie (2006) mentions wrestling is used by elite rugby players as part of their training regimen to improve general strength and power. Eddie Jones, the England rugby union coach since 2015, has used wrestling as a conditioning exercise for his players. In my view, the tetrad was a training cycle for all athletes in preparation for competition and not just for wrestlers.

CHAPTER 5 SUMMARY

Physical fitness was an important aspect of life in ancient Greece. There is limited evidence regarding the methods of training in ancient Greece. The literary works of Philostratus, Galen, and Lucian on athletics provide us with some insights to the types of exercises used to improve fitness and athletic condition. Blundell's work contains a great body of ancient knowledge on athletics gathered from older sources. Increased specialization resulted in fleshy, over-muscled bodies, gracelessness, and ill health and was condemned by the likes of Plato and Galen.

Galen defined hygiene as the therapeutic art concerning the body. He stated that for the best constitution of the body, the individual requires moderate exercise, which is best for the preservation of health. Galen defined three categories of exercise. The first category was called vigorous exercises, performed with strength but without speed. These were essentially a type of exercise to improve muscular strength. The second category of exercises he classified as rapid without being vigorous and violent. This second category comprised speed exercises developed to improve speed mostly, but not strength. The third category of exercises were violent exercises, which were described as a combination of vigor and rapidity. This exercise combined strength and speed (i.e., power). Galen's category of exercise suggests a knowledge of sports-specific training. The first category trains for strength required in the heavy events such as wrestling, the second category for speed required in sprinting, and the third category for power necessary for the throwing events such as the discus. Galen, in his short treatise, described a Roman ball game of interception called Harpastum. He believed that the exercise with the small ball was beneficial to health as well as training both speed and strength.

The bodily ideal achieved by the ancient Greeks could only be achieved through resistance training. There were a variety of weight-training-type exercises designed by the Greeks to develop and strengthen the muscles, which suggested a rudimentary understanding of the progressive overload principle. Halteres were an early form of dumbbell used for strengthening. Specialized jump training was used to improve speed and strength. Rope climbing strengthened the upper body.

There were several types of running exercises for training speed and endurance. Walking was used for health but not by athletes. Athletes were trained to jump a ditch or any other obstacle, sometimes carrying weights such as halteres or plummets, which were used to improve strength. Throwing the quoit aimed to improve strength to the inferior extremities and lumbar region.

The Greeks recognized the importance of diet for health and treating illness. Athletic trainers supervised a diet of porridge, cheese, figs, and meal cakes. The runner Dromeus may have been the first athlete to conceive of a meat diet. The objective of the meat diet was to produce the bulk and strength supposedly necessary in the heavy events.

The tetrad training cycle was possibly devised after 146 BC and applied to all athletes, particularly at that time of the Roman imperial period. The tetrad system described by Philostratus was a specific sequence of training days for athletes, including a preparatory day, intense day, recovery day, and middling day. This system incorporated different exercise intensities, rest, and technical aspects of training. It was organized around modern theories of periodization and demonstrated a knowledge to vary intensity levels of exercise and produce a training effect. An alternative interpretation of the tetrad system suggests the preparatory day did not include any exercise, but a form of restoration therapy involving massage techniques to prepare the athlete for the following intense day of training. The third day was not a recovery day but consisted of moderate-intensity exercise. The fourth day was allotted to one of the heavy events, such as wrestling, and used as a conditioning exercise rather than for technical training only.

CHAPTER 6:

THE GREEK BODY AND PHYSICAL CULTURE

He shone among the other pentathletes as the bright moon in the middle of the month outshines the stars; in this way he showed his wondrous body to the great ring of watching Greeks...

—Bacchylides *Ep.* 9. 20–23

6.1: The Greek Body

The Greek ideal represented an ambiguous and paradoxical relationship between the physical body and the divine god or athlete. Winckelmann (1756)[48] suggested the ancient Greeks were superior to the modern man at the time in physical strength and beauty, a fact he attributed to their overall physical culture and superior forms of exercise (Stocking, 2014). Before Winckelmann, the Renaissance saw a fascination with Greek imagery and the illustration of the muscular Greek physique. There was also the searches for and discovery of ancient Greek and Roman manuscripts in this period.

---

48. Johann Winckelmann was an eighteenth-century antiquary. He complied the history of the art of antiquity from Roman copies of lost Greek originals. He never visited Greece.

The Library of Alexandria,[49] which had stored such books, had long since been destroyed. Several hundred books found their way to Florence in the first three decades of the fifteenth century from private collectors. These included complete versions of Aristotle's *Politics* and Herodotus's *Histories* as well as parts of Homer's *Odyssey*. These books became hugely influential in Renaissance Europe and led to changes to the education system in Florence. As mentioned in chapter 1, ancient Greek physical culture occupied an important place in the education of everyday life of all citizens. A highly organized system was developed for the training of youths, military training, preparation for festivals, and the Olympic Games.

Gymnasia flourished in all Greek cities and were also intellectual centers. The value of exercise was appreciated both by the state and by individuals. Physicians were aware of the role of exercise in the prevention and treatment of illness. This superiority in training techniques was observed in Greek sculpture. Winckelmann explained, "Their bodies received great and manly shape through exercise, which the Greek masters gave to their sculptures" (Stocking, 2014).

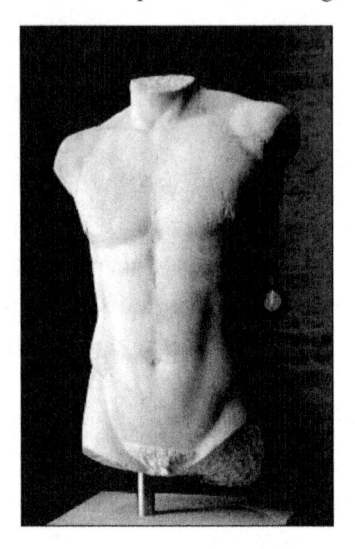

Figure A: Torso of Apollo, probably after a statue of Onatas from Aegina (ca. 460 BC). Image in the public domain.

---

49. The Library of Alexandria was established by Ptolemy II (285–246BC). The Ptolemies had attempted to amass all the Greek texts in existence (Fox, 2006).

The ancient Greeks developed beautiful and physical body forms (Taylor, 1880). Male beauty, according to Bacchylides, was athletic, hard, and powerful. Galen suggested that legitimate and genuinely true beauty consisted of good complexion, good flesh, and proportion of parts (Galen, *Thrasybulus* 10). Those who attended the gymnasium aimed to achieve physical excellence and beautiful bodies. The values of bodily strength and endurance were maintained as essential factors of manliness. Images of classical bodily perfection have survived into our modern times. Figure A shows a muscular male torso with defined abdominal muscles. It was in the muscles of the trunk rather than of the limbs where the real strength lay, and careful hardening of these muscles distinguishes early Greek sculpture from all other art. In the sixth century BC, the idea of manly virtue was encapsulated in the statue type known as a kouros, a "young man." This basic form with arithmetically calculated proportions was borrowed from Egypt, but the difference was that these statues were nude. The Greek kouros was composed to demonstrate the essential elements of manhood: broad shoulders, developed biceps and pectoral muscles, and flat stomach, with a clear division of torso and pelvis, powerful buttocks, and thighs (Jenkins, 2015). These anatomical details were stylized and based more on the notion of the ideal rather than on observation. By the end of the sixth century BC, the kouroi became more realistic and anatomically correct. It was Greek nudity that provided the opportunities to observe the well-conditioned body and portray it accurately (Miller, 2004).

Polyclitus of Argos was a sculptor active in the middle to late fifth century BC. His most famous work was the *Doryphoros*, or *Spear-Bearer*. He was also responsible for the statue of Pythocles, a pentathlete from Elis (Pausanias, 6.7.10).

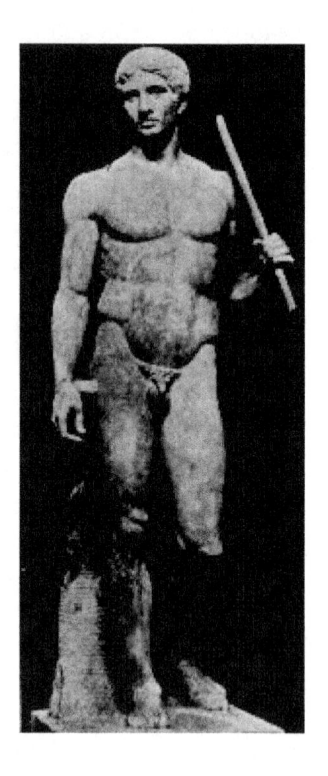

Figure B: Doryphoros (Spear-Bearer). Image in the public domain, PD-US-expired.

The key feature of his sculptures was the well-balanced muscular proportion of the human form. He also wrote a treatise, *Canon*, which is now lost about how to represent the ideal physique in bronze or stone using a system of mathematical calculations. A standard of an aesthetically successful body was constructed in terms of tautness, symmetry, and balance. Philostratus, with reference to Polyclitus's art of sculpture, described the ideal characteristics to be considered. He suggested a model of proportionality between the upper and lower quadrants of the body as well as posterior and anterior: "The ankle should agree in its measurement with the wrist, the forearm should correspond to the calf and the upper arm with the thigh, the buttock with the shoulder, and the back should be examined by comparison with the stomach" (Phil, *Gym* 25). How did these statues match the natural physique achieved by the athlete, and does Greek athletic sculpture reflect the ancient training regimens designed to build these muscular bodies? It is generally agreed that Polyclitus's theory of proportion is separate from natural anatomical presentation. His statue of Doryphoros is viewed as a sculpture rather than a representation of anatomical reality (Stocking, 2014).

Early inscriptions on athletic monuments emphasize that statues reproduced the likeness and size of the victors. Preference was given for the mesomorphic body type in ancient Greece as shown in Figure A. Athletic art of the fifth century BC was dominated by the search for the ideal. Ancient sculpture indicated the superiority of the Greeks achieved through physical exercise but may have also represented a physical impossibility that could only exist in a divine capacity. Isocrates the Greek orator (436–338 BC) stated, "No one can make the nature of his body resemble the statues or paintings" (Stocking, 2014). Spivey (2012) suggests that the ancient Greek sculptors of the fifth century BC collaborated and competed in creating a stereotype of the winning athlete's body. This was a muscular physique achieved by hard training and then refined by the sculptors with mathematical calculations.

The works of Polyclitus and Myron[50] sought to portray men not as they were but as they should be. These statues were not real men but a synthesis of parts to create the ideal. The *Riace Bronzes*, also called the *Riace Warriors*, are two full-size Greek bronzes of naked bearded warriors, cast about 460–450 BC and discovered off the coast of Riace Marina, Italy. It has been suggested that these statues were casted from the same basic prototype (more or less). Statue A portrays a younger warrior, with statue B indicating the more mature-looking of the two. In my opinion, these bronzes represent two different athletes, with one athlete having a more defined and thicker rectus abdominis muscle. I believe some Greek and Roman art and sculpture were true representations of the athletic body.

To distinguish between representations of athletic events, early sculptors would put into the hands of a statue a discus or a pair of jumping weights for the pentathlete or boxing thongs for the boxer, to indicate in what event victory had been achieved. Later statues represented the athlete in a typical position, such as a boxer sparring with an imaginary opponent or a pentathlete swinging the discus.

---

50. Myron was a fifth-century BC Athenian artist and contemporary of Polyclitus. His work fell between 480 and 440 BC, and he was famous in antiquity for statues of athletes.

Figure C: Discobolus, by Lancellotti Massimo. Photograph by Marie-Lan Nguyen, 2006. Image in the public domain.

The original *Discobolus* was a bronze statue of a discus thrower sculptured by Myron in 460 BC. Myron produced many statues of Olympic victors to commemorate their victories. Many of these statues at Olympia were melted down or broken up following the Roman conquest because of their depictions of nudity. The original *Discobolus* is lost, but it is known through literary references and descriptions as well as Roman copies, particularly the Lancellotti *Discobolus* (Spivey, 2012). The Lancellotti *Discobolus*, shown in Figure C, is a marble Roman copy made in AD 140 after the bronze original by Myron. This is believed to be the most accurate copy. The *Discobolus* has been assumed to depict a Greek male athlete about to throw the discus, and he would have been a pentathlete. The pentathlete was an all-around athlete with no particularly overdeveloped muscle group. The sculptor Myron's work between 480 and 440 BC does not commemorate the athletic victory but focuses more on the study of the athlete in motion. Myron's *Discobolus* combines stability and motion. At the top of the backward swing, there appears to be a momentary pause, which suggests stability, while the contorted posture of the trunk and the ropelike pull of the right arm implies the movement that has preceded it and a stronger movement yet that is to follow. Aristotle, in his *Rhetoric*, observed that the pentathletes were the most beautiful, being trained for both power and speed events. The pentathletes had a physical type most likely to exhibit muscle balance, symmetry, and measured proportions (Spivey, 2012). Philostratus suggested the pentathlete should be tall and compact but not excessively muscled or underdeveloped either (Phil, *Gym* 31). The *Discobolus* is one of the most famous of ancient Greek images. In ancient Greece, it created an idealized image of the Olympic Games, which became the model to strive for.

6.2: Applied Anatomy[51]

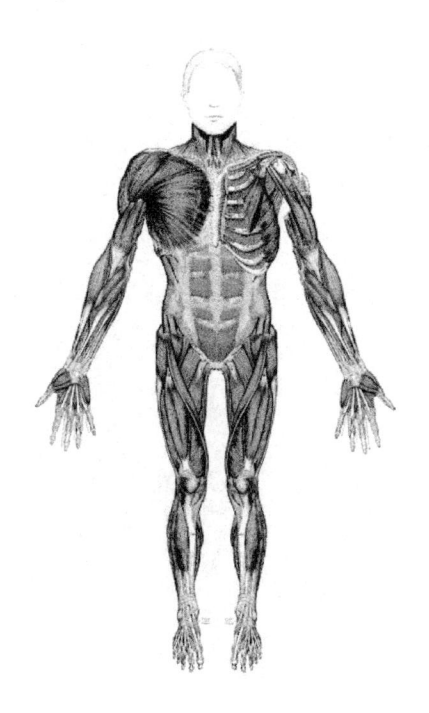

Figure D: The anterior abdominal muscles. Image in the public domain.

---

51. Anatomical descriptions were sourced from *Gray's Anatomy*, 38th edition, and Palastanga et al. (1995).

The anterior abdominal muscles consist of the rectus abdominis, or "six-pack" seen in Figure D (the muscles shaded in red). The rectus abdominus is a paired muscle running vertically on each side of the anterior wall of the abdomen. The six-pack sections of rectus abdominis are separated into distinct muscle bellies by a tendinous intersection of connective tissue. The two parallel muscles are separated by a midline band of connective tissue called the linea alba. The rectus abdominus is an important postural muscle and has a role in respiration. It acts as a flexor of the lumbar spine, demonstrated by the "crunch" sit-up. The external oblique muscle curves around the lateral and anterior parts of the abdomen. It is the most superficial of the three sheets of muscle of the anterior abdominal wall (Figure E).

This muscle is an ipsilateral lateral flexor (side-bending) and a contralateral rotator of the trunk. Hence, the right external oblique would bend to the right and rotate to the left.

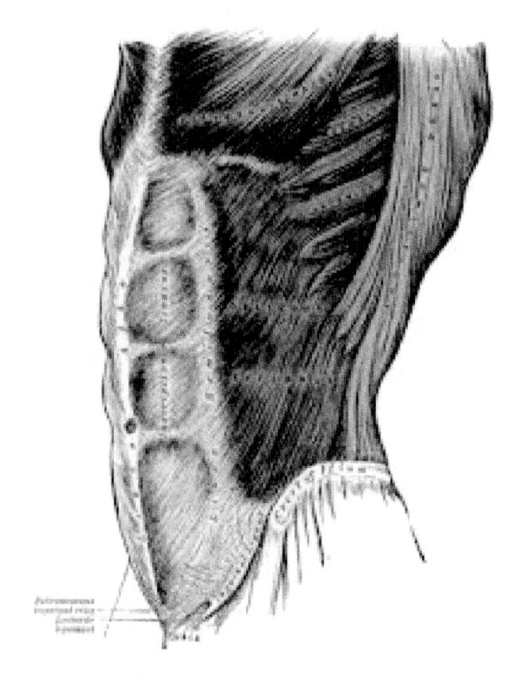

Figure E: The external oblique muscle. Image in the public domain.

Fibers of the external oblique muscle give rise to an aponeurosis (fascia), which is a strong tendinous sheet. The lower border of the aponeurosis stretches between the pubic tubercle and anterior superior iliac spine. This forms the inguinal ligament, also called the Poupart's ligament. The inguinal ligament is curved along its length, with the convexity pointing toward the thigh, where is it continuous with the fascia lata. This ligament in adults is 12–14 cm in length and inclined at 35–40 degrees to the horizontal. The lateral half of the ligament is more oblique, whereas the medial half gradually widens toward its attachment to the pubis, where it becomes more horizontal. The internal oblique muscle lies deep to the external oblique, as shown in Figure F.

This muscle causes ipsilateral rotation and side-bending of the trunk. It acts with the external oblique muscle of the opposite side to achieve the torsional movement of the trunk.

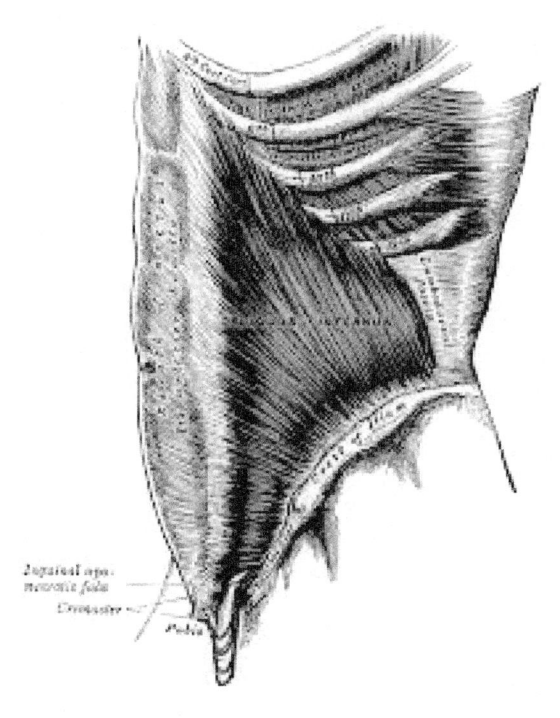

Figure F: The internal oblique muscle. Image in the public domain.

Achieving the "six-pack" or abdominal muscle definition, as seen in Figure J on page 150 is dependent on the overall body fat a person has. Genetically, some individuals will store less body fat around their abdominal muscles, whereas others will store excess fat around their stomachs. Improving abdominal mass with exercise can improve definition and muscle thickness, but it is not possible to achieve this definition with exercise alone or "spot reduction." Spot reduction refers to the claim that fat can be targeted from a specific area of the body through exercise of specific muscles in the desired area, in this case exercising the abdominal muscles. The crunch abdominal exercise for example has been found to be more superior to the standard sit-up for activation of the rectus abdominis muscle (Beim et al., 1997). The focus for achieving abdominal muscular definition should be an overall fat loss. A body-fat percentage of below 10 percent in males (below 16 percent in females) will reveal definition in the lower abdomen muscles (Fleck, 1983). The average body-fat percentage for adult males is 18 to 24 percent and 25 to 31 percent for females. Athletes, on average, will have generally a lower percentage of body fat than nonathletes, ranging from 6 to 13 percent. This will depend on the type of athletic event. For example, runners have a body-fat percentage between 6.3 and 7.7 percent, whereas wrestlers are between 5 and 10.7 percent (Doxey, 1984). Heavy resistance training and HIIT are more superior forms of exercise for burning fat and increasing metabolism. Boutcher (2010) suggests that high-intensity intermittent exercise may be more effective at reducing subcutaneous and abdominal body fat than other forms of exercise. This may be due to increased exercise and postexercise fat oxidation and decreased postexercise appetite. Nutrition is also important for muscular definition and fat reduction. Protein is key for losing fat and for overall weight loss.

Fiber can also boost weight loss and burn fat. Howarth et al. (2010) found that an increased fiber intake, whether given as higher-fiber foods or as a fiber supplement, results in increased satiety and/or increased hunger, leading to weight loss. Typical foods high in fiber include fruit, whole grains, vegetables, nuts, and beans/legumes. A Mediterranean diet like that of the ancient Greeks has been found to be effective for weight loss, higher intake of fiber, and a decrease in waist circumference. A typical Mediterranean diet with restricted calories may include moderate fats, such as olive oil and nuts. This diet is rich in vegetables and low in red meat, with poultry and fish replacing beef and lamb (Shai et al., 2008).

THE FIRST PHYSICAL CULTURISTS

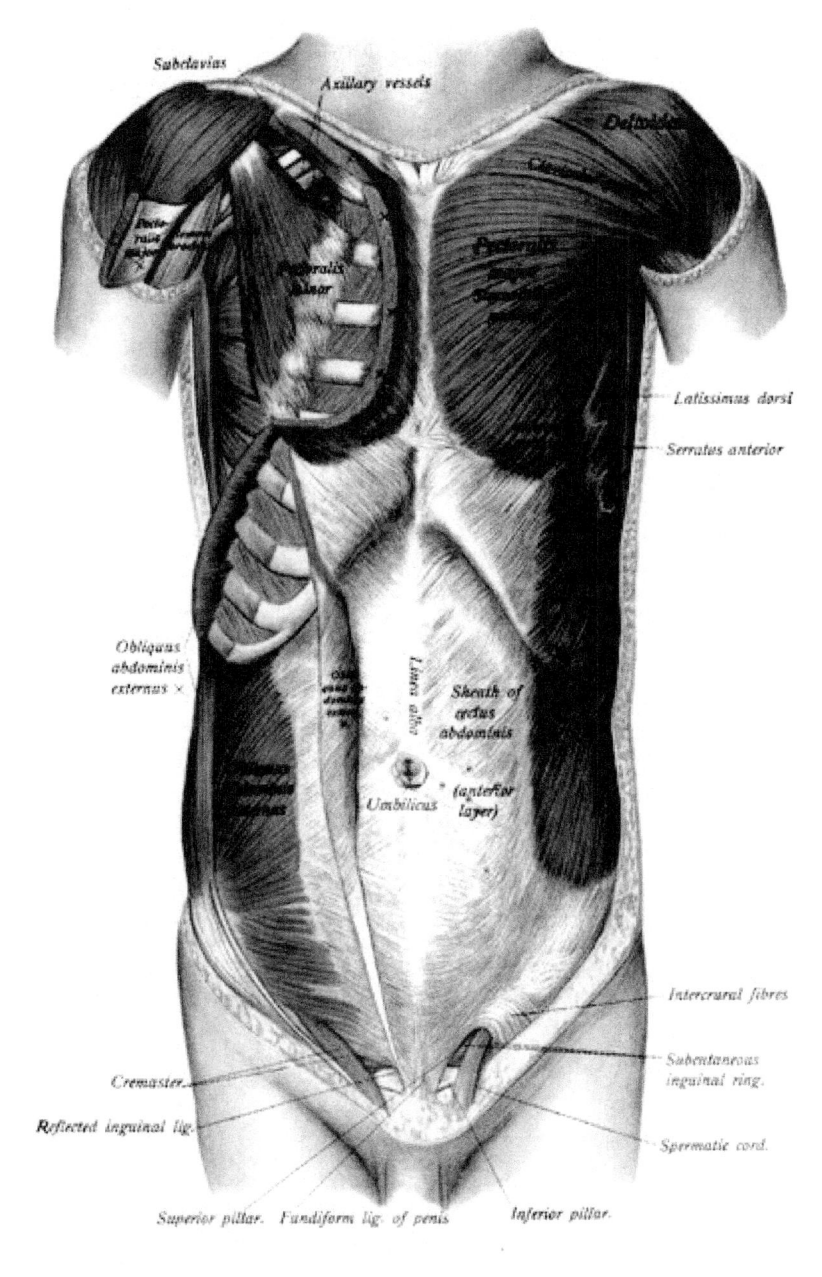

Figure G: The human torso representing the anterior muscles including pectoralis major and minor. Image in the public domain.

Figure G shows the major muscles of the human torso, which are represented very accurately in ancient Greek sculpture without significant exaggeration (Figure I). In addition to the anterior muscles are the chest (pectoral and serratus muscles) and shoulder muscles (deltoid).

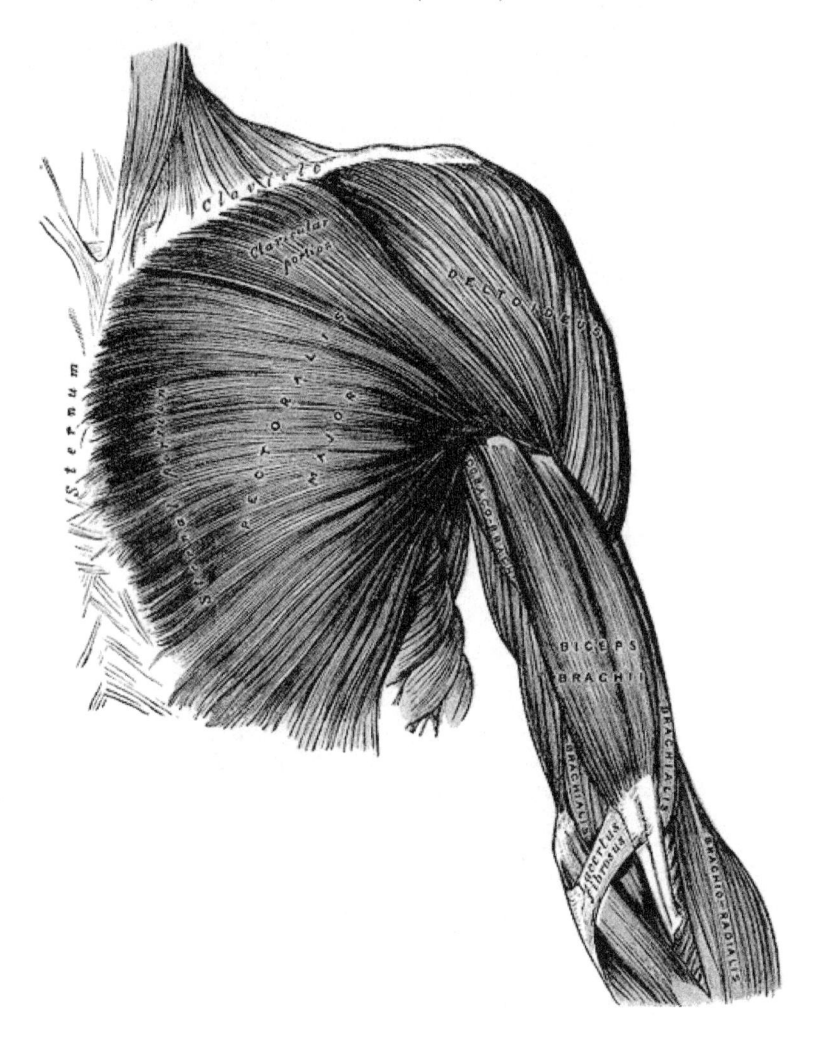

Figure H: The superficial muscles of the upper body including pectoralis major and deltoid. Image in the public domain.

A well-developed chest or pecs is one of the more popular goals of physical culturists and athletes. The pectoralis major, shown in Figures G and H, is a thick, fan-shaped muscle found on the upper half of the anterior surface of the thoracic wall. This muscle arises from the clavicle (collarbone), sternum (breastbone), and ribs converging as a tendon to attach to the humerus. The clavicular fibers may be prolonged into the deltoid tendon. The whole muscle assists in adduction and medial rotation of the humerus at the shoulder joint. The pectoralis major is one of the major climbing muscles. If the arms are fixed above the head, this muscle can be used to pull the trunk upward, assisted by the latissimus dorsi muscle. The pectoralis minor is a thin triangular muscle lying deep in the pectoralis major muscle (Figure G). This muscle arises from the ribs attaching to the coracoid process of the scapular. The pectoralis minor assists serratus anterior (see below) in drawing the scapular forward and around the chest wall. Two of the best chest-development exercises that target both the pectoralis major and minor muscles are the decline bench press and dips.

Akagi et al. (2014) found with electromyographic studies that the pectoralis major contributes to the bench press exercise, as do the deltoid and triceps brachii muscles. The bench press is a resistance exercise that has been widely used to optimize the performance of the upper extremities, including the pectoral muscles with an aim to increase muscle strength, hypertrophy, or athletic performance (de Araújo Farias et al., 2017). A training volume of three sets of ten repetitions at 75 percent 1 RM bench press increases the overall size of pectoralis major (Akagi et al., 2014). The dumbbell bench press has been shown to elicit significantly greater pectoralis major activity (de Araújo Farias et al., 2017). Marcolin et al. (2015) also found that the narrow-based variant of the push-up emphasized pectoralis major and triceps muscle activity.

The serratus anterior muscle is an important muscle in sport performance. This muscle, shown in Figures E and G, is a large, flat muscular sheet sandwiched between the ribs and the scapular. From extensive attachments, serratus anterior inserts into the medial border of the scapular. Serratus anterior is major protractor of the pectoral girdle and is involved in all thrusting, pushing, and punching movements. Hence, more advanced development of this muscle is seen in boxers. It is also one of the primary muscles responsible for maintaining normal rhythm and shoulder motion.

Lack of strength or endurance of the serratus anterior allows the scapular to rest in a downwardly rotated position, causing the inferior border to become more prominent. Correct positioning of the humerus in the glenoid cavity, known as scapulohumeral rhythm, is critical to the proper function of the shoulder joint (glenohumeral joint) during overhead motion. If the normal scapulohumeral rhythm is disturbed, this may alter the positioning of the glenoid relative to the humeral head, resulting in injury. Exercises that elicit the greatest electromyographic activity from the serratus anterior muscle were found to be the push-up plus, serratus anterior punch, and dynamic hug, which are all up to ninety degrees of humeral elevation (Decker et al., 1999). Exercises above ninety degrees of humeral elevation are also advocated to improve serratus anterior function, such as the wall slide (Hardwick et al., 2006). The wall slide begins by slightly leaning against the wall with the ulnar border of the forearms (little finger side) in contact with the wall, elbows flexed at ninety degrees and shoulders abducted at ninety degrees in the scapular plane. From this position, the arms slide up the wall in the scapular plane while leaning into the wall. This exercise produces serratus anterior activity above 120 degrees (Hardwick et al., 2006).

The push-up plus starts with the standard press-up position with extended elbows, but the aim is to continue rising by protracting the scapular, then returning to the starting position by retracting the scapular and flexing the elbows. The serratus anterior punch involves standing with the knees slightly bent and a split stance. Then, using resistance bands or pulleys while maintaining elbow extension, with the arm at shoulder height and the humerus rotated at forty-five degrees, the scapular is protracted and retracted. This exercise shows greater activation of the serratus anterior than the forward punch. The dynamic hug starts with the elbow flexed at forty-give degrees, arm abducted at sixty degrees, and medial rotation at forty-five degrees. A hugging action is performed by horizontally flexing the humerus. A conditioned serratus anterior muscle is important for sports such as swimming, tennis, and throwing events. During throwing as well as pushing and punching movements, the pectoralis major acts to move the humerus forcefully, while the serratus anterior and pectoralis minor simultaneously protract the shoulder girdle. A fatigued serratus anterior muscle will reduce scapular rotation and protraction, which will cause the humeral head to translate anteriorly as well as superiorly, possibly leading to shoulder impingement and rotator cuff tears (Decker et al., 1999).

The deltoid muscle shown in Figure H is a triangular muscle that gives the shoulder its rounded contour. It can be divided into three parts: anterior, posterior, and middle. The muscle fibers of deltoid insert into the deltoid tuberosity on the lateral aspect of the humeral midshaft. The anterior part of the deltoid is a strong flexor, and the medial rotator of the humerus assists the pectoralis major in this movement, while the posterior part is a strong extensor and lateral rotator acting with the latissimus dorsi muscle. The middle multipennate fibers of the deltoid are the principal abductors of the arm. The anterior deltoid is activated by barbell and dumbbell shoulder or military press exercises. Sixty to seventy percent of a maximum voluntary isometric contraction of the anterior deltoid is achieved during a plyometric push-up (clapping) and a one-armed push-up. Dunnick et al. (2015) found that the free-weight bench press significantly increases activation of both the anterior and middle deltoids compared to the use of a chest-press machine at higher exercise intensities. The middle and posterior deltoids are trained with the rowing exercise and prone horizontal abduction at one hundred degrees (Escamilla et al., 2009).

The bicep muscle is shown with relative bulk and definition in the *Spear-Bearer* statue (Figure B). This is a muscle that all physical culturists train for hypertrophy to emphasize their muscular physique. The biceps brachii muscle shown in Figure H is a large fusiform muscle in the flexor compartment of the upper arm. It has two attached parts or heads. The short head arises from the coracoid apex of the scapula. The long head starts within the capsule of the shoulder arising from the supraglenoid tubercle of the scapula. The two tendons lead into two elongated bellies, which form a single muscle attaching as a flattened tendon at the radial tuberosity. The biceps brachii muscle acts as a flexor of the elbow but is also a powerful supinator of the forearm. When the elbow is at ninety degrees, maximum power is achieved for both flexion and supination.

The brachialis is often a forgotten muscle. This is the main flexor of the elbow. This muscle arises from the shaft of the humerus and inserts into the tuberosity of the ulna. The straight barbell and alternating dumbbell curls are generally used to train the bicep muscle. Kidgell et al. (2010) found that a progressive resistance program of biceps curls (flexion-extension movements using a dumbbell with the forearm supinated) just after four weeks resulted in a 28 percent increase in 1 RM posttraining due to neuromuscular adaptation. Oliveira et al. (2009) reported that standing dumbbell curls and sitting dumbbell curls with the trunk inclined backward are recommended for biceps' force improvement. An undulated curling bar has been found to exhibit the highest level of EMG activity for both the biceps brachii and brachialis muscles. Chin-ups up to ninety-degree elbow flexion with supination of the forearm is also an effective exercise for training the bicep muscle; the maximum power of the muscle is achieved in this position.

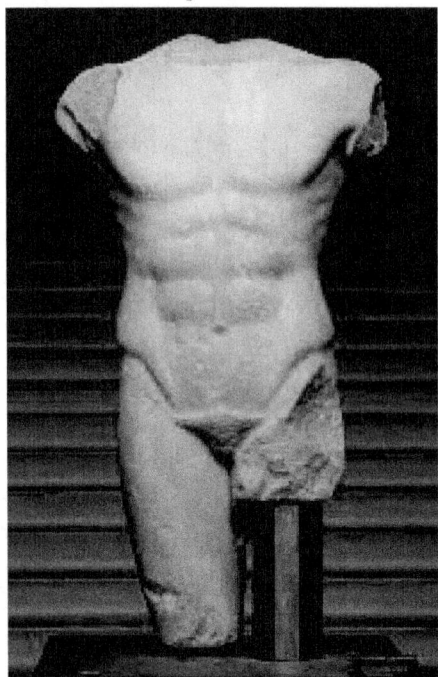

Figure I (left): Male torso between ca 480 and 470 BC Torso Miletus, Louvre. Photograph by Marie-Lan Nguyen, 2006. Image in the public domain. Figure J (right): Muscular Torso. (Madrid, Orgullo 2010 - Torso con bandera de España. This image was originally posted to **Flickr** *by Brocco Lee at https://www.flickr.com/photos/69772513@N00/4774040630. It was reviewed on 2 August 2010 by* **FlickreviewR** *and was confirmed to be licensed under the terms of the cc-by-sa-2.0. No changes to the image were made).*

In my view, the only exception to nonexaggerated anatomical representations in Greek sculpture is the inguinal ligament. The Roman phrase *Supra Verum* is translated as the hyperreal. Stocking (2014) believes that our only written explanation of the visual formula in Greco-Roman sculpture thought to be supra verum are the hyperdeveloped lower abdominal muscles that wrap around the iliac crest, known as the iliac furrow, formed by the inguinal ligament. This is more popularly known as Apollo's belt. This feature is more pronounced in Greek statues like the *Doryphoros* in Figure B. In this example, the "belt" has a greater curvature and a thickened or hypertrophied rather than thinned appearance. It continues to wrap around the back rather than represent its attachment to the pubis. Philostratus may refer to this anatomical exaggeration when he states, "the chest should curve outward similarly to the parts beneath the hip joint" (Phil, *Gym* 25).

The musculature of the upper body shown in the statue from antiquity in Figure I closely matches muscular physique in modern times (Figure J). The rectus abdominus is clearly visualized, with the sections of the muscle separated into distinct muscle bellies. The midline band of connective tissue or linea alba, as well as the inguinal ligament, are also seen. It appears that in Figure I, the inguinal ligament is inclined within thirty-five to forty degrees to the horizontal without exaggeration in my opinion. A well-developed pectoralis major muscle or chest and serratus anterior are also visualized in the statue.

Figure K: Heracles and his child Telephos. Marble. Roman copy of the first–second century CE after a Greek original of the fourth century BCE. Found in Tivoli, Italy. Photograph by Marie-Lan Nguyen, 2007. Image in the public domain.

This text has focused mainly on the upper torso, but Figure K depicting Heracles shows the lower-limb musculature. The most prominent muscles for muscular development of the lower extremities are the quadriceps and triceps surae (calf muscles), shown in Figures K, L and N, respectively. The quadriceps femoris, known as the great extensor muscle of the leg, covers all the front and sides of the femur. It can be divided into four parts. The rectus femoris arises from the ilium and travels down the middle of the thigh (Figure L). The other three arise from the shaft of the femur and surround it from the trochanters and the condyles. In front is the vastus intermedius, the medial is vastus medialis, and the lateral is vastus lateralis (Figure M).

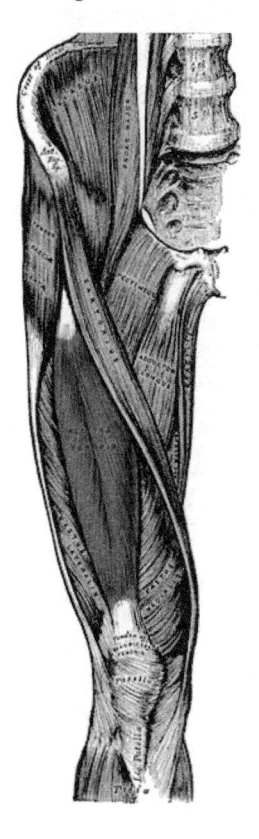

Figure L: The muscles of the anterior thigh highlighting rectus femoris in red. Image in the public domain.

    The rectus femoris crosses both hip and knee joints, whereas the three vasti muscles cross the knee joint only. The tendons of the four components of quadriceps unite in the lower part of the thigh to form a strong tendon attached to the base of the patella and form the ligamentum patellae (Figures L and M). The ligamentum patellae runs from the apex of the patella to the tibial tuberosity, acting as the tendon of the quadriceps femoris muscle. The articularis genus is a small muscle that is usually distinct from vastus intermedius but can blend with it.

The function of articularis genus is to prevent the synovial membrane becoming trapped and affecting the normal movements of the knee joint.

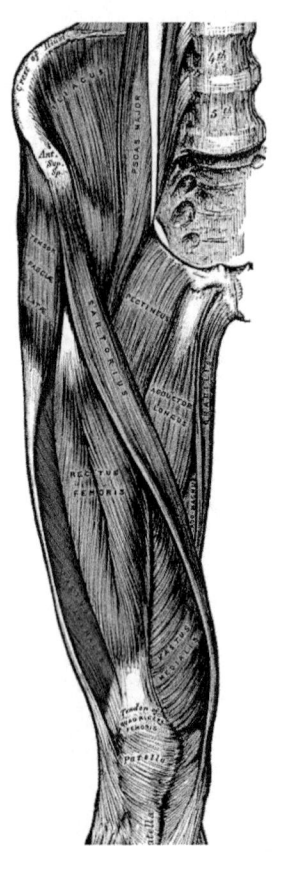

Figure M: The muscles of the anterior thigh highlighting vastus lateralis in red. Image in the public domain.

Quadriceps femoris is the main extensor of the knee joint. The rectus femoris crosses in front of the hip and is therefore a flexor of that joint. The vasti muscles have different roles in extension of the knee during various ranges. Vastus medialis, for example, is more active during the final range of knee extension and may act to resist the lateral movement of the patella. The bilateral squat is the most popular exercise for quadriceps muscle development and knee rehabilitation programs (Slater and Hart, 2017). The barbell back squat has the bar or load behind it, whereas in the front squat the load is in the front. The front squat emphasizes the higher activation of vastus lateralis and rectus femoris, but the activation of these muscles is lower in the back squat. Vastus medialis is activated equally in both squats. Alternative exercises to build up the quadriceps muscles without using weights include the single leg squat, alternating forward lunge, and mountain climber. Conventional resistance training increases the neuronal input of the agonist muscles, leading to an increase in muscle strength.

Progressive resistance training eventually leads to muscle hypertrophy. Plyometric training, as mentioned in chapter 4, closely resembles the ballistic movement patterns involved in athletic performance. For example, plyometric training has been reported to increase maximal vertical jump. In individuals participating in plyometric training, both type I and type II muscle fibers'[52] cross-sectional area (CSA) increases have been observed (Potteiger et al., 1999). Vissing et al. (2008) compared the changes in muscle strength, power, and morphology of the lower-limb muscles induced by plyometric training versus conventional resistance weight training. The conventional resistance training (CRT) consisted of the leg press and knee extensions to train the quadriceps muscles. The plyometric training (PT) consisted of jumping exercises. Following a twelve-week training program, gains in maximal muscle strength were similar between the two exercise groups, whereas muscle power increased almost exclusively with PT. The CSA of the quadriceps muscle in both legs combined increased by 8.4 cm^2 in the CRT and by 7.5 cm^2 in the PT group, but there were no significant differences between the groups.

---

52. Muscle fibers were originally divided into types by histochemical analysis as types I, IIA, and IIB. Type I is slow and has more endurance capabilities, whereas Type IIb is fast, generating more power. Type IIA is a hybrid of types I and II (Scott et al., 2001).

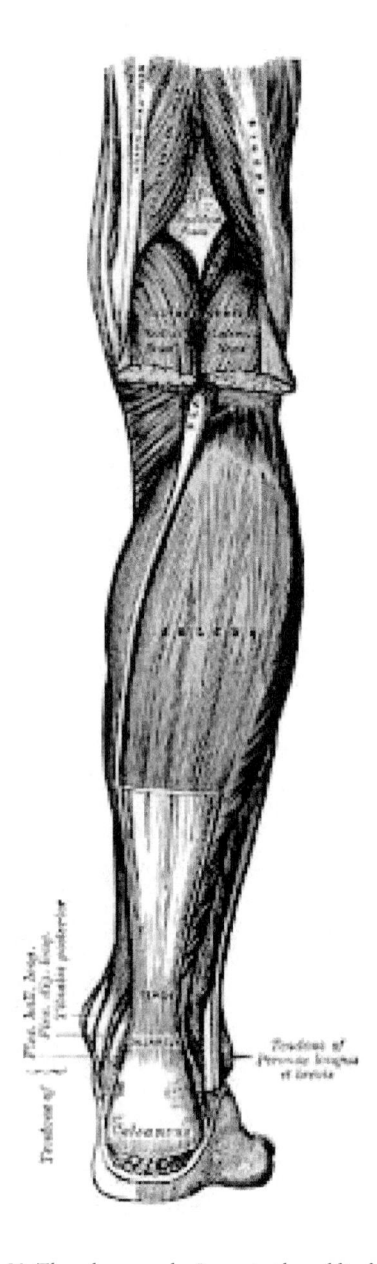

Figure N: The soleus muscle. Image in the public domain.

The triceps surae muscle complex or calf muscle shown in Figure N is traditionally the hardest muscle to develop and train for hypertrophy. The statue of Hercules from antiquity in Figure K shows well-developed calf muscles. The muscles in the posterior compartment of the lower leg form: superficial and deep groups. The muscles of the superficial group form the bulk of the calf consist of gastrocnemius, plantaris, and soleus. Their main function is the plantar flexion of the foot. The gastrocnemius is the most superficial of the muscle group and forms the belly of the calf. It arises from two heads shown in Figure N, which are connected to the condyles of the femur by a strong, flat tendon. The gastrocnemius muscle belly extends to the midcalf, where it starts to insert into an aponeurosis. The aponeurosis receives the tendon of soleus to form the tendon of Achilles. The Achilles tendon is the thickest and strongest tendon in the body. It attaches to the posterior surface of the calcaneus. The soleus muscle (Figure N) is a broad, flat muscle situated immediately deep or anterior to gastrocnemius. It arises from the head and shaft of the fibula and the medial border of the tibia. The soleus is covered proximally by gastrocnemius, but below the midcalf, it is broader than the tendon of gastrocnemius and is accessible on both sides. The two heads of gastrocnemius together with soleus form a tripartite muscle mass sharing the Achilles tendon and sometimes termed the triceps surae.

These muscles, as mentioned, are chief plantar flexors of the foot. Gastrocnemius acts as the propelling force in walking, running, and leaping, acting mainly at the ankle. It is also a flexor of the knee. The soleus muscle is suited more as a postural muscle, as it prevents the leg from falling forward under the influence of body weight. This postural role of soleus is suggested by its high content of type I muscle fibers, which are slow and fatigue resistant.

A standard exercise for training the calf muscle is the calf or heel raise. Heel raises are recommended with the knee straight for gastrocnemius and bent for soleus. Soleus activity has been found to be 4 percent greater when tested in forty-five-degree knee flexion compared to zero-degree knee flexion, whereas both heads of gastrocnemius are 5 percent lower in forty-five-degree knee flexion (Herbert-Losier et al., 2012). Hence seated heel raises target the soleus, as the gastrocnemius muscle contracts less when the knee is bent. The donkey heel raise is suggested as one of the better exercises for training the calf muscles. This involves a bilateral heel or calf raise on a small block with lumbar flexion, which increases the stretch at the triceps surae muscle complex. Training exercises to improve calf power include pick jumps, sprints, and Olympic lifts. The pick jump consists of small bilateral leg jumps forward and then backward with a weight held above the head. Olympic lifts include the clean and press with a half squat. It has been found that the single leg jump elicits the greatest calf-muscle activation, followed by the single-heel raise, with the seated heel raise showing the least amount of muscle activation (Mullaney et al., 2011). High-intensity resistance exercise at 80 percent 1 RM has been found to be an effective method for gaining muscular size and strength at the calf muscle. It would seem also that plyometric training (PT) would be an effective method of developing the calf muscle, as single leg jumps elicit higher calf muscle activation. Kubo et al. (2007) compared CRT and PT for the calf muscles. The PT involved hopping and drop-jump training. It was found that after a twelve-week training program, a 5 percent gain in whole-muscle CSA for the calf muscles was equally induced by CRT and PT.

6.3: Achieving the Ideal Body

The norm to aspire to in ancient Greece was a body with broad shoulders, contoured thorax, firm waist, and powerful thighs, as represented in classical sculpture. These sculptors, in my opinion, shown in Figures A, I, and K show balanced, well-proportioned muscular forms derived from actual Greek athletes and not a representation of the ideal. These exemplary muscular bodies were achieved as described in chapter 5 by their concepts of exercise training, including the progressive overload principle and Mediterranean diet to increase lean muscle mass and increase muscular strength. It was Philostratus who provided a holistic approach to training and practical hints. Boxers in ancient Greece would have had a well-developed serratus anterior muscle and shoulder muscles as well as toned abdominal muscles. Philostratus suggested the best type of stomach for a boxer is slim, for these athletes are light and have good breathing. Wrestlers, according to Philostratus, should have a body shape that is the same as a well-proportioned athlete (Phil, *Gym* 34—35). He also suggested that stocky athletes of small stature but strong and heavily built were best suited to wrestling.

Muscular development and low body fat were achieved with early plyometrics, such as jumping, exercises with the ball, sprint training, use of the punching bag, as well as sparring. The punching bag was part of the equipment in the ancient Greek gymnasium and is a good exercise for burning fat as well as for pectoral, shoulder, and core muscle development (i.e., rectus abdominis, internal and external obliques, and *erector spinae* muscles). This training was followed very vigorously with the correct diet. Rope climbing, as described by Galen, would help develop the pectoral muscles.

Throwing the quoit or lifting the plummet over their heads or shoulders would train the deltoid muscles as well as the arms of lower extremities. Epictetus, a stoic philosopher in the first century AD, indicated that athletes develop their shoulders using the halteres (*Discourses*, Book II, 4). Hanging from a piece of wood for as long as possible or doing pull-ups would have been used to develop the upper limb and biceps muscle. Jumping exercises such as leaping from a low to a high place or jumping on one leg would have increased quadriceps as well as calf-muscle power and hypertrophy.

That being said, by the late fifth century BC, there was a disproportionate physical development brought on by sporting specialization. It was mentioned in antiquity that athletes who trained for the wrestling, boxing, and the pankration events resulted in fleshy, overmuscled bodies, gracelessness, and ill health. According to Philostratus, it was desirable to have a free-standing neck like that of a beautiful and proud horse associated with athletic training rather than a sunken neck into the shoulders, which was linked with brute strength (Phil, *Gym* 35). The sunken neck to the shoulders could be referring to the bulky athletic statues in the Hellenistic period and onward (Rusten and König, 2014). Anatomically, this could refer to the overdeveloped musculature of the back and neck such as large upper trapezius muscles. This may be a description of a wrestler's physique in the Hellenistic period, although Stocking (2014) suggests this "yoked neck" could be also be that of a manual laborer. I believe this most likely to be a description of a wrestler. In modern wrestlers, the cervical muscles are strongly involved with well-developed cervical extensor muscles to maintain the neck and head in a fixed position against the opponent's force (Chaabene et al., 2017). Galen mentioned that these athletes had too much heaviness of the body.

Figure O: Marble statue of the so-called Apollo Lykeios, AD 130–161, Roman. Image in the public domain.

Although I have given examples that ancient Greek statues represented the real athlete and these muscular torsos could be achieved with training, it has been suggested previously that the statue of Doryphoros is a mathematically perfect body, both balanced and symmetrical but beyond reality. Apollo's belt was excessively defined in Greek sculpture, as shown in Figure O, which is an unrealistic anatomical feature. Athletic artwork in ancient Greece also displayed distortion or scarring arising from injury, perhaps representing the brutality and violence of ancient sport (König, 2010).

One example of distortion was the cauliflower ear, which was an identifying sign of an athlete. The cauliflower ear appeared in many early and late classic works. The so-called Thermae boxer in Figure P (third to second centuries BC), for example, displays this feature. Swollen ears were common in Hellenistic works but also appear on representations of gods and demigods. Herakles is frequently shown with such an ear. The cauliflower ear was something to be avoided if possible, as ear guards were used in training.

Figure P: So-called Thermae Boxer: athlete resting after a boxing match. Bronze, Greek artwork of the Hellenistic era, third to second centuries BC. Image in the public domain.

6.4: Physical Culture from Ancient Greece to the Twentieth Century

This book suggests the ancient Greeks were the first physical culturists, and they were. No other civilization in antiquity cultivated their bodies like the Greeks. Lucian mentioned "young men aglow with such splendid condition, they are neither lean and emaciated nor heavy (full-bodied) but symmetrical in their lines" (Lucian, *Anacharsis* 42). Lucian also quoted that athletes had sweated away the useless and superfluous part of their tissues, but what made for strength and elasticity is left upon them uncontaminated by what is worthless, and they maintain it vigorously (Lucian, *Anacharsis* 42). From the fifth century BC, there was a heightened interest in Athens on the facets of masculinity and bodily culture by their citizens. The athletic program of the Panathenaia (the grand religious and athletic festival of ancient Athens) included an event called *euandria*, a term translated as "manly excellence" or "manly beauty." The euandria was a competitive event in which well-built and muscular men engaged in a physical performance, possibly involving displays of group fitness and coordination (Papakonstantinou, 2012). The prize-winning body in the euandria would earn a substantial gift, such as oxen. A prize was also given for the love of training.

The manliness contest in Athens also included senior categories. Another version of the contest was held at Elis. This was called Krisiskallous, "the judgment of the beautiful," and was to the glory of the goddess Athena. Another similar contest was staged at Tanagra in Boeotia beside the altar of the god Hermes (Kriophoros) or Hermes the Ram-Bearer. The winner of the contest that showed the most beauty was given the privilege to carry a ram around the city walls in Hermes's honor. Thus, the appearance of a beautiful man could be claimed as something that was pleasing to the eyes of the gods (Spivey, 2012).

Athletes would apply yellow dust to their bodies, making them gleam and making it more pleasant to look at the well-trained body (Phil, *Gym* 56). There was also evidence from inscriptions of several gymnasia in ancient Greece that held a range of institutional competitions promoting outstanding bodily beauty. This would have encouraged those to train and motivate attendance at the gymnasia. This included the euexia, which was a kind of physique competition emphasizing general fitness and a good state of bodily condition, or hexis (Crowther, 1991). These competitions were a test of muscular development and posture with marks awarded for tone, definition, and symmetry. The level of fitness, health appearance, and bodily attributes would be acquired after long periods of training and dieting. This is comparable to bodybuilding contests in the twentieth century. The athletic bodies of participants in the euandria and euexia contests evoke representations of athletic physique in Epinikian poetry, as well as the art of the sixth and fifth centuries BC.

Were these muscular bodies presented at these contests, models that all citizens in Athens and the Greek world aspired to? There were criticisms for overtrained athletic bodies, fitness, and appearance contests in civic festivals. Not all athletes had the perfect body or symmetry, as mentioned in 6.3. Xenophon suggested the body should not be like long-distance runners who develop their legs at the expense of the shoulders, nor like boxers, who develop their chest and shoulders at expense of the legs; he rather had the view of giving the body a balanced development by exercising it in every part (Xenophon, *Symposium* 2.32–33).

Strengthening exercises for muscular development declined after the fall of Rome. There are few references to resistance training until the eighteenth century. New exercise systems and gymnastics had developed in the early decades of the nineteenth century in Europe and America, which evolved from Greek revivalism. The end of the eighteenth century saw the emergence of local strongmen at taverns who would demonstrate feats of strength, such as lifting large rocks or pulling wagons as well as wrestling. Milo of Croton was probably one of the first recorded strongmen, equivalent to those of the eighteenth to twentieth centuries. It was said that Milo carried his own statue into the Altis. He would hold a pomegranate so fast that no one could take it from his hand, yet he held it so daintily that he did not crush it. In another feat of strength, he used to stand on a greased quoit and jeer at those who charged at him and tried to push him off. He also used to bind a ribbon around his forehead and break it by swelling his veins. It is said that Milo came to an unfortunate end and was killed by wild beasts. In the woods one day, Milo found a tree that was split and kept open with wedges. He attempted to pry the tree with his own hands, but the wedges slipped, and Milo's hands were trapped, with him ending up as prey for the wolves (Pausanias, 6.14.6–8).

In the nineteenth century, there were two integrated traditions: muscular showmanship and physical fitness. The roots of muscular showmanship lay in the circus, strongman shows, and military training. Physical training was for health benefits. It was Dio Lewis, a physician, who developed a new form of gymnastics in the 1860s and lectured widely on the importance of physical education for health. Physical culture shifted from feats of strength to the display of the perfect muscular body (Toon and Golden, 2002). Athletic training literature from the nineteenth century showed a desire to transform marble into flesh. Ancient sculpture, mainly from Roman reproductions and not Greek originals, were objects of imitation for the public to aspire to achieving the ideal physique. Arnold Schwarzenegger once said, "At the end of the 19th century a new interest in muscle building arose, not muscle as a means of survival or defending one-self, but a return to the Greek ideal, muscular development as a celebration of the human body" (Stocking, 2014).

In the 1850s George Barker Windship contributed to America's first weight-training boom. He quoted, "Strength is health," and realized that huge feats of strength could not be achieved by ordinary exercises of the gymnasium. Daniel Savage patented the first graduated dumbbell in 1860, which allowed weight to be increased or decreased. Windship improved the design of the dumbbell in 1865 using flat, metallic disks that were simpler in construction and quickly adjustable, which he patented (Todd, 1995). This dumbbell closely resembles those that are used today. In contrast to Galen, who suggested that training to excess was harmful, Windship advocated heavy lifting. Following his sudden death at forty-two, though, this concept became less popular.

Eugen Sandow (1867–1925) was a famous professional strongman who introduced German physical culture and the naturalist movement to the United States. Sandow's initial inspiration for pursuing physical culture came from seeing Greco-Roman sculpture as a child. He compared his own body to this sculpture, and this inspired him to pioneer the practice of modern bodybuilding. He then went on to inspire the young to exercise and promoted health. It was Robert Jefferies Roberts who coined the term *bodybuilding* in 1881. He became the director of the Boston Young Men's Christian Association (YMCA). The YMCA, founded in 1844, saw sports as a means for enhancing Christian values and facilitated the popularity of weight training.

Bernarr Macfadden (1868–1955) was a significant figure in the physical culture movement of the twentieth century. He told a familiar story of his transformation from a frail weakling to a strongman using his exercise regimen. Macfadden gained his strength from boxing and wrestling. He was a self-promoter and publisher of the magazine *Physical Culture*, which began circulation in 1899 and continued for over fifty years. He staged the first physique contest for males and females in the United States. His catchphrase was "Weakness is a crime; don't be a criminal." *Physical Culture* covered aspects of healthy living such as nutrition, dance, and natural healing.

Macfadden's regimen was a combination of weight training, diet, and health theories (Reich, 2010). Macfadden advocated all the muscles of the body should be exercised to maintain health. Underexercising was one of the causes of disease. Other causes of disease, according to Macfadden, included heredity, mental influences, contagion, improper diet, overstrain or understrain, physical, mechanical, and chemical causes (Macfadden, 1911). Macfadden may have taken his ideas and concepts from the ancient Greeks or may have been influenced by them. He commented that the science of bodybuilding was a feature of ancient Greek religion, and as a result, they developed the human body to the highest degree of perfection. Their shared idea that physical health is the first and best step toward mental and moral health. Macfadden quoted Aristotle on the Greek idea of providing healthful play exercises for children and the youth, which should be promoted in modern cities of the United States. Aristotle said, "The education of the body must precede that of the intellect, we must surrender our children in the first instance to the gymnastic and the art of the trainer" (Aristotle, *Politics* V 3). Macfadden, though, believed that it was better to exercise outdoors and the muscles should be exercised moderately. For it was Galen who quoted Hippocrates on his suggested health program: "Work, food, drink, sleep, love, all in moderation" (Robinson, 1955). To Macfadden, the gymnasium was unnatural but a necessity in modern civilization. Calisthenics he classified as free-movement exercises without apparatuses to promote gracefulness and strength. The horse and parallel bars were types of gymnastic equipment recommended by Macfadden for developing the arms, chest, shoulders, and trunk muscles, including the latissimus dorsi muscle (Macfadden, 1911). The punching bag was a common and popular form of apparatus in the gymnasium, as it was in Galen's time, for developing speed. Macfadden believed that building a powerful physique was not merely for the sake of health, vitality, and resisting power. A perfect physique should be achieved by all-around exercise aiming at a symmetrical and uniform development of the whole.

Macfadden gives reference to ancient Greek sculpture of the Greek ideal, showing strong and symmetrical male figures. Macfadden regarded weightlifting as a form of advanced training. He explained that after one has thoroughly strengthened and hardened every part of the body by ordinary exercises, then he or she is ready for the practice of weightlifting. He outlined a dumbbell workout of twelve exercises. It was recommended that a new exerciser should limit his or her workout to five or ten minutes a day, adding two to three minutes daily until a half-hour routine was achieved. Each movement was to be continued until the muscle or muscles began to tire. As the muscles began to harden, the advanced trainer could continue each exercise until extreme fatigue set in. Macfadden stated that the building of strength requires that one exert his strength vigorously, though not straining, and requires a progressive increase in resistance. Galen had defined strengthening exercises as vigorous, "when a man works out violently but without speed" (Galen, *Hygiene* II 9). As mentioned in chapter 5, the ancient Greeks had known about the concept of progressive resistance through the story of Milo, also quoted by Galen. Macfadden suggested extended repetition of a light movement to improve endurance but not strength. He also recommended combining speed and strength which Galen classed as violent, "when he works out violently with speed" (Galen, *Hygiene* II 9).

In sports, Macfadden suggested one should aim first to gain a perfect degree of strength and symmetry through all-around physical culture methods, but a concept recognized by the ancient Greeks of sport-specific training was advocated. For example, in boxing, one could gain stamina, endurance, and strength by distance running, special gymnastic exercises and other activities, as well as the actual practice of boxing. Again, as with the ancient Greeks, Macfadden regarded wrestling as the best activity for building vigorous manhood, for it demanded both strength and endurance. It was not a sport for the weakling, he said. Macfadden was forward thinking for his time, as he suggested that weight-training exercises be combined with exercises for speed and flexibility to counteract the tendency to become slow—for example, bag punching, sprinting, jumping, and boxing. Many sports coaches in the 1940s, concerned with mainly swimming and track events, believed that exercise with weights produced muscle tightness and a decrease in speed. It was not until the 1950s when more research into the effects of weight training on speed, power, and endurance showed that it did not produce detrimental effects associated with muscle tightness. As mentioned in chapter 4, the development of strength through a systematic program of weight training would be accompanied by increased coordination and speed of movement (Mastley et al., 1953). In all professional sports, weight training is integral in the athletes' exercise regimens.

Charles Atlas (1893–1972) was inspired by Sandow and Macfadden's *Physical Culture* magazine. Atlas (born as Angelo Siciliano) was a major exponent of the physical culture movement that spread throughout the United States. Atlas won the contest for "the world's most handsome man" in 1921 based on facial appearance, bodily form, and development. The contest's judge was Bernarr Macfadden (Reich, 2010). His philosophy was to modify behavior through exercise, diet, and discipline with the emphasis on strength, health, and "perfect manhood" (Toon and Golden, 2002). His fitness plan aimed to improve both body and mind through a series of twelve lessons. His lessons were holistic, including positive thinking, imagery, nutrition, and other lifestyle changes.

Atlas developed the dynamic tension method. The technique involved flexing the muscles hard while also moving. The muscles of a body part are tensed, and then that body part is moved against tension in the form of body weight (Reich, 2010). Alan Calvert (1875–1944) a pioneer in weight training, opened the Milo Barbell Company in 1902 and promoted progressive resistance exercise using adjustable barbells and dumbbells (Beckwith, 2006). Calvert also understood that resistance training enhanced athletic performance.

Joe Weider (1920–2013) was regarded as the father of bodybuilding. He worked on Calvert's routines and improved on them to build a huge bodybuilding and fitness empire. Weider developed his own system, the Weider system, in the 1930s and 1940s but would continue to add new principles to it. This system introduced new methods, such as forced repetitions and supersets. These methods varied the degree of intensity of effort as well as the length of rest intervals between sets and between individual repetitions. Weider also stressed the importance of recuperation and rest, which are just as important as the training session itself (Weider and Reynolds, 1989). A period of rest was an integral part of the tetrad system for athletic training in antiquity (see chapter 5). The Weider system was a great success, producing some of the greatest bodybuilders of all time, including Arnold Schwarzenegger and Frank Zane. These men were the embodiment of muscularity with near-perfect proportion and symmetry, but it was the ancient Greeks who had achieved this perfect physical form more than two thousand years before.

CHAPTER 6 SUMMARY

It had been suggested the ancient Greeks were superior to the modern man in physical strength and beauty. This was attributed to their overall physical culture and superior forms of exercise. Physical culture occupied an important place in the education of everyday life of all citizens in ancient Greece. Those who attended the gymnasium aimed to achieve physical excellence and a beautiful body. The superiority in training techniques was observed in Greek sculpture. Images of classical bodily perfection have survived into our modern times. Greek nudity provided the opportunities to observe the well-conditioned body and portray it accurately in sculpture. It has been suggested that the muscular physique achieved by hard training was then refined by the sculptors with mathematical calculations. This current work suggests that some of Greek and Roman art and sculpture were true representations of the athletic body. The only exception to nonexaggerated anatomical representations in Greek sculpture are the hyperdeveloped lower abdominal muscles, which wrap around the iliac crest, known as Apollo's belt. This feature is more pronounced in Greek statues. The cauliflower ear was an identifying sign of an athlete and a display of distortion in Greek sculpture. By the late fifth century BC, there was a disproportionate physical development of athletes brought on by sporting specialization.

The anterior abdominal muscles consist of the rectus abdominis or "six-pack," which is depicted in Greek statues. This muscle definition is dependent on having a low body-fat percentage. This can be achieved by a combination of specific training for burning fat and increasing metabolism, as well as a Mediterranean diet. A well-developed chest or pecs is one of the more popular goals of physical culturists and athletes. Two of the best chest-development exercises that target both the pectoralis major and minor muscles are the decline bench press and dips. The serratus anterior muscle is an important muscle in sport performance, with more advanced development of this muscle seen in boxers. The deltoid muscle is a triangular muscle that gives the shoulder its rounded contour. The anterior deltoid is activated by barbell and dumbbell shoulder or military press exercise, whereas the free-weight bench press significantly increases activation of both anterior and middle deltoids. The biceps muscle is trained to emphasize muscular physique and is developed by straight barbell or alternating dumbbell curls. The quadriceps femoris is the main extensor of the knee joint. This muscle can be developed by conventional resistance training and plyometrics. The calf muscle is traditionally the hardest muscle to develop and train for hypertrophy. A standard exercise for training the calf muscle is the calf or heel raise. Plyometric training is also an effective method of developing the calf muscle. In ancient Greece, muscular development and low body fat were achieved with early plyometrics such as jumping, doing exercises with the ball, sprint training, using the punching bag, sparring, rope climbing, throwing the quoit, or lifting the plummet.

The ancient Greeks were the first physical culturists achieving their good body condition with hard work and sacrifice. There were several competitions held throughout Greece from the fifth century BC promoting outstanding bodily beauty. Some athletes in the heavy events had unusual physiques and conditions, which not all Greeks aspired to. The end of the eighteenth century saw the emergence of local strongmen. New exercise systems and gymnastics had developed in the early decades of the nineteenth century in Europe and America, which evolved from Greek revivalism.

In that period, physical culture shifted from feats of strength to the display of the perfect muscular body returning to the ancient Greek ideal. Eugen Sandow inspired the young to exercise and promoted health in the United States. Bernarr Macfadden was a significant figure in the physical culture movement of the twentieth century. He was inspired by the ancient Greeks. His influence lead to the likes of Joe Weider, whose training system produced some of the greatest bodybuilders of all time.

EPILOGUE

The ancient Greeks' appreciation of the body and focus on health as well as fitness may be unparalleled in history. The Greeks believed that development of the body was equally as important as the development of the mind. They believed that exercise was important for good health and could cure health problems. The desire to improve the human body and to increase their abilities through physical exercise as well as specialized training were purely ancient Greek inventions. Their ideal was to achieve a beautiful, well-balanced body through physical culture. They were the first physical culturists and founded the Olympic Games, which have lasted over a thousand years. The trainers in ancient Greece were able to distinguish between the quantity and quality of exercise. They knew details about exercise intensity, speed, and power as well as the certain types of physiques to suit each sporting event. They were able to increase muscular size through training and diet. This showed an awareness of the physiological effects of exercise and how to adapt them to the needs of every individual.

Finally, although this is probably my last major project, I believe it has been my best one. Revisiting those exercise concepts from sport science, I have also learned more about ancient Greek athletics and their training techniques. I have presented this work in a simple and easily readable form. I have admired the civilization that gave us democracy, philosophy, and the foundations of physical training. In ancient Greece, the gymnasium was a place for physical development and learning. The gymnasium was always a sanctuary to maintain my physical and mental health. Maybe I have come full circle; perhaps we all do at some point. There are always other possibilities. Explore them and start a new journey. Do not worry about the judgments of others; judge yourself, do your best, and achieve what you set out to do. Peace and long life!

ACKNOWLEDGMENTS

Once again, I would like to thank all those scholars who have helped me compile this book. In working on this project, I have been dependent on the work of others. The books, journals, and internet publications I have read are listed in the following bibliography.

BIBLIOGRAPHY

Acevedo, E. O. and Goldfarb, A. H., 1989. Increased training intensity effects on plasma lactate, ventilatory threshold, and endurance. *Medicine & Science in Sports & Exercise, 21*(5), pp. 563–568.

Adams, F., 1844. *The seven books of Paulus Aegineta*, vol. 1. Syndenham Society: London.

Adams, K., O'Shea, J. P., O'Shea, K. L., and Climstein, M., 1992. The Effect of Six Weeks of Squat, Plyometric and Squat-Plyometric Training on Power Production. *Journal of Applied Sport Science Research, 6*(1), pp. 36–41.

Adams, T. M., Worley, D., and Throgmartin, D., 1987. The effects of selected plyometric and weight training on muscular leg power. *Track Field Q Rev, 87*, pp. 45–47.

Adams, W. L., 2014. *Sport, Spectacle, and Society in Ancient Macedonia. A companion to Sport and Spectacle in Greek and Roman Antiquity*. John Wiley & Sons: West Sussex, pp. 332–347.

Akagi, R., Tohdoh, Y., Hirayama, K. and Kobayashi, Y., 2014. Relationship of pectoralis major muscle size with bench press and bench throw performances. *The Journal of Strength & Conditioning Research, 28*(6), pp. 1778–1782.

Alvar, B., Wenner, R. and Dodd, D. J., 2010. The effect of daily undulated periodization as compared to linear periodization in strength gains of collegiate athletes. *The Journal of Strength & Conditioning Research, 24*(Suppl. 1), p. 1.

American College of Sports Medicine, 2009. American College of Sports Medicine stand. Progression models in resistance training for healthy adults. *Medicine & Science in Sports & Exercise, 41*(3), pp. 687–708.

Amirthalingam, T., Mavros, Y., Wilson, G. C., Clarke, J. L., Mitchell, L., and Hackett, D. A., 2017. Effects of a modified German volume training program on muscular hypertrophy and strength. *The Journal of Strength & Conditioning Research, 31*(11), pp. 3109–3119.

Arabaci, R., 2008. Acute effects of pre-event lower limb massage on explosive and high-speed motor capacities and flexibility. *Journal of Sports Science & Medicine, 7*(4), pp. 549–555.

Baar, K., Nader, G. and Bodine, S., 2006. Resistance exercise, muscle loading/unloading and the control of muscle mass. *Essays in Biochemistry, 42*, pp. 61–74.

Badian, E., 2000. Darius III. *Harvard Studies in Classical Philology, 100*, pp. 241–267.

Barrow, H. M., 1983. *Man and Movement: Principles of Physical Education*. 3rd ed. Lea & Febiger: Philadelphia.

Barrow, H. M. and Brown, J., 1988. *Man and Movement: Principles of Physical Education*. 4th ed. Lea & Febiger: Philadelphia.

Bartolomei, S., Hoffman, J. R., Merni, F. and Stout, J. R., 2014. A comparison of traditional and block periodized strength training programs in trained athletes. *The Journal of Strength & Conditioning Research, 28*(4), pp. 990–997.

Beale, A., 2011. *Greek Athletes and the Olympics*. Cambridge University Press: Cambridge.

Beckwith, K. A., 2006. *Building strength: Alan Calvert, the Milo Bar-bell Company, and the modernization of American weight training* (Doctoral dissertation).

Beim, G. M., Giraldo, J. L., Pincivero, D. M., Borror, M. J. and Fu, F. H., 1997. Abdominal strengthening exercises: a comparative EMG study. *Journal of Sport Rehabilitation, 6*(1), pp. 11–20.

Bernstein, I., 2014. *Musculoskeletal Health in Ealing: Chapter for Ealing Joint Strategic Needs Assessment 2014*. [Online] Available from: http://www.ealingccg.nhs.uk/media/9881/Ealing_JSNA_MSk_Health_pre-pub_201409-06.pdf.

Berryman, J. W., 2012. Motion and rest: Galen on exercise and health. *The Lancet, 380*(9838), pp. 210–211.

Bertani, R. F., Campos, G. O., Perseguin, D. M., Bonardi, J. M., Ferriolli, E., Moriguti, J. C. and Lima, N. K., 2018. Resistance Exercise Training Is More Effective than Interval Aerobic Training in Reducing Blood Pressure During Sleep in Hypertensive Elderly Patients. *The Journal of Strength & Conditioning Research, 32*(7), pp. 2085–2090.

Best, T. M., Hunter, R., Wilcox, A., and Haq, F., 2008. Effectiveness of sports massage for recovery of skeletal muscle from strenuous exercise. *Clinical Journal of Sport Medicine*, *18*(5), pp. 446–460.

Billat, L.V., 2001. Interval training for performance: a scientific and empirical practice. *Sports Medicine*, *31*(1), pp. 13–31.

Bishop, D., Girard, O. and Mendez-Villanueva, A., 2011. Repeated-sprint ability—Part II. *Sports Medicine*, *41*(9), pp. 741–756.

Blundell, J. W. F., and Mercuriale, G., 2001. *The Muscles and Their Story, from the Earliest Times; Including the Whole Text of Mercurialis, and the Opinions of Other Writers Ancient and Modern, on Mental and Bodily Development.* By John W. F. Blundell, Chapman and Hall, 193, Piccadilly.

Bobbert, M. F., Mackay, M., Schinkelshoek, D., Huijing, P. A. and van Ingen Schenau, G. J., 1986. Biomechanical analysis of drop and countermovement jumps. *European Journal of Applied Physiology and Occupational Physiology*, *54*(6), pp. 566–573.

Bonfante, L., 1989. Nudity as a costume in classical art. *American Journal of Archaeology*, *93*(4), pp. 543–570.

Borg, G. A., 1982. Psychophysical bases of perceived exertion. *Medicine & Science in Sports & Exercise*, *14*(5), pp. 377-381.

Bouguezzi, R., Chaabene, H., Negra, Y., Ramirez-Campillo, R., Jlalia, Z., Mkaouer, B., and Hachana, Y., 2018. Effects of different plyometric training frequency on measures of athletic performance in prepuberal male soccer players. *The Journal of Strength & Conditioning Research*, *34*(6), pp. 1609–1617.

Bourne, N. D., 2008. *Fast science: A history of training theory and methods for elite runners through 1975* (Doctoral Thesis).

Boutcher, S. H., 2010. High-intensity intermittent exercise and fat loss. *Journal of Obesity*, *868*, pp. 23–31.

Bradbury, D. G., Landers, G. J., Benjanuvatra, N., and Goods, P. S., 2018. Comparison of Linear and Reverse Linear Periodized Programs with Equated Volume and Intensity for Endurance Running Performance. *The Journal of Strength & Conditioning Research*. *34*(5), pp. 1345-1353.

Bradley, W. J., Cavanagh, B. P., Douglas, W., Donovan, T. F., Morton, J. P., and Close, G. L., 2015. Quantification of training load, energy intake, and physiological adaptations during a rugby preseason: a case study from an elite European rugby union squad. *The Journal of Strength & Conditioning Research, 29*(2), pp. 534–544.

Broberg, S., Katz, A., and Sahlin, K., 1988. Propranolol enhances adenine nucleotide degradation in human muscle during exercise. *Journal of Applied Physiology, 65*(6), pp. 2478–2483.

Brooks, G.A., 2000. Intra-and extra-cellular lactate shuttles. *Medicine & Science in Sports & Exercise, 32*(4), pp. 790–799.

Bryan, C. P., 1930. *The Papyrus Ebers: Translated from the German Version.* Geoffrey Bles: London.

Callaghan, M. J., 1993. The role of massage in the management of the athlete: a review. *British Journal of Sports Medicine, 27*(1), pp. 28–33.

Callaghan, P., 2004. Exercise: a neglected intervention in mental health care? *Journal of Psychiatric and Mental Health Nursing, 11*(4), pp. 476–483.

Chaabene, H., Negra, Y., Bouguezzi, R., Mkaouer, B., Franchini, E., Julio, U., and Hachana, Y., 2017. Physical and physiological attributes of wrestlers: an update. *The Journal of Strength & Conditioning Research, 31*(5), pp. 1411–1442.

Cheung, K., Hume, P.A., and Maxwell, L., 2003. Delayed onset muscle soreness. *Sports Medicine, 33*(2), pp. 145–164.

Christopoulos, G. A., Yalouris, N., and Szymiczek, O., 2003. *The Olympic Games in Ancient Greece: Ancient Olympia and the Olympic Games.* Ekdotike Athenon: Athens.

Cormie, P., McGuigan, M. R., and Newton, R. U., 2011. Developing maximal neuromuscular power: part 2-training considerations for improving maximal power production. *Sports Medicine, 41*(2), pp. 125–146.

Coxe, J. R., 1846. *The writings of Hippocrates and Galen: epitomised from the original Latin translations.* Lindsay and Blakiston: Philadelphia.

Crowther, N. B., 1977. Weightlifting in antiquity: achievement and training. *Greece & Rome, 24*(2), pp. 111–120.

Crowther, N. B., 1985. Studies in Greek Athletics. Part II. *The Classical World, 79*(2), pp. 73–135.

Crowther, N. B., 1991. *Euexia, Eutaxia, Philoponia: three contests of the Greek gymnasium.* Zeitschrift für Papyrologie und Epigraphik, *85*(1991), pp. 301–304.

Dawson, I., 2005. *Greek and Roman Medicine.* Hodder Wayland: New York.

de Araújo Farias, D., Willardson, J. M., Paz, G. A., Bezerra, E. D. S., and Miranda, H., 2017. Maximal Strength Performance and Muscle Activation for the Bench Press and Triceps Extension Exercises Adopting Dumbbell, Barbell, and Machine Modalities Over Multiple Sets. *The Journal of Strength & Conditioning Research, 31*(7), pp. 1879–1887.

Decker, M. J., Hintermeister, R. A., Faber, K. J. and Hawkins, R. J., 1999. Serratus anterior muscle activity during selected rehabilitation exercises. *The American Journal of Sports Medicine, 27*(6), pp. 784–791.

DeLorme, T. L., and Watkins, A. L., 1948. Techniques of Progressive Resistance Exercise. *Archives of Physical Medicine and Rehabilitation 29*(5), pp. 263–273.

De Souza, E. O., Tricoli, V., Rauch, J., Alvarez, M. R., Laurentino, G., Aihara, A. Y., Cardoso, F. N., Roschel, H., and Ugrinowitsch, C., 2018. Different patterns in muscular strength and hypertrophy adaptations in untrained individuals undergoing nonperiodized and periodized strength regimens. *The Journal of Strength & Conditioning Research, 32*(5), pp. 1238–1244.

de Villarreal, E. S. S., Kellis, E., Kraemer, W. J., and Izquierdo, M., 2009. Determining variables of plyometric training for improving vertical jump height performance: a meta-analysis. *The Journal of Strength & Conditioning Research, 23*(2), pp. 495–506.

Dhahbi, W., Chaouachi, A., Padulo, J., Behm, D. G., and Chamari, K., 2015. Five-meter rope-climbing: a commando-specific power test of the upper limbs. *International Journal of Sports Physiology and Performance, 10*(4), pp. 509–515.

Diamond, L. B., Casaburi, R., Wasserman, K., and Whipp, B. J., 1977. Kinetics of gas exchange and ventilation in transitions from rest or prior exercise. *Journal of Applied Physiology, 43*(4), pp. 704–708.

Doxey, G. E., 1984. Body composition assessment and methodology in nonathletic and athletic adolescent and adult males and females. *Journal of Orthopaedic & Sports Physical Therapy, 5*(6), pp. 336–347.

Drees, L., 1968. *Olympia: gods, artists, and athletes.* Pall Mall Press: London.

Dunnick, D. D., Brown, L. E., Coburn, J. W., Lynn, S. K., and Barillas, S. R., 2015. Bench press upper-body muscle activation between stable and unstable loads. *The Journal of Strength & Conditioning Research, 29*(12), pp. 3279–3283.

Duthie, G. M., 2006. A framework for the physical development of elite rugby union players. *International Journal of Sports Physiology and Performance, 1*(1), pp. 2–13.

Egan, R., 2007. How the Pentathlon Was Won: Two Pragmatic Models and the Evidence of Philostratus. *Phoenix, 61*, pp. 39–54.

Elekuvan, R. M., 2014. Effectiveness of fartlek training on maximum oxygen consumption and resting pulse rate. *International Journal of Physical Education, Fitness and Sports, 3*(1), pp. 85–88.

Escamilla, R. F., Yamashiro, K., Paulos, L., and Andrews, J. R., 2009. Shoulder muscle activity and function in common shoulder rehabilitation exercises. *Sports Medicine, 39*(8), pp. 663–685.

Fleck, S. J., 1983. Body composition of elite American athletes. *The American Journal of Sports Medicine, 11*(6), pp. 398–403.

Fleck, S., 2011. Non-linear periodization for general fitness & athletes. *Journal of Human Kinetics, 29*(Special Issue), pp. 41–45.

Fleck, S. J., and Kraemer, W., 2014. *Designing resistance training programs*. 4th ed. Human Kinetics: Australia.

Foran, B., 2001. *High-performance sports conditioning*. Human Kinetics: Champaign, Illinois.

Forman, T. C., Nichols, A. W., and LaBotz, M., 2006. The Use of Traditional Hawaiian Lomilomi Massage by Intercollegiate Athletes. *Clinical Journal of Sport Medicine, 16*(5), p. 436.

Foster, C., Wright, G., Battista, R. A., and Porcari, J. P., 2007. Training in the aging athlete. *Current Sports Medicine Reports, 6*(3), pp. 200–206.

Fox, R. L., 2006. *The Classical World: An Epic History of Greece and Rome*. Penguin Random House: UK.

Franchini, E., Brito, C. J., Fukuda, D. H., and Artioli, G. G., 2014. The physiology of judo-specific training modalities. *The Journal of Strength & Conditioning Research, 28*(5), pp. 1474–1481.

Franchini, E., Cormack, S., and Takito, M. Y., 2019. Effects of High-Intensity Interval Training on Olympic Combat Sports Athletes' Performance and Physiological Adaptation: A Systematic Review. *The Journal of Strength & Conditioning Research*, 33(1), pp. 242–252.

Galloway, S. D. R., and Watt, J. M., 2004. Massage provision by physiotherapists at major athletics events between 1987 and 1998. *British Journal of Sports Medicine*, 38(2), pp. 235–237.

Gardiner, E. N., 1904. Further notes on the Greek jump. *The Journal of Hellenic Studies*, 24, pp. 179–194.

Gardiner, E. N., 1930. *Athletics in the Ancient World*. Dover Publications: New York.

Gardner, P., 1880. The Pentathlon of the Greeks. *The Journal of Hellenic Studies*, 1, pp. 210–223.

Gasibat, Q., and Suwehli, W., 2017. Determining the benefits of massage mechanisms: A review of literature. *Rehabilitation Sciences*, 2(3), pp. 58–67.

Gesler, W. M., 1993. Therapeutic landscapes: theory and a case study of Epidauros, Greece. *Environment and Planning D: Society and Space*, 11(2), pp. 171–189.

Ghalioungui, P., 1963. *Magic and Medical Science in Ancient Egypt*. Hodder and Stoughton: London.

Gibala, M. J., and McGee, S. L., 2008. Metabolic adaptations to short-term high intensity interval training: a little pain for a lot of gain? *Exercise and Sport Sciences Reviews*, 36(2), pp. 58–63.

Goldsworthy, A., 2007. *Caesar*. Weidenfeld & Nicholson: London.

Graham, D., 1890. *A treatise on massage, Theoretical and Practical: Its history, mode of application and effects, indications and contra-indications, with results in over fifteen hundred cases*. J. H. Vail & Company: New York.

Green, R. M., 1951. *A translation of Galen's hygiene: De Sanitate Tuenda*. Charles C Thomas: Springfield.

Hackney, A. C., 2006. Stress and the neuroendocrine system: the role of exercise as a stress-or and modifier of stress. *Expert Review of Endocrinology & Metabolism*, 1(6), pp. 783–792.

Haff, G. G., and Nimphius, S., 2012. Training principles for power. *Strength & Conditioning Journal, 34*(6), pp. 2–12.

Hardwick, D. H., Beebe, J. A., McDonnell, M. K. and Lang, C. E., 2006. A comparison of serratus anterior muscle activation during a wall slide exercise and other traditional exercises. *Journal of Orthopaedic & Sports Physical Therapy, 36*(12), pp. 903–910.

Harmon, A. M., 1961. *Lucian with an English Translation iV.* Harvard University Press: Massachusetts.

Harris, H. A., 1964. *Greek Athletics and Athletics.* Hutchinson and Co. LTD: London.

Harris, H. A., 1972. *Sport in Greece and Rome* (Vol. 16). Cornell University Press: Ithaca, New York.

Hébert-Losier, K., Schneiders, A. G., García, J. A., Sullivan, S. J., and Simoneau, G. G., 2012. Influence of knee flexion angle and age on triceps surae muscle activity during heel raises. *The Journal of Strength & Conditioning Research, 26*(11), pp. 3124–3133.

Hilbert, J. E., Sforzo, G. A., and Swensen, T., 2003. The effects of massage on delayed onset muscle soreness. *British Journal of Sports Medicine, 37*(1), pp. 72–75.

Hobbelen, J. H. S., Tan, F. E., Verhey, F. R., Koopmans, R. T., and de Bie, R. A., 2012. Passive movement therapy in severe paratonia: a multicenter randomized clinical trial. *International Psychogeriatrics, 24*(5), pp. 834–844.

Howarth, N. C., Saltzman, E., and Roberts, S. B., 2001. Dietary fiber and weight regulation. *Nutrition Reviews, 59*(5), pp. 129–139.

Hugh, M. L., 2004. Mercuriale, Ligorio, and the Revival of Greek Sports in the Renaissance. *Seventh International Symposium for Olympic Research*, Chapter 2. pp. 13-24.

Hukkanen, E., and Häkkinen, K., 2017. Effects of sparring load on reaction speed and punch force during the precompetition and competition periods in boxing. *The Journal of Strength & Conditioning Research, 31*(6), pp. 1563–1568.

Issurin, V. B., 2010. New horizons for the methodology and physiology of training periodization. *Sports Medicine, 40*(3), pp. 189–206.

Jakeman, J. R., McMullan, J., and Babraj, J. A., 2016. Efficacy of a four-week uphill sprint training intervention in field hockey players. *The Journal of Strength & Conditioning Research, 30*(10), pp. 2761–2766.

Jarvis, M. M., Graham-Smith, P., and Comfort, P., 2016. A methodological approach to quantifying plyometric intensity. *The Journal of Strength & Conditioning Research, 30*(9), pp. 2522–2532.

Jenkins, I., 2015. *Defining Beauty, the body in ancient Greek art*. The British Museum Press: London.

Jensen, R. L., and Ebben, W. P., 2007. Quantifying plyometric intensity via rate of force development, knee joint, and ground reaction forces. *The Journal of Strength & Conditioning Research, 21*(3), pp. 763–767.

Jiménez, A., 2009. Undulating periodization models for strength training & conditioning. *Motricidade, 5*(3), pp. 1–5.

Johnson, I., 2016. *Galen: Hygiene Books 1–4*. Harvard University Press: London.

Johnson, I., 2018. *Galen: Hygiene Books 5–6, Thrasybulus, On exercise with a small ball*. Harvard University Press: London.

Johnson, I., 2018. *Galen: On the constitution of the art of medicine, the art of medicine, a method of medicine to Glaucon*. Harvard University Press: London.

Johnson, W., 1866. *The Anatriptic Art: A history of the Art*. Simpkin Marshall and Co: London.

Jones, A.M., and Carter, H., 2000. The effect of endurance training on parameters of aerobic fitness. *Sports Medicine, 29*(6), pp. 373–386.

Jones, T.W., Smith, A., Macnaughton, L. S., and French, D. N., 2017. Variances in strength and conditioning practice in elite Rugby Union between the northern and southern hemispheres. *The Journal of Strength & Conditioning Research, 31*(12), pp. 3358–3371.

Jüthner J., and Brein, F., 1968. *Die athletischen Leibesübungen der Griechen II: Einzelne Sportarten*. Graz: Hermann Böhlaus.

Karampatsos, G., Terzis, G., and Georgiadis, G., 2011. Muscular strength, neuromuscular activation, and performance in discus throwers. *Journal of Physical Education and Sport, 11*(4), pp. 369–375.

Kavanaugh, A., 2007. The Role of Progressive Overload in Sports Conditioning. Conditioning Fundamentals. *NSCA's Performance Training Journal, 6*(1), pp. 15–17.

Khammassi, M., Ouerghi, N., Hadj-Taieb, S., Feki, M., Thivel, D., and Bouassida, A., 2018. Impact of a 12-week high-intensity interval training without caloric restriction on body composition and lipid profile in sedentary healthy overweight/obese youth. *Journal of Exercise Rehabilitation, 14*(1), pp. 118–125.

Kidgell, D. J., Stokes, M. A., Castricum, T. J., and Pearce, A. J., 2010. Neurophysiological responses after short-term strength training of the biceps brachii muscle. *The Journal of Strength & Conditioning Research, 24*(11), pp. 3123–3132.

Kilit, B., and Arslan, E., 2019. Effects of high-intensity interval training vs. on-court tennis training in young tennis players. *The Journal of Strength & Conditioning Research, 33*(1), pp. 188–196.

Laursen, P. B., and Jenkins, D. G., 2002. The scientific basis for high-intensity interval training. *Sports Medicine, 32*(1), pp. 53–73.

Lee, H. M., 1993. Wrestling in the "Repêchage" of the Ancient Pentathlon. *Journal of Sport History, 20*(3), pp. 277–279.

Leger, L. A., and Lambert, J., 1982. A maximal multistage 20-m shuttle run test to predict VO2 max. *European Journal of Applied Physiology and Occupational Physiology, 49*(1), pp. 1–12.

Leger, L. A., Mercier, D., Gadoury, C., and Lambert, J., 1988. The multistage 20 metre shuttle run test for aerobic fitness. *Journal of Sports Sciences, 6*(2), pp. 93–101.

Lehmann, C. M., 2009. Early Greek athletic trainers. *Journal of Sport History, 36*(2), pp. 187–204.

Lenoir, M., De Clercq, D., and Laporte, W., 2005. The "how" and "why" of the ancient Greek long jump with weights: A five-fold symmetric jump in a row? *Journal of Sports Sciences, 23*(10), pp. 1033–1043.

Leonard, F. E., 1915. *Pioneers of modern physical training.* Association Press: New York.

Lievens, M., Bourgois, J., and Boone, J., 2020. Periodization of plyometrics: is there an optimal overload principle? *Journal of Strength & Conditioning Research.*

Limacher, M., Piña, I. L., Stein, R. A., Williams, M., and Bazzarre, T., 2000. Resistance exercise in individuals with and without cardiovascular disease: benefits, rationale, safety, and prescription an advisory from the committee on exercise, rehabilitation, and prevention, council on clinical cardiology, American Heart Association. *Circulation, 101*(7), pp. 828–833.

Lorenz, D. S., Reiman, M. P., and Walker, J. C., 2010. Periodization: current review and suggested implementation for athletic rehabilitation. *Sports Health, 2*(6), pp. 509–518.

Lynch, J. P., 1972. *Aristotle's School; a Study of a Greek Educational Institution.* Univ. of California Press: Berkeley.

Macfadden, B., 1912. *Macfadden's Encyclopedia of physical culture* (Vol. 5). Physical Culture Publishing Company: New York.

Makaruk, H., and Sacewicz, T., 2011. The effect of drop height and body mass on drop jump intensity. *Biology of Sport, 28*(1), pp. 63–67.

Mancinelli, C. A., Davis, D. S., Aboulhosn, L., Brady, M., Eisenhofer, J., and Foutty, S., 2006. The effects of massage on delayed onset muscle soreness and physical performance in female collegiate athletes. *Physical Therapy in Sport, 7*(1), pp. 5–13.

Marcolin, G., Petrone, N., Moro, T., Battaglia, G., Bianco, A., and Paoli, A., 2015. Selective activation of shoulder, trunk, and arm muscles: a comparative analysis of different push-up variants. *Journal of Athletic Training, 50*(11), pp. 1126–1132.

Marindin, G. E., 1890. The game of 'Harpastum' or 'Pheninda.' *The Classical Review, 4*(4), pp. 145–149.

Markovic, G., and Mikulic, P., 2010. Neuro-musculoskeletal and performance adaptations to lower-extremity plyometric training. *Sports Medicine, 40*(10), pp. 859–895.

Marriott, H. E., and Lamb, K. L., 1996. The use of ratings of perceived exertion for regulating exercise levels in rowing ergometry. *European Journal of Applied Physiology and Occupational Physiology, 72*(3), pp. 267–271.

Masley, J. W., Hairabedian, A., and Donaldson, D. N., 1953. Weight training in relation to strength, speed, and co-ordination. *Research Quarterly. American Association for Health, Physical Education and Recreation, 24*(3), pp. 308–315.

Masterson, D. W., 1976. The ancient Greek origins of sports medicine. *British Journal of Sports Medicine, 10*(4), pp. 196–202.

Mattern, S. P., 2008. *Galen and the Rhetoric of Healing.* The John Hopkins University Press: Baltimore.

Mattern, S. P., 2013. *The Prince of Medicine: Galen in the Roman Empire.* Oxford University Press: UK.

Matthews, V., 1994. *The Greek Pentathlon Again.* Zeitschrift fur Papyrologie und Epigraphik, *100*, pp. 129–138.

Matveev, L. P., and Zdornyj, A. P., 1981. *Fundamentals of sports training.* Progress Publishers: Moscow.

McDonnel, M., 1993. Athletic Nudity among the Greeks and Etruscans: The Evidence of the "Perizoma Vases." *Publications de l'École Française de Rome, 172*(1), pp. 395–407.

McEvoy, K. P., and Newton, R. U., 1998. Baseball throwing speed and base running speed: The effects of ballistic resistance training. *The Journal of Strength & Conditioning Research, 12*(4), pp. 216–221.

McEwen, B. S., 2005. Stressed or stressed out: what is the difference? *Journal of Psychiatry and Neuroscience, 30*(5), pp. 315–318.

McInman, A. D., and Grove, J. R., 1991. Peak moments in sport: A literature review. *Quest, 43*(3), pp. 333–351.

Mercurialis, H., 1967. 1569. *De Arte Gymnastica.* Medicina Rara: Stuttgart.

Mikalson, J. D., 1975. *The Sacred and Civil Calendar of the Athenian Civil Year.* Princeton University Press: Princeton.

Miller, S. G., 1991. *Arete: Greek sports from ancient sources.* University of California Press: Berkeley.

Miller, S. G., 2004. *Ancient Greek Athletics.* Yale University Press: London.

Minetti, A. E. and Ardigo, L. P., 2002. Halteres used in ancient Olympic long jump. *Nature, 420*(6912), pp. 141–142.

Monedero, J., and Donne, B., 2000. Effect of recovery interventions on lactate removal and subsequent performance. *International Journal of Sports Medicine, 21*(8), pp. 593–597.

Montero, Á. M., 2020. Sports training in Ancient Greece and its supposed modernity. *Journal of Human Sport & Exercise, 15*(1), pp. 163–176.

Mouratidis, J., 2010. The length of the running race in the ancient pentathlon. *Nikephoros: Zeitschrift für Sport und Kultur im Altertum, 23*, pp. 57–69.

Mullaney, M., Tyler, T. F., McHugh, M., Orishimo, K., Kremenic, I., Caggiano, J., and Ramsey, A., 2011. Electromyographic analysis of the triceps surae muscle complex during Achilles tendon rehabilitation program exercises. *Sports Health, 3*(6), pp. 543–546.

Myer, G. D., Kushner, A. M., Brent, J. L., Schoenfeld, B. J., Hugentobler, J., Lloyd, R. S., Vermeil, A., Chu, D. A., Harbin, J., and McGill, S. M., 2014. The back squat: A proposed assessment of functional deficits and technical factors that limit performance. *Strength & Conditioning Journal*, 36(6), pp. 4–27.

Neufer, P. D., 1989. The effect of detraining and reduced training on the physiological adaptations to aerobic exercise training. *Sports Medicine*, 8(5), pp. 302–320.

Newby, Z., 2005. *Greek athletics in the Roman world: victory and virtue.* Oxford University Press: Oxford.

Newton, R. U., and Kraemer, W. J., 1994. Developing explosive muscular power: Implications for a mixed-methods training strategy. *Strength & Conditioning Journal*, 16(5), pp. 20–31.

Norton, K., Norton, L., and Sadgrove, D., 2010. Position statement on physical activity and exercise intensity terminology. *Journal of Science and Medicine in Sport*, 13(5), pp. 496–502.

Nunn, J. F., 1997. *Ancient Egyptian Medicine.* British Museum Press: London.

Oliveira, L. F., Matta, T. T., Alves, D. S., Garcia, M. A., and Vieira, T. M., 2009. Effect of the shoulder position on the biceps brachii EMG in different dumbbell curls. *Journal of Sports Science & Medicine*, 8(1), pp. 24–29.

Özdemirkiran, T. and Ertekin, C., 2011. Cremaster muscle motor unit action potentials. *Clinical Neurophysiology*, 122(8), pp. 1679-1685.

Palastanga, N., Field, D., and Soames, R., 1995. *Anatomy and Human Movement: Structure and Function.* 2nd ed. Butterworth Heinemann: Oxford.

Paleologos, C., 1961. Origin of the modern theory of training. *Track and Field Quarterly Review*, 8, pp. 26–29.

Papakonstantinou, Z., 2012. The athletic body in classical Athens: Literary and historical perspectives. *The International Journal of the History of Sport*, 29(12), pp. 1657–1668.

Patrucco, R., 1972. *Lo sport nella Grecia antica* (Vol. 1). L. S. Olschki Editore: Florence.

Phillips, D. J., and Pritchard, D., 2003. *Sport and festival in the ancient Greek world.* The Classical Press of Wales: Swansea.

Pitta, R. M., Pinto Montenegro, C. G., Rica, R. L., Bocalini, D. S., Tibana, R. A., Prestes, J., Stone, W. J., and Figueira Jr., A. J., 2019. Comparison of the Effects of Linear and Non-Linear Resistance Training Periodization on Morphofunctional Capacity of Subjects with Different Fitness Levels: A Systematic Review. *International Journal of Exercise Science, 12*(4), pp. 666–690.

Pleket, H. W., 1975. Games, prizes, athletes, and ideology. Some aspects of the history of sport in the Greco-Roman world. Stadion. *Zeitschrift Für Geschichte des Sports und der Korperkultur, 1*(1), pp. 49–89.

Plummer, E. M., 1897. Athletic Games among the Homeric Heroes. *American Physical Education Review, 2*(4), pp. 197–208.

Plummer, E. M., 1898a. II. The Olympic Games in Ancient Times. *American Physical Education Review, 3*(1), pp. 1–18.

Plummer, E. M., 1898b. III. The Olympic Games in Ancient Times. *American Physical Education Review, 3*(2), pp. 93–106.

Pollock, M. L., Franklin, B. A., Balady, G. J., Chaitman, B. L., Fleg, J. L., Fletcher, B., Limacher, M., Piña, I. L., Stein, R. A., Williams, M., and Bazzarre, T., 2000. Resistance exercise in individuals with and without cardiovascular disease: benefits, rationale, safety, and prescription an advisory from the committee on exercise, rehabilitation, and prevention, council on clinical cardiology, American Heart Association. *Circulation, 101*(7), pp. 828–833.

Poppendieck, W., Wegmann, M., Ferrauti, A., Kellmann, M., Pfeiffer, M., and Meyer, T., 2016. Massage and performance recovery: a meta-analytical review. *Sports Medicine, 46*(2), pp. 183–204.

Posadzki, P., Smith, T. O., and Lizis, P., 2009. Lomi Lomi as a massage with movements: a conceptual synthesis? *Alternative Therapies in Health & Medicine, 15*(6), pp. 44–49.

Potach, D.H., and Chu, D. A., 2000. *Plyometric Training*. In T. R. Baechle & R. W. Earle (eds.), Essentials of Strength Training and Conditioning, pp. 413–456. Human Kinetics: Champaign, Illinois.

Potteiger, J. A., Lockwood, R. H., Haub, M. D., Dolezal, B. A., Almuzaini, K. S., Schroeder, J. M. and Zebas, C. J., 1999. Muscle power and fiber characteristics following 8 weeks of plyometric training. *The Journal of Strength & Conditioning Research, 13*(3), pp. 275–279.

Powell, O., and Wilkins, J., 2003. *Galen: On the properties of foodstuffs*. Cambridge University Press: Cambridge.

Pritchard, D., 2003. Athletics, education, and participation in classical Athens. In D. J. Phillips & D. Pritchard (eds.), Sport and festival in the ancient Greek world, pp. 293–350. The Classical Press of Wales: Swansea.

Puhvel, J., 1984. *Hittite etymological dictionary: Words beginning with H* (Vol. 3). Walter de Gruyter: Berlin.

Ramírez-Campillo, R., Andrade, D. C., and Izquierdo, M., 2013. Effects of plyometric training volume and training surface on explosive strength. *The Journal of Strength & Conditioning Research, 27*(10), pp. 2714–2722.

Ramírez-Campillo, R., Henríquez-Olguín, C., Burgos, C., Andrade, D. C., Zapata, D., Martínez, C., Álvarez, C., Baez, E. I., Castro-Sepúlveda, M., Peñailillo, L. and Izquierdo, M., 2015. Effect of progressive volume-based overload during plyometric training on explosive and endurance performance in young soccer players. *The Journal of Strength & Conditioning Research, 29*(7), pp. 1884–1893.

Ramsbottom, R., Brewer, J., and Williams, C., 1988. A progressive shuttle run test to estimate maximal oxygen uptake. *British Journal of Sports Medicine, 22*(4), pp.141–144.

Ratamess, N., Alvar, B., Evetoch, T., Housh, T., Kibler, W., and Kraemer, W., 2009. Progression models in resistance training for healthy adults [ACSM position stand]. *Medicine & Science in Sports & Exercise, 41*(3), pp. 687–708.

Reich, J., 2010. The World's Most Perfectly Developed Man: Charles Atlas, Physical Culture, and the Inscription of American Masculinity. *Men and Masculinities 12*(4), pp. 444–461.

Reisner, G. A., 1905. *The Hearst medical papyrus hieratic text in 17 facsimile plates in collotype, with introduction and vocabulary* (Vol.1). J. C. Hinrichs: Leipzig.

Renshaw, J., 2015. *In search of the Greeks*. Bloomsbury Publishing. London.

Renson, R., 2019. How could ancient Greek athletes jump 16 meters and why modern athletes not? A multidisciplinary approach to unravel the technique of the ancient Greek halma. *Olimpianos—Journal of Olympic Studies, 3*, pp. 1–27.

Rhea, M. R., Ball, S. D., Philips, W. T. and Burkett, L. N., 2002. A comparison of linear and daily undulating periodized programs with equated volume and intensity for strength. *The Journal of Strength & Conditioning Research, 16*(2), pp. 250–255.

Rimmer, E., and Sleivert, G., 2000. Effects of a plyometrics intervention program on sprint performance. *The Journal of Strength & Conditioning Research, 14*(3), pp. 295–301.

Robinson, R. S., 1955. *Sources for the History of Greek Athletics.* Ares Publishers: Chicago.

Robergs, R. A., and Roberts, S. O., 1997. *Exercise physiology. Exercise, performance, and clinical applications.* Mosby-Year Book: St. Louis.

Rognmo, Ø., Hetland, E., Helgerud, J., Hoff, J., and Slørdahl, S.A., 2004. High intensity aerobic interval exercise is superior to moderate intensity exercise for increasing aerobic capacity in patients with coronary artery disease. *European Journal of Cardiovascular Prevention & Rehabilitation, 11*(3), pp. 216–222.

Rugg, S., and Sternlicht, E., 2013. The effect of graduated compression tights, compared with running shorts, on counter movement jump performance before and after submaximal running. *The Journal of Strength & Conditioning Research, 27*(4), pp. 1067–1073.

Rusten, J., and König, J., 2014. *Philostratus: Heroicus, Gymnasticus, Discourses 1 and 2.* Harvard University Press: London.

Sankey, S. P., Jones, P. A., and Bampouras, T., 2008. Effects of two plyometric training programmes of different intensity on vertical jump performance in high school athletes. *Serbian Journal of Sports Sciences, 2*(4), pp. 123–130.

Scanlon, T., 2008. The Heraia at Olympia Revisited. *Nikephoros: Zeitschrift für Sport und Kultur im Altertum 21*, pp. 159–196.

Scanlon, T. F., 2014a. *Sport in the Greek and Roman Worlds, Volume 1: Early Greece, the Olympics, and Contests.* Oxford University Press: Oxford.

Scanlon, T. F., 2014b. *Sport in the Greek and Roman Worlds, Volume 2: Greek Athletic Identities and Roman Sports and Spectacle.* Oxford University Press: Oxford.

Schoenfeld, B. J., Wilson, J. M., Lowery, R. P. and Krieger, J. W., 2016. Muscular adaptations in low-versus high-load resistance training: A meta-analysis. *European Journal of Sport Science, 16*(1), pp. 1–10.

Scott, W., Stevens, J., and Binder-Macleod, S. A., 2001. Human skeletal muscle fiber type classifications. *Physical Therapy, 81*(11), pp. 1810–1816.

Selye, H., 1976. Forty years of stress research: principal remaining problems and misconceptions. *Canadian Medical Association Journal, 115*(1), pp. 53–56.

Shai, I., Schwarzfuchs, D., Henkin, Y., Shahar, D. R., Witkow, S., Greenberg, I., Golan, R., Fraser, D., Bolotin, A., Vardi, H., and Tangi-Rozental, O., 2008. Weight loss with a low-carbohydrate, Mediterranean, or low-fat diet. *New England Journal of Medicine, 359*(3), pp. 229–241.

Shephard, R. J., 2012. The Developing Understanding of Human Health and Fitness: 2. Early city life. *Health and Fitness Journal of Canada 5*(1), pp. 27–46.

Shephard, R. J., 2012. The Developing Understanding of Human Health and Fitness: 3. The Classical Era. *Health and Fitness Journal of Canada, 5*(2), pp. 3–29.

Simopoulos, A. P., 1989. Nutrition and fitness. *JAMA, 261*(19), pp. 2862–2863.

Skiadas, P. K., and Lascaratos, J. G., 2001. Dietetics in ancient Greek philosophy: Plato's concepts of healthy diet. *European Journal of Clinical Nutrition, 55*(7), pp. 532–537.

Slater, L.V., and Hart, J. M., 2017. Muscle activation patterns during different squat techniques. *Journal of Strength & Conditioning Research, 31*(3), pp. 667–676.

Spencer, W. G., 1935. *Aulus Cornelius Celsus: On Medicine.* Vol. 1. Books 1-4. Harvard University Press: Cambridge.

Spivey, N., 2012. *The Ancient Olympics.* Oxford University Press: Oxford.

Stellingwerff, T., 2012. Case study: nutrition and training periodization in three elite marathon runners. *International Journal of Sport Nutrition and Exercise Metabolism, 22*(5), pp. 392–400.

Stickland, M. K., Petersen, S. R., and Bouffard, M., 2003. Prediction of maximal aerobic power from the 20-m multi-stage shuttle run test. *Canadian Journal of Applied Physiology, 28*(2), pp. 272–282.

Stocking, C. H., 2014. Greek Ideal as Hyperreal: Greco-Roman Sculpture and the Athletic Male Body. *Arion: A Journal of Humanities and the Classics, 21*(3), pp. 45–74.

Stocking, C. H., 2016. The Use and Abuse of Training "Science" in Philostratus' Gymnasticus. *Classical Antiquity, 35*(1), pp. 86–125.

Stöggl, T., and Sperlich, B., 2014. Polarized training has greater impact on key endurance variables than threshold, high intensity, or high volume training. *Frontiers in Physiology, 5*(33), pp. 1–9.

Sullivan, R., 1995. A Brief Journey into Medical Care and Disease in Ancient Egypt. *Journal of the Royal Society of Medicine*, 88(3), pp. 141–145.

Sutherland, W. B., 1917. *Physical Culture: The Bruce Sutherland system*. Thomas Nelson and Sons: London.

Suzuki, M., Umeda, T., Nakaji, S., Shimoyama, T., Mashiko, T., and Sugawara, K., 2004. Effect of incorporating low intensity exercise into the recovery period after a rugby match. *British Journal of Sports Medicine*, 38(4), pp. 436–440.

Sweet, W. E., 1983. A new proposal for scoring the Greek Pentathlon. *Zeitschrift für Papyrologie und Epigraphik*, 50, pp. 287–290.

Sweet, W. E., 1987. *Sport and recreation in ancient Greece: A sourcebook with translations*. Oxford University Press: Oxford.

Taipale, R. S., Mikkola, J., Nummela, A., Vesterinen, V., Capostagno, B., Walker, S., Gitonga, D., Kraemer, W. J., and Häkkinen, K., 2010. Strength training in endurance runners. *International Journal of Sports Medicine*, 31(7), pp. 468–476.

Tavares, F., Smith, T. B., and Driller, M., 2017. Fatigue and Recovery in Rugby: A Review. *Sports Medicine (Auckland, NZ)*, 47(8), pp. 1515–1530.

Taylor, G. H., 1880. Health by Exercise: What Exercises to Take and how to Take Them, to Remove Special Physical Weakness. *Embracing an Account of the Swedish Methods, and a Summary of the Principles of Hygiene*. American Book Exchange.

Todd, J., 1995. From Milo to Milo: A history of barbells, dumbbells, and Indian clubs. *Iron Game History*, 3(6), pp. 4–16.

Tomlinson, R. A., 1983. *Epidauros*. Granada Publishing: London.

Toon, E., and Golden, J. L., 2002. "Live Clean, Think Clean, and Don't Go to Burlesque Shows": Charles Atlas as Health Advisor. *Journal of the History of Medicine and Allied Sciences*, 57(1), pp. 39–60.

Vallance, J. T., 1990. *The Lost Theory of Asclepiades of Bithynia*. Clarendon Press: Oxford.

van der Kruk, E., van der Helm, F. C. T., Veeger, H. E. J., and Schwab, A. L., 2018. Power in sports: A literature review on the application, assumptions, and terminology of mechanical power in sport research. *Journal of Biomechanics*, 79, pp. 1–14.

Vissing, K., Brink, M., Lønbro, S., Sørensen, H., Overgaard, K., Danborg, K., Mortensen, J., Elstrøm, O., Rosenhøj, N., Ringgaard, S. and Andersen, J. L., 2008. Muscle adaptations to plyometric vs. resistance training in untrained young men. *The Journal of Strength & Conditioning Research, 22*(6), pp. 1799–1810.

Waterfield, R., and Waterfield, K., 2013. *The Greek Myths: Stories of the Greek Gods and Heroes vividly retold.* Quercus: London.

Weerapong, P., Hume, P. A., and Kolt, G. S., 2005. The mechanisms of massage and effects on performance, muscle recovery and injury prevention. *Sports medicine, 35*(3), pp. 235–256.

Weider, J., and Reynolds, B., 1989. *Joe Weider's Ultimate Bodybuilding: The Master Blaster's Principles of Training and Nutrition.* Contemporary Books: Chicago.

Weltman, A., 1995. *The blood lactate response to exercise.* Human Kinetics: Champaign, Illinois.

Whipp, B. J., Ward, S. A., Lamarra, N., Davis, J. A., and Wasserman, K., 1982. Parameters of ventilatory and gas exchange dynamics during exercise. *Journal of Applied Physiology, 52*(6), pp. 1506–1513.

White, G. E., West, S. L., Caterini, J. E., Battista, A. P. D., Rhind, S. G., and Wells, G. D., 2020. Massage Therapy Modulates Inflammatory Mediators Following Sprint Exercise in Healthy Male Athletes. *Journal of Functional Morphology and Kinesiology, 5*(1), p. 9.

Whitehead, M. T., Scheett, T. P., McGuigan, M. R., and Martin, A. V., 2018. A Comparison of the Effects of Short-Term Plyometric and Resistance Training on Lower-Body Muscular Performance. *The Journal of Strength & Conditioning Research, 32*(10), pp. 2743–2749.

Wilkins, J. and Hill, S., 2006. *Food in the ancient world.* Blackwell Publishing: Malden, USA.

Williams, P. L., Bannister, L. H., Berry, M. M., Collins, P., Dyson, M., Dussek, J. E., and Ferguson, M. W., 1995. *Gray's Anatomy: The anatomical basis of medicine and surgery.* 38th ed. Churchill Livingston: New York.

Winwood, P. W., Keogh, J. W., and Harris, N. K., 2011. The strength and conditioning practices of strongman competitors. *The Journal of Strength & Conditioning Research, 25*(11), pp. 3118–3128.

Wood, M., 2005. *In search of the Trojan War.* BBC Books: London.

Yallouris, N., 1979. *The Eternal Olympics: The Art and History of Sport*. Caratzas Brothers: New York.

Young, D. C., 1984. *The Olympic myth of Greek amateur athletics*. Ares Publishers: Chicago.

Young, D. C., 2008. *A brief history of the Olympic games*. John Wiley & Sons: Hoboken.

Zainuddin, Z., Newton, M., Sacco, P., and Nosaka, K., 2005. Effects of massage on delayed-onset muscle soreness, swelling, and recovery of muscle function. *Journal of Athletic Training*, 40(3), pp. 174–180.

Zanon, S., 1989. Plyometrics: past and present. *New Studies in Athletics*, 4(1), pp. 7–17.

Zaras, N., Spengos, K., Methenitis, S., Papadopoulos, C., Karampatsos, G., Georgiadis, G., Stasinaki, A., Manta, P., and Terzis, G., 2013. Effects of strength vs. ballistic-power training on throwing performance. *Journal of Sports Science & Medicine*, 12(1), pp. 130–137.

Zupan, M. F., Arata, A. W., Dawson, L. H., Wile, A. L., Payn, T. L. and Hannon, M. E., 2009. Wingate anaerobic test peak power and anaerobic capacity classification for men and women intercollegiate athletes. *The Journal of Strength & Conditioning Research*, 23(9), pp. 2598–2604.

INDEX

abdomen 95, 123, 142, 144
Academy XVII, 56
Achilles 41-44, 60, 85
Achilles tendon 157, 186
aerobic 70, 72, 75, 78, 80, 101-102, 118, 128, 132, 176, 183-184, 187, 190- 191
Agamemnon 8, 42, 44-45
Ajax 43, 47
Alan Calvert 167
alarm phase (GAS) 75-76, 113
aleipteior 61-63, 126
aleiptes XIV, 57, 61
Alexander Aphrodisias 125
Alexander the Great XVIII, 9-11, 16
amateur XIII, 12, 14, 17, 111, 194
amortization 74
amphora 9, 33, 39, 44
anaerobic 31, 70, 72, 91, 118, 194
anaerobic threshold 70, 72, 80-81
anatomy XIV-XV, XXI, 59, 63, 85, 141, 187, 193
anatrochasmos 101
Antyllus 96, 99
aphalmos 98
apodyterium 55
Apollo 8, 40, 56, 104, 137
Apollo's belt 151, 160, 169
aponeurosis (fascia) 143, 157
apotherapeutic 123-124
apotherapy 119-120, 123-124, 126-128
Archaic period 3, 16
archery XI, 2, 42, 44, 46, 51
Arete 7, 186
aristocrat(s) 1, 8, 12, 17
Aristotle XVIII, 5, 10-11, 26, 32, 34, 53, 56, 60, 85, 125, 136, 141, 165, 185
armed combat 42, 44, 51

army 1-2, 4, 9-10, 85, 106
Arnold Schwarzenegger 164, 168
aryballos 57, 63
Asclepiades of Bithynia XVIII-XIX, 62, 88, 122, 192
Asclepius 9-10
Athena 9, 21, 43, 45, 162
Athenaeus of Naucratis 49, 105, 109
Athenaeus (physician) 53
Athenian(s) XVII, XX, 4, 9, 11, 21, 26, 40, 56, 106, 136, 186
Athens XVII-XVIII, XX, 4, 7, 9, 11, 16, 21, 38, 40-41, 92, 102, 162-163, 178, 187, 189
athlete(s) XII-XXI, 7-8, 10-14, 17, 19-24, 26-34, 36-40, 45, 47, 51, 55-63, 66, 69-78, 81, 84, 87-99, 101-105, 107-120, 123- 132, 134-135, 137-140, 144, 147, 158- 163, 167, 169-170, 175-176, 178-181, 185, 188-190, 193-194
athlete's diet XVI, 61, 107-110
athlete's equipment 55, 57
athletic training XX-XXI, 10-11, 59, 87, 112, 114, 119, 123, 159, 164, 167, 185, 194
Automedes of Phlious 27-28
Bacchylides 21, 27-28, 135, 137
balbis 31, 33-34
ball games 94, 128
ballistic training/exercises 69, 93, 155, 186, 194
barbarians XX, 22-24
barbell(s) 65, 149, 154, 167, 169-170, 179, 192
barley 105-106, 108
bathing 85, 122-123
beans 106, 144
bench press 78, 92, 104, 132, 147, 149, 169 175, 179-180
Bernarr Macfadden XV, 164, 167, 170
bodybuilding 163-165, 167, 193
body-fat percentage 144, 169
boxing 1-2, 4, 12-13, 16, 20-21, 29-30, 36-38 41-43, 45-46, 51, 55-56, 60, 86, 89-90, 94, 118, 130-131, 139, 159, 161, 165- 166, 182
Brauron 49, 52
bread 105-106, 108-110
Bronze Age 2-3, 16, 46-47
bull leaping 2, 16
cadet training 11, 16
calf (animal) 97
calisthenic 96, 165

cap 47, 58, 63
carbohydrates 107-109
cauldrons 5, 41
cauliflower ears 13, 161, 169
Celsus XVIII-XIX, 61-62, 85, 102, 105, 121-123, 191
cestus 37
chariot racing XIII, 4, 20, 24, 46, 50-52
Charles Atlas 167, 189, 192
cheese 106-109, 134
Chionis of Sparta 32-33
city-states XIII, 3, 6, 9, 16, 24
coaches 12, 93, 101, 166
cold baths XIX, 129
competition(s) X-XI, XIV-XV, 2, 4-5, 9, 11, 14, 19-20, 22, 24, 29-30, 36-37, 44-45, 51, 57-59, 61, 63, 73, 83, 90, 93, 99, 119-120, 125-126, 128-129, 132, 162, 170, 182
concentric 74, 90-91, 98
conisterium 55
continuous training 72, 78, 80, 101
coryceum (punching bag) 55
countermovement jump (CMJ) 74, 91, 177
creatine kinase 130
crunch (sit-up) 142, 144
cryotherapy 129
cycling 73, 116, 127-128
Daly Thompson 14
dancing 4, 46
Darius III 10, 176
Delphi 5, 7-9, 20, 32, 40, 54
diaulos 23, 32, 38, 43, 101
Diomedes 42, 100
Discobolus 104, 140-141
discus XX, 4, 11, 25-29, 32, 34-35, 42, 44-49 51, 59, 93-95, 104, 133, 139-140, 183
disease XVIII, 60, 76, 88, 111, 121-122, 165, 184, 188, 190, 192
diskos 5
dislocations 61, 124
doctor(s) XVII, XIX, 61, 84, 88, 102, 129
dolichos 38-39, 109
DOMS (delayed onset muscle soreness) 126-127, 130
Dorians 2, 9

Doryphoros (Spear-bearer) 137-139, 149, 151, 160
drop jumps 74, 93
dumbbell 31, 48, 74, 81, 95-96, 133, 147, 149-150, 164, 166-167, 169-170, 179, 187, 192
duration 31, 68, 72, 80, 85-86, 93, 97, 101-102 113, 129
eccentric 74, 90, 98
education XI-XII, 3, 9, 11, 15, 54, 60, 83, 136, 164-165, 169, 176, 180, 183, 185, 188-189
Egypt 1-2, 95, 121, 137, 181, 187, 192
Ekplethrism 101-102
Eleans 5-6, 36, 50
Elis 5-6, 19-20, 27, 31, 38, 46-47, 50, 56, 115, 137, 162
endurance X, XIV, 40, 66-67, 70-71, 73, 78-80, 90, 92, 101-102, 111, 116-118, 128, 131-132, 134, 137, 148, 155, 166-167, 175, 177, 183, 189, 191-192
Epeius 44, 59
epheboi XVIII, 11, 44, 55, 57
ephedros 30
Epinikion 21, 51
equestrian 7, 10, 15, 20, 51
Erasistratus 85, 88, 105
ergometer (cycle) 70, 73
Etruscan(s) 24, 26, 35, 186
euandria 162-163
euexia 60-61, 162-163, 179
Eugen Sandow 164, 170
exercise intensity 68-70, 72, 78, 80, 98, 101, 110, 116-117, 119, 131, 171, 187
exercise prescription X, 76
exhaustion phase (GAS) 75-76, 81, 97, 113-114
Fartlek 72, 80, 180
fat(body) XV, 94, 105, 109, 144, 159, 169-170, 177
fat(diet) 107, 144, 191
fatigue 26, 30, 67, 70, 76, 78, 88, 113-114, 123, 126-127, 157, 166, 192
female XIV, XVII, XX, 14, 24, 41-42, 48-52, 78, 144, 165, 179, 185
fencing 61-62
festivals XIII, XXI, 1, 3, 5, 7, 9, 11-12, 16, 31, 42, 54, 63, 85, 105, 109, 136, 163
figs 106-109, 134
first triad 26, 28
fish 105-107, 110, 144
follis 89-90
football/soccer 73, 81, 98, 177, 189
footraces XVII, 5, 20, 30-31, 42, 49, 51-52

force (related to exercise) 59, 65, 69, 71, 73-74, 80, 86, 90-92, 98, 102-103, 111, 150, 157, 159, 182-183
Frank Zane 168
frequency 67-68, 74, 76-77, 89, 97, 102, 129, 177
frictions 120-126, 128
funeral games 2, 4-5, 10, 25, 41, 44, 46, 51
Galen IX, XII, XIV, XVII, XVIII-XXI, 48, 53, 59-62, 84-95, 98-99, 101-108, 111-112, 114, 119-125, 127, 131-133, 137, 159, 164-166, 176, 181, 183, 185, 189
garland 8, 20
GAS (general adaptation syndrome) 75-76, 81, 97, 113
Geometric period 2
Gerenus 114, 120
glove (boxing) 37, 43-44
glucose 31, 108
gods 3, 6, 16, 85, 106, 161-162, 179, 193
Greek diet 105-107
Greek physique 11, 135
Greek revivalism XV, 163, 170
Greek trainers XIV, 59
gymnasium XI, XIV, XVII, XX, 9, 13, 22-24, 31, 49, 53-63, 87, 92-94, 99, 102-104, 114-115, 120, 125, 130, 137, 159, 164-165, 169, 171, 179
gymnastes XIV, 59-63
gymnastics XVII, XXI, 4, 48, 60-61, 65, 83-85, 87, 104, 107, 163-164, 170
halma (jump) 31, 34, 189
haltere XX, 31-34, 96, 103-104, 133-134, 159, 186
halterobolia 96
harpastum 90, 94-95, 133, 185
health IX-XI, XV-XIX, XXI, 1, 8, 13, 59-61, 84-88, 94-95, 101-103, 105, 107, 112, 123, 126, 128, 133-134, 159, 163-165, 167, 170-171, 176, 178, 184-186, 188, 191, 192
heavy events XIII, 20, 30, 36, 38, 51, 55, 86, 94, 109, 114, 131, 133-134, 170
heavyweights 13, 108
Hector 41, 100
heel raise(s) 73, 157-158, 170, 182
Hellanodikai XX, 19, 115, 129
Hellenistic period 9, 11-12, 16, 55, 57, 61, 159
Hephaestion 10
Hera 5, 48-50, 52, 100
Herac(k)les 4, 31, 86, 152, 161
Heraia 48-50, 52, 190

Hermes 31, 86, 162
Herodicus of Selymbria 60, 84
Herodotus 8, 27, 40, 47, 136
hexis 88, 112, 162
high-intensity 66, 70, 72, 77-78, 80-81, 107, 117-118, 126-127, 130-131, 144, 158, 177, 181, 183-184
high-volume 77-78, 81, 116-117
HIIT 72-73, 80-81, 117-118, 144
himantes 37, 44
hippios 38
Hippocrates XVI-XVII, XIX, 53, 60, 62, 84-85, 87-89, 102, 105, 111-112, 121-123, 125, 165, 178
hippodrome 24-25
Hisarlik 47
Hittite 2, 16, 189
Homer XI-XII, XIV, XVI, 1-4, 8, 16, 25, 41-47, 51, 53, 55, 59, 61, 100, 106, 136, 188
honey 105-108, 121
hoplite phalanx 54
hoplite race 39-40
horizontal jump 32, 91
humerus 147-149
humors XVI, XVIII, 61, 85, 88, 106, 108
Hygiene XVII-XVIII, XXI, 60, 84, 88-90, 92, 94, 105-108, 119-121, 123-125, 132-133, 166, 181, 183, 192
hypertrophy 66-68, 78, 97, 147, 149, 155, 157, 159, 170, 176, 179
hysplex 42
Iliad XI, XIV, 1, 4-5, 8, 41-44, 46-48, 51, 85, 100, 104
illness XV-XVI, 13, 84, 88, 90, 105, 134, 136
inflammation 123-124, 126-127
inguinal ligament 23, 143, 151
injury 23, 74, 95, 98, 113, 117, 128, 148, 161, 193
intense day 110, 119-120, 125, 134
interval training XIV, 72, 78, 80, 110, 117, 177, 181, 183-184
iron 34, 44-47, 97, 104, 192
Iron age 3
Isocrates 60, 139
isotonic 74
Isthmia 8, 38, 42
Isthmian Games XVII, 7

Jason and the Argonauts 25-26
javelin 4, 11, 25-29, 35-36, 41-42, 44, 46, 48, 51, 59, 63, 104
Joe Weider 167, 170, 193
judges 9, 19-20, 37, 51
Judo 118, 180
jumping XX, 26, 31-34, 50, 54, 69-70, 74, 90-96, 98, 103, 118, 130-131, 139, 155, 159, 166, 170
jump squat 70, 74, 81
kampter 25, 38, 43
King Iphitus 5
knee joint 153-154, 170, 183
kouros 24, 137
Lacedaemonians 4, 53, 56
lactate threshold 116-118
Lev Matveev 77, 111
ligament(s) 23, 66, 124, 128, 143, 151
ligamentum patellae 153
linea alba 142, 151
load(s) 66-72, 74-78, 81, 92-94, 97-98, 100, 111, 113, 115, 127, 129, 155, 177, 180, 182, 190
loincloth(s) 22-24, 43
Lomilomi massage 128, 180
low-intensity 66, 72, 77-78, 81, 116, 129
low-volume 68, 77-78, 81, 117
Lucian XII, XIV, XX, 12, 23, 40, 51, 53, 55-58, 84, 91-92, 99, 101-103, 124, 130-131, 133, 162, 182
lumbar 104, 134, 142, 157
Lyceum XVIII, XX, 56, 92
Lycurgus of Sparta 48
maltho 56
marathon race 40-41, 117, 191
Martial 89, 95
massage XVII, XIX, 57, 61-62, 114, 120-128, 131, 134, 176-178, 180-182, 185, 188, 193-194
masseur 61, 63, 123
meal cakes 108, 134
meat 12, 105-109, 134, 144
Mediterranean diet 144, 158, 169
Mercuriale 86-87, 96, 103-104, 177, 182

Mesopotamia(ns) XX, 1-2, 16
MET (metabolic equivalent) 70, 80
metabolic stress 67
metu 121
middling day 119, 130, 134
military XIII, 2-3, 10-11, 16, 23, 38-39, 51, 54, 87, 100
military (exercise/training) 2, 11, 16, 54, 63, 87, 104, 136, 149, 164, 169
Milo of Croton 97, 111, 163
Minoan 2, 16, 47
mixed-training 69, 128
mosaics 11, 95
muscle fibers 23, 66, 78, 123, 126, 149, 155, 157
muscles named
    biceps brachii 137, 149-150, 159, 169, 184, 187
    brachialis 149-150
    calf 73, 138, 152, 157-159, 170
    cremaster 23, 187
    deltoid 67, 146-147, 149, 159, 169
    erector spinae 159
    external oblique 142-143, 159
    gastrocnemius 157
    gluteal 67
    internal oblique 23, 143
    latissimus dorsi 67, 147, 149, 165
    pectoralis major 145-149, 151, 169, 175
    pectoralis minor 147-148
    quadriceps 39, 67, 78, 152-155, 159, 170
    rectus abdominus 142, 151
    rectus femoris 152-155
    serratus anterior 147-148, 151, 158, 169, 179, 182
    soleus 156-157
    triceps surae (calf) 152, 157-158, 182, 186
    vastus intermedius 153
    vastus lateralis 153-155
    vastus medialis 153-155
music(al) XVII, 4, 9-10, 34, 65, 83
Mycenaean 2, 41, 46
Myron 139-140
Nemea 7-8, 27, 38, 42

Nemean Games 7, 37
Nestor 41
neuromuscular 65, 76-77, 97, 116, 150, 178, 183
nudity XIII, XVII, 22-24, 51, 54, 63, 137, 140, 169, 177, 186
nutrition 105, 107, 124, 144, 165, 167, 182, 191, 193
Odysseus 43, 45, 47
Odyssey XIV, 41, 44-47, 51, 59, 136
oil (olive) XIV, 4, 9-10, 21-22, 24, 55, 57-58, 61, 63, 105-107, 121, 123-125, 144
Olympia XIX-XX, 4-8, 10, 12, 15, 19-21, 23, 25, 27, 30-32, 38-39, 44, 46-50, 56, 58, 96, 100, 109, 114-115, 129, 140, 178-179, 190
Olympiad 4-5, 8, 23, 30-32, 36, 38-39, 51, 97
Olympic Games XIII-XV, XIX, XXI, 4, 6-8, 12, 16-17, 19-20, 24, 26, 35, 40-44, 46-48, 50-51, 72, 115, 129-130, 136, 141, 171, 178, 188, 194
Olympic ode 4-5, 19, 21, 60
(One) 1 RM 66-70, 78, 93, 132, 147, 150, 158
oracle 5, 8-9, 20
Oribasius 87, 89, 96, 122
overtraining syndrome 97, 113
oxen 41, 97, 100, 162
oxygen-uptake kinetics 70-71, 80
paedotribe XIV, 59-63, 84, 86, 125-126
paganica 90
pain IX-X, 23, 67, 88, 121-123, 127, 181
painful 37, 45, 121
palaestra(e) 9, 24, 36, 49, 54-55, 58, 62, 86-87, 103, 130-131
palaistrophulus 62
Panathenaic Games 9
Panhellenic Games 7-8, 16
pankration XX, 20, 29-30, 36, 38, 51, 55, 61, 86, 92, 100, 108-110, 130-131, 159
passive movement(s) 126, 128, 182
Patroclus 2, 4, 41, 46, 51
Paulus Aegineta 122, 125, 175
Pausanias XII, XIX-XXI, 5, 12, 14, 19-21, 23, 25, 27, 32, 37, 40, 48-50, 56, 96, 100, 109, 115, 137, 163
peak performance 75, 112
peak power 70, 194
pederasty XIII, 22, 51, 54, 63
pentathlon XIII, XVI, XVIII, 14, 20, 25-32, 35-36, 43, 51, 93, 130, 180-181, 184, 186, 192
Pericles 9

periodization XIV-XV, 75, 77-78, 81, 93-94, 97, 111, 113, 115-116, 134, 175, 180, 182-185, 188, 191
    linear 77-78, 81, 175, 180
    nonlinear 77, 81
    reverse linear 77-79, 177
    undulating 78, 116, 183
periodos 7
peritrochasmos 101
Persia(ns) 1, 3-4, 8, 10, 24, 32, 40
petaurum 99
Phaeacian Games 45, 47
Phayllos 32-35
Pheidippides 40
Philip II 6-7 9, 10
philosopher(s) XVI-XVIII, 10, 13, 55-56, 108, 125, 159
Philostratus XII, XIV-XV, XXI-XXII, 12, 25, 32-40, 55, 58-59, 61, 84, 96, 101, 108, 110-111, 113-115, 118-120, 124-125, 129-131, 133-134, 138, 141, 151, 158-159, 180, 190-191
physical culture X-XII, XV, 135-136, 162, 164-167, 169-171, 185, 189, 192
physical education XI-XII, 3, 9, 11, 164, 176, 180, 183, 185, 188
physical fitness X, 1, 16, 83, 118, 133, 163
Pindar 4-5, 9, 13, 15, 19, 21, 51, 60
Plataea 39-40
Plato XII, XVII-XVIII, 7, 13, 17, 14-15, 17, 21-22, 26, 48, 53, 56, 59-61, 65, 84, 86-87, 105-107, 132-133, 191
Plato's Republic XVII, 13, 21-22, 48, 60, 65, 106
plethrium 56
Pliny 108-109, 122
plummets 103, 134
Plutarch 10, 40, 44, 48, 85, 87, 106-107
plyometrics XIV-XV, 73-74, 81, 93, 159, 170, 184, 190, 194
poetry 4, 21, 46, 55, 163
polarized training 117, 191
Polyclitus of Argos 137-139
Polydamas XX, 100
porridge 108, 134
powder(s) XIV, 55, 58, 63, 107
power XIV, 6, 66, 69-71, 73-74, 80-81, 86, 90-94, 98-99, 102-103, 111, 128, 131-133, 141, 149-150, 155, 158-159, 165, 167, 171, 175, 178-179, 182, 187-188, 191-192, 194

precompetition 90, 128, 182
preparatory day 110, 113, 119-120, 125, 134
preparatory exercise 120, 124-126, 128
prizes XIII, XX, 3, 5, 7-9, 11-13, 16, 19-21, 25, 40-41, 47, 49, 62, 86, 188
professionalism XIII, 12-15, 17
progressive overload XIV, 71, 80, 97-98, 111, 133, 158, 183
protein(s) 107-109, 144
punch 37, 90, 148, 182
punching bag(s) 55, 89, 159, 165, 170
Pythagoras 109-109
Pythian Games 7-8
quoit 5, 44, 92-93, 99, 104, 134, 159, 163, 170
race in armor 20, 39, 51
rapid exercise (Galen) 86, 89-90, 94, 133
rating of perceived exertion (RPE) 116-117
recovery 62, 67, 71-73, 76-77, 97, 101, 110-113, 115, 119, 127-130, 134, 177, 186, 188, 192-194
recovery day 110, 119, 130, 134
regimen(s) X, XII, XVII, 4, 13, 61, 66, 75, 78, 81, 83-84, 89, 97, 102, 105, 109-110, 112-113, 115, 117-118, 132, 138, 165, 167, 179
relaxation 110, 114, 120, 123, 129
Renaissance 86, 135-136, 182
repechage 27, 184
repetitions 66-68, 71, 74-75, 77-78, 80-81, 89, 94, 111, 116, 147, 167
resistance phase (GAS) 75-76, 97, 113
resistance training 65, 73-75, 92-93, 96, 99, 133, 144, 155, 163, 167, 170, 175, 180, 186, 188-190, 193
restoration therapy 119-120, 123, 125, 128, 134
Roman(s) XI, XIII, XV, XVIII-XIX, XXI, 5, 11-12, 16, 21, 37, 48, 50, 59, 89-90, 95-96, 104, 106, 110, 120, 130, 133-135, 139, 140, 151-152, 164, 169, 175, 179, 185, 187-188, 190-191
Roman empire 11-12, 17, 185
Roman imperial period 95, 110, 130, 134
Rope climbing 99, 133, 159, 170
rubbing(s) 62, 121-123, 125-126
rugby union 14, 74, 107, 109, 128-130, 132, 178, 180, 183, 192
running XIII, XVII-XVIII, XX, 2, 14, 23, 26, 28, 30-31, 33, 35, 38-40, 42, 45, 48-50, 54, 56-57, 59, 70-73, 78, 80, 86, 89, 91, 94-95, 101-102, 116, 118, 130, 134, 157, 166, 177, 186, 190

running economy 71, 78, 91, 118
running track(s) 31, 49, 54
sacred 5-6, 20, 40, 47, 51, 56, 85, 186
sacrifices 7, 20, 85
scapular 147-148
scholars 20, 34, 46, 173
sculptors XIX, 139, 158, 169
Selye 75-76, 81, 97, 113, 190
semeion 31
set(s) 66-68, 71, 74-75, 77, 80-81, 89, 94, 111, 147, 167, 179
shadowboxing 37, 89, 94
shuttle run 101-102, 184, 189, 191
Sifan Hassan 14
six-pack 142, 144, 169
skamma 31-32, 43, 54-56, 131
skiing 116
Socrates 24, 59
soldier(s) 4, 6, 24, 39, 42, 54, 99-100, 103
Solon XX, 9, 92
sparring 37, 55, 139, 159, 170, 182
Spartans 3-4, 6, 16, 22, 36, 40
spear 44-45, 54
specialization XV, 12, 14, 17, 59, 63, 86, 133, 159, 169
spectators 20, 27, 38
speed XII, XVIII, 21, 31, 60, 66, 71-73, 89-95, 97-98, 101-102, 128, 133-134, 141, 165-167, 171, 176, 182, 185-186
sphairisterion 62
spheristici XIV, 62-63
spine X, 99
Spondophoroi 6
sponge 58, 63
sport(s) IX-XI, XIII-XVII, XXI, 1-3, 11-14, 16, 22-24, 26-27, 35-36, 41, 45-46, 54, 59, 61, 63, 65-67, 69, 72-75, 80-81, 89, 91-93, 101, 112, 115-116, 118-119, 126, 128, 130, 132, 147-148, 161, 164, 166-167, 169, 171, 175-194
sports-specific training XIV, 94, 133
sprinting 31, 54, 69, 73-74, 90-91, 94, 102, 118, 133, 166
squat 67, 69-70, 74, 78, 81, 91-92, 127, 132, 154-155, 158, 175, 187, 191
stadia 8, 10, 16, 39, 102
stadion race 4, 9, 14, 20-21, 23, 26, 28-32, 34, 38-39, 49, 91, 94, 101

Strabo 10
strengthening XIV-XV, 65-67, 75, 78, 81, 95-97, 99-100, 103-104, 121-122, 133, 163, 166, 176
stress(or) 67, 71-73, 75-77, 81, 97-98, 111, 113-114, 116, 126, 181, 190
stretch-shortening cycle 74, 90
strigil 10, 58, 63
strongman 97, 99-100, 164-165, 193
supercompensation 76, 81, 97, 112-113, 115
superfluities 123-124
surgeon XIX, XXI, 96, 119
Sutherland XI
Swedish massage 126
swelling 121, 163, 194
swimming 1, 129, 148, 166
synoris 25
teacher XVIII, 62-63, 84
tendon(s) 66, 74, 121, 123-124, 147, 149, 153, 157, 186
tennis 12, 26, 57, 118, 148, 184
tethrippon 4, 25, 46
Tetrad XV-XVI, XXI, 110-111, 113-120, 124-126, 128-132, 134, 167
The Jump XIII, XVIII, XX, 25-28, 31-34, 45, 90, 98, 103
Theogenes 7, 109
Theokoloi 20
Theon of Alexandria 84, 119-120, 123, 125, 128
Thrasybulus XXI, 59-61, 85-86, 88, 112, 119-120, 137, 183
throwing XX, 2, 11, 27, 32, 35, 44-45, 47-48, 54, 59, 63, 69, 86, 92-96, 98-100, 104, 118, 133-134, 148, 159, 170, 186, 194
Thucydides 4, 9, 22, 106
training volume XIV, 68, 71, 77-78, 80-81, 98, 117, 147, 189
trigon 95
tripod 5, 41-42, 46
Trojan Horse 44
Trojan war 3, 9, 45, 47, 84, 193
Troy 47
truce(s) 5-6, 9, 16, 38-39
Tryphon 84, 119-120, 123, 128
vase paintings XI, 22, 25, 32-33, 35, 49
vegetables 105-108, 144
vegetarian 105, 109

velocity 65, 69-71, 80, 91-93
vertical jumps 74, 81, 91, 155, 179, 190
vigorous exercise (Galen) 89, 92, 114, 133, 166
violent exercise (Galen) 86, 92, 123, 133, 166
Vitruvius XIV, 54-56, 63, 130
VO2max 70, 79-80, 101-102, 118, 127
walking 54, 85-86, 101-102, 122, 134, 157
war(s) XIII, XVII, 1, 3-4, 6, 13, 16-17, 22, 24, 35, 42, 48, 51, 54, 59, 85, 87, 106
warfare 39, 46
warlike 26, 87, 103
weightlifting 2, 166, 178
wheat 105-106
Winckelmann 135-136
Windship 164
wine XIX, 107-109, 122
wreaths 4, 6, 49
wrestling XI, XIII, XVII, XX, 1-2, 4, 11, 13, 20, 26-31, 36-39, 41-43, 45-46, 48-49, 51-52, 54-56, 59-63, 86, 89, 92, 94-95, 97, 99-100, 108, 114, 116, 118-120, 125, 130-134, 158-159, 165-166, 184
wrestling bout(s) 11, 20, 27, 36, 38, 43, 72, 89
wrestling school 49, 52, 54, 60-61, 89, 94-95, 99-100, 132
Xenophanes 12, 17
Xenophon (athlete) 14
Xenophon (historian) 24, 83, 109, 163
Xerxes 8
xystarches XIV, 62-63
Zeus XIII, 4-5, 7-8, 16, 20-21, 51

Printed in Great Britain
by Amazon